TSE TSAN TAI
(1872–1938)

Dr Dong Wang

TSE TSAN TAI (1872–1938)

An Australian-Cantonese Opinion Maker in British Hong Kong

The Asian Studies Collection

Collection Editor
Dr Dong Wang

The author and publisher extend their gratitude to the academic reviewers of this book.

First published in 2023 by Lived Places Publishing.

All rights reserved. No part of this publication may be reproduced, stored in a retrieval system, or transmitted in any form or by any means, electronic, mechanical, photocopying, recording or otherwise, without prior permission in writing from the publisher.

The authors and editors have made every effort to ensure the accuracy of information contained in this publication, but assume no responsibility for any errors, inaccuracies, inconsistencies and omissions. Likewise, every effort has been made to contact copyright holders. If any copyright material has been reproduced unwittingly and without permission the Publisher will gladly receive information enabling them to rectify any error or omission in subsequent editions.

Copyright © 2023 Lived Places Publishing

British Library Cataloguing in Publication Data
A CIP record for this book is available from the British Library

ISBN: 9781915271846 (pbk)
ISBN: 9781915271860 (ePDF)
ISBN: 9781915271853 (ePUB)

The right of Dong Wang to be identified as the Author of this work has been asserted by them in accordance with the Copyright, Design and Patents Act 1988.

Cover design by Fiachra McCarthy
Book design by Rachel Trolove of Twin Trail Design
Typeset by Newgen Publishing UK

Lived Places Publishing
Long Island
New York 11789

www.livedplacespublishing.com

Abstract

Who was Tse Tsan Tai? Insurrectionist? Socialite? Patriot? Public Intellectual?

Born and raised in Australia and trained in Anglo-Hong Kong's civil service, Tse Tsan Tai (1872–1938) was all of these and more. A first native media man and anti-Qing patriot, he advocated independent thinking and a free China. Through his words, this book explores a composite identity, touching on themes of diaspora, religion, colonialism, civil society, science, and revolution in Hong Kong, Australia, Qing and Nationalist Chinas, and of our time.

Ideal reading for students of Asian Studies, East Asian Studies, Diaspora Studies, Chinese and Hong Kong History, International Relations, Indo-Pacific Studies, Colonial Studies, Cultural History, Sociology, and related courses, this fascinating book uses biography to ask the question: what were the original ideals for republicanism in China?

Keywords

Colonialism; East Asia; cultural history; diaspora; revolution; biography; identity; republicanism; Qing; race; sociology; Christianity

Acknowledgments

Hong Kong (HK) has been close to my heart and mind. In 2001–2002, I worked at Lingnan University HK (Tuen Mun) to help found its history department on a teaching fellowship funded by the US Lingnan Foundation based at Yale University at the time. Hong Kong is the place where I rediscovered myself, powered by professional calling, before I came back to the United States to work at Gordon College on the North Shore of Boston in 2002. Two decades afterwards, hopes and efforts for a democratic China are renewed in the unfolding story of Tse Tsan Tai (1872–1938) in British Hong Kong. Intellectual support from John Fitzgerald, David Parker, Flemming Christiansen, Kathryn Myers, Kristin Stapleton, David Kenley, William Tsutsui, Lynn White, III, Paul Dunscomb, and the Alaska World Affairs Council is acknowledged herewith.

Dong Wang, NW Germany, December 25, 2022.

Epigraph

Since I belong to no party and have no political enemies, I shall gladly welcome contributions toward this history from all friends and colleagues, irrespective of nationality or party, as I am conscious of the fact that many important historical details must have escaped my memory or remain hidden from my knowledge.

– Tse, 1924, conclusion

Contents

Introduction		x
Learning objectives and discussion topics		xxviii
Chapter 1	"A native of Sydney"	1
Chapter 2	The 1911 Revolution: a Christianized democratic China?	21
Chapter 3	"The world's great problem solved"	53
Chapter 4	Where business, culture, politics, and advocacy converged	69
Chapter 5	Conclusion: Chinas and the curse?	97
Chapter 6	Historical documents reading: excerpts of Tse Tsan Tai's writings	101
Notes		219
Bibliography		231
Index		241

Introduction

Tse Tsan Tai (Xie Zuantai 謝纘泰 1872–1938, also known as James Ah See) is perhaps best known for his 1899 cartoon "The Situation in the Far East" (Tse, 1899) and as Hong Kong's first native media man who cofounded the influential and still existing *South China Morning Post* (SCMP) in 1903. Owned by the Alibaba Group of the People's Republic of Chaina (PRC) since 2016, SCMP has been widely considered as a PRC soft-power promoter.

This book tells the story of Tse, an Australian-Cantonese public intellectual who lived his entire adult life in British Hong Kong. Critically reading his words, we explore how mixed heritage, diaspora, religion, democracy, colonialism, and revolution impacted identity, while considering the roots of republicanism in nineteenth- and twentieth-century Chinas.

Born and raised in Australia and trained in British Hong Kong's civil service, Tse Tsan Tai established the *South China Morning Post* in 1903 together with Alfred Cunningham (1870–?).[1] A leading anti-Qing insurrectionist in Hong Kong, he worked alongside the major figures, Chinese and foreign, in the movements leading up to the 1911 Revolution and the first Republic of China (1912–1928) in Nanjing and Beijing. A sophisticated socialite, an acerbic debater, and the inventor of aluminum airships, he put his mastery of English to use in public opinion pieces and newspaper polemics. The life course he steered between revolutions, the print media, contemporary science, Christian faith, Cantonese patriotism, independence, freedom, business, and cultural preservation made him a vibrant witness to the constantly changing identities that defined his age and place. Tse's words throw a fresh light on the original meanings of the Chinese Republic, a possibility still very much alive today.

Tse Tsan Tai's life and place invite scrutiny as well. Neither is typical – the man was just as unusual as Hong Kong is unique. However, the period between the 1890s and the 1930s produced constellations that are worth examining. What they called "Far East", and we now refer to as "East Asia" were and are still again the site of a major geopolitical shift. Hong Kong was and again today is in focus when it comes to determine the reach of empires and the issues of nationalism, democracy, autocracy, and freedom are again in the air. It is essential for us to carefully study dimensions of nationalism, racism, the Christian faith, and universalism as they were used by Tse and others in British Hong Kong and China at the time.

Divided into six chapters, this book is organized around four themes in the first four chapters: place (mainly Sydney, Hong Kong, and Canton); revolution and politics; religion and universalism; and business and culture. Juxtaposing Tse's own words with other sources and discussions, core histories are teased out. Chapter 5 serves as a conclusion, followed by Chapter 6 consisting of lengthy excerpts from Tse's works. My aim is to provide substantive insights into British Hong Kong and China arising from sources written by Tse and others. An edited collection of Tse's works, some facsimiles, as well as links to further resources can be found at https://wellingtonkoo.org.

Note on sources and style

Tse Tsan Tai at the age of 65 deemed his chief legacy to include his *The Chinese Republic. Secret History of the Revolution*, his argument that the biblical Garden of Eden was in Xinjiang (Chinese Turkestan), and his synthesis of historical China's art civilization. He selected items on these themes from among his many newspaper contributions, mainly to the English language press that burgeoned on the China coast at the time, and pamphlets he had had printed by Kelly & Walsh. He bundled them, together with an issue of *United China Magazine* from October 1933 which also reprinted some of his works – containing his stylistic, careful handwritten corrections in red ink. He entrusted the package to a British woman two years his senior, Miss Clara Beatrice Mitchell (1870–1947), on her way from mainland China via Hong Kong back home to Leeds in Yorkshire. Tse gave Mitchell a written permission to have them published in Britain, suggesting they "ought to sell in millions, when properly advertised" (Tse, 1937b).

This full set of publications, which Tse Tsan Tai authorized in 1937 for publication in Toto, constitutes an important source for this book. In the event, Mitchell's illness and the ravages of World War II thwarted the publication plan, and the material came into my possession after spending ninety years in an attic somewhere in Britain.

Tse and Mitchell seemed to have hit it off instantly at what seems to have been their first encounter in 1937: "I am still wondering how we could have sat & talked for 6 hours, when you called to see me at Noon yesterday. & [sic] no doubt the exchanges of views

Bankers:
The Hongkong & Shanghai Banking
Corporation,
Hong Kong.

Address:
The Tai Hing Mining Company,
No. 232, Hennessy Road,
Hong Kong.

I, the undersigned hereby authorize Miss Clara B. Mitchell to obtain the best possible terms and conditions for the printing and publishing of my following three books and supplementary pamphlets by a leading London Publishing Firm for sale in Great Britain, her Colonies and Dominions, the United States of America, and other countries of the world, together with translation rights:

Revised Edition (1937).

1. "The Creation: The Real Situation of Eden: and the Origin of the Chinese" with supplementary "Map of Asia". (1914).
   also
   Supplementary Pamphlets Nos. 1 to 12, and also No. 13 to No. 49.

2. Ancient Chinese Art.

3. A Short History of the Chinese Revolution.

Terms and conditions to be submitted for my approval.

Tse Tsan Tai

Hong Kong, 1 September 1937.

P.S. A few suitable illustrations dealing with the Upheaval of Central Asia and the Subsidence of the "Pacific" Continent, and Prehsitoric Discoveries, might be included at the discretion of the Publishers.

Note. These three books ought to sell in millions, when properly advertised.

Figure 1 Tse Tsan Tai's written permission for Miss Clara B. Mitchell, in Dong Wang's possession.

re Religion & other matters was mutually interesting". (Tse, 1937c) We also know that Mitchell returned home to Leeds around 1938 and convalesced for two years from ill-health "caused by her experiences when the Japanese attacked [Shanghai on August 13-November 26, 1937]" (Lui, October 19, 1940).

Mitchell, a single lady and teacher at Quarry Mount School in Leeds who had at least since 1921 rented out accommodation to a Chinese student lodger in her house on Meanwood Road in Leeds,[2] went to China upon her retirement and stayed there for about eight years before she headed home when the Japanese invaded Shanghai in 1937. We do not know what Mitchell did in China. Although she was a schoolteacher by profession, her bilingual business card indicates that she held a master's degree in technology (MTSc, 英國工科碩). A Chinese book found with the papers, *Happy Family* by female activist Frances W. Liu (劉王立明, 1897–1970), carries the author's personal dedication to Mitchell, dated September 15, 1933, but I am afraid that these are the only sparse straws to clutch at when seeking for motives and context. Neither do we know who introduced her to Tse nor why he entrusted her with the task of getting his work published. No matter whether their encounter was sheer historical contingency or part of a larger scheme, Tse took the opportunity offered seriously, for the careful selection and arrangement of his works and detailed instructions for their publication reveal, as we shall see, his deeply concerned verdict on the direction Chinese politics had taken.

They are therefore not just normal historical sources charting the lifetime of a protagonist; they add important information on how Tse himself at one given time chose to curate his own legacy, a point confirmed by both omissions and meticulous handwritten corrections and insertions in the material.³

Name, place, and quotation styles

Names of Chinese protagonists are mainly rendered in the original format used in historical sources, followed, on the first occasion, by any aliases, pinyin transcription where known, traditional Chinese characters where known, as well as birth and death years. I avoid normalizing formats of names in direct quotations, so while I use the correct Wade-Giles format in the running texts, for example, "Kang Yu-wei," it may in quotations be rendered "Kang Yu Wei" to follow the original.

Chinese geographical names are in pinyin transcription, except in direct quotations, where they are included in the original format. Hong Kong and Macau are in the classical postal transcription. In quotations, the old form "Hongkong" is retained where appropriate. Emphases in quotations are original if not marked as "emphasis added".

Chapter outline

The opening chapter charts how Tse's life (1872–1938) among heterogeneous diasporic Australian-Cantonese Chinese communities, secret societies, and colonial Hong Kong shaped his engagement with Qing China. Both person and places were essentially composite: Tse, an Australian-born Cantonese Christian of anti-Qing reform and revolutionary stock, British Hong Kong civil servant, cartoonist, political conspirator, cofounder of South China's oldest still published newspaper, and socialite who knew how to spread his message; Australia's Sydney and Melbourne areas, home to the largest ethnic, political, social, trading, and mining groups of Cantonese and other Chinese Australians, who played a crucial role in building the Republic of China; colonial Hong Kong, an entrepôt, a global hub, free port, gateway city, and a place of contending interests and crossed purposes. Our story is about a man who conducted a cosmopolitan life as a virtuoso in multiple registers. British Hong Kong – a place that still seeks its roots and role models in a constantly changing and vibrant diversity. Tse Tsan Tai was in favor of British monarchical democracy, was mostly silent on historical Australian white racism, and did not object to British colonialism in Hong Kong and in Australia, yet framed some of his views in explicit racist terms.

Chapter 2 examines Tse's account of revolutionary movements that ultimately toppled China's last dynasty, the Qing (1644–1911), and led to the founding of the Republic of China, and its Hong Kong-based precursors, providing fresh insights and firsthand perceptions of important events that many contemporary historians have treated as mere stepping stones on the path toward major historical turning points.

Chapter 3 reveals Tse's other identity as a Christian dreamer of one humanity with sino-centric traits. Tse's short book, *The Creation: The Real Situation of Eden, and the Origin of the Chinese* (1914), reinterpreted the biblical Genesis as a mythology of the historical "Far East" (East Asia). Tse claimed that the Garden of Eden was the Tarim Basin (i.e. today's Xinjiang where the People's Republic of China's first atomic test took place on October 16, 1964), and mapped the biblical narratives onto Chinese origin myths.

Chapter 4 examines Tse as an avid shaper of public opinion in the English language press in East Asia who locked horns with opinion makers in Hong Kong, Australia, Qing and Nationalist China, Britain, and the United States, and explores his fusion of business, culture, heritage, science, politics, and diverse mix of associates within the media and cultural circles on the China coast.

The book concludes with Chapter 5, covering Tse Tsan Tai's afterlife in Australia, Hong Kong, and the PRC. In Australia, Tse has been considered a son of Sydney, a paragon of Australian Chinese heritage, and an antidote to the White Australia lore. By contrast, Nationalist and Communist Chinese statehoods alike have reincarnated him as a patriotic hero to the degree that his Christian, civil liberty, and anti-Party identities were erased. Is history a double-edged sword? An uncomfortable mirror of the present? The straight path from the past to the present? Or something we need to dress up so that it justifies us?

Antiquities and geoculture

Tse's "free China" cause that amounted to a violent racist campaign against the Manchus, who were singled out and blamed for China's modern misery, unveils how he was suspended between a sino-centric, racial bias, and color-blind faith in universal love and one humanity. Yet his rhetoric placed the universal "we" at the apex of passion, reason, and morals, while masking partisan opinion and preference as scientific truths. The following intermezzo may indicate how this worked.

He himself probably never became aware of it, but in 1905 an Italian advocate of cultural nationalism circulated Tse's vigorous commentary on the pillage of national treasures among the participants in one of the most symbolic international congresses:

> An interesting little incident was the circulation during the Congress of printed slips of paper, presented by an Italian Countess. These papers contained a protest by a Chinaman, Mr Tse Tsan Tai, against the removal of great works of art from their places of discovery, the taking of any relics to museums in other countries than that to which they naturally belong.
>
> (Dapp, 1905)

These words were part of Isabel Frances Dapp's report on the first International Congress of Classical Archaeology held in Athens in 1905. Her disdain for the Italian countess as well as for Tse probably reflected the general reaction at the conference to Tse's and the countess's message, for the majority of scholars and connoisseurs gathered there regarded Romano-Hellenic classical antiquity as the common ground of modern civilization and were convinced that national museums and private collections had a natural duty and right to put on display the original heritage of universal culture and save it from local savagery. At the time, Tse Tsan Tai's appeal was shrugged off as odd, but it was put on record.

Why would an Italian countess sow Tse's protest in such barren soil? British-Italian Evelyn Lillian Haseldine Carrington, Countess Martinengo-Cesaresco (1852–1931), a prolific and erudite historian of the Italian Risorgimento and avid scholar of Italian folklore championing nationalist and liberal cultural currents in

Italy and Greece, used Tse's statement to make a provocative political gesture (Hopkin, 2017). Likely without Tse's knowledge, she had his letter to the editor of the *Daily Graphic* in London reprinted and distributed it at the conference. The letter, also published in the *Westminster Gazette* under the title "Plundering Ancient Monuments. A Dignified Protest from Hong Kong" (December 15, 1904, p. 10), can be seen below from the 1905 conference proceedings, where it was printed under the title "On the Removal of Works of Art and Relics":

> Mr Tse Tsan Tai writes from Hong Kong, that he has read with growing concern the constant reports of archaeological discoveries and the desecration of the ancient pyramids, temples, etc. in Egypt, the Euphrates Valley, Ancient Greece, and Italy, and the wholesale removal of works of art, sepulchral remains and relics, etc., to swell the collections of the museums of Europe and America.
>
> 'These acts of vandalism … should henceforth be suppressed, and I appeal to every historian, bibliologist, archaeologist, and Egyptologist to advocate that the plundering and destruction of these ancient monuments and historical remains should immediately cease.
>
> An international society should be founded for the protection of all ancient monuments and relics of civilization, no matter in what country they may be discovered, and none of the relics should be removed from the country to which they belong.
>
> All the important and valuable works of art and relics which are at present exhibited in the museums

of Europe and America should be restored to the countries from which they have been taken, and be stored, catalogued, and protected in special buildings to be erected for their reception in accordance with the laws of this society.

If the different museums of the world should require any particular relics it is possible to get replicas made in stone, metal, or plaster, and, if this is impossible, photography can be resorted to. Thus will the monuments and remains of ancient civilisation be preserved in their entirety, and be saved from loss and destruction.

Would the peoples of modern Europe and America relish the idea of their sacred edifices and tombs being plundered and robbed of their contents at any time in the distant future? This morbid craving for archaeological collections is contrary to the high ideals of civilization, and should be checked before it is too late.

In order to add to our knowledge of the earth and its history, archaeological excavations should be encouraged throughout the world, but the relics which are brought to light should not, on any account, be removed. They should be treasured in a building to be built on the spot.'

(Tse, 1905)

Tse's sharp pen was later vindicated. He drew attention to a cause that is today regulated by international conventions on world heritage alongside global efforts to clamp down on the smuggling of and the black markets for antiques and works of art. Embodying the perennial tension between nationalism and internationalism in cultural heritage, Tse predated by a decade the fledgling attempts of the early Chinese Republic to counter the removal of China's national treasures by foreign museums and collectors (Wang, 2020a, ch. 6). That he imagined the establishment of an "international society" to deal with art and relics is testimony to the staying power of peace and cultural heritage protection pulses. The international community did, after two destructive world wars and other misery, eventually make such an organization come true in the form of UNESCO's World Heritage Center, the International Council on Monuments and Sites, and others.

Here, Tse – as always – snatched the initiative by standing on the side of high ideals of civilization, knowledge, and science, while in the abstract blaming the US and European art elites for their morally low – criminal (plunder) and addictive (morbid craving) – behavior. Tse took side with effect, leaving it to his opponents to expose themselves as bigots (seen in the expressions of "little incident", "Italian Countess", and "protest by a Chinaman").

Agency and worldview

Living in a context where omnipresent ethnic, nationalist, religious, and racial differences were situationally negotiated, blurred, and morphed, Tse's human condition is perhaps best summed up as what Benedict Anderson terms "colonial cosmopolitanism" (Anderson, 2018, pp. 171–177). Like everybody else around him, Tse simultaneously lived out multiple language registers, cultural and religious expressions, social roles, and political convictions. Each of these identities was subject to social dynamics outside the local colonial setting, yet within it amalgamated into evolving constellations of intersectional opportunities and sense of normality, diversity, and convergence.

Applying Anderson's notion to trace or "reimagine" the biographical complexity of historical protagonists, we gain a potent tool to understand and better explain their world views and activities. Anderson examined the literary-political biography of Kwee Thiam Tjing of Java. Kwee (郭添清, 1900–1974), known as Tjamboek Berdoeri, was born of Chinese stock in what is now Indonesia and was a vociferous Indonesian patriot during the last twenty years of the Dutch colonial rule (1816–1941) before Japan's occupation (1941–1945). Here I shall discuss Tse's opinion-shaping activities within the evolving situations in Australia, Hong Kong, mainland China, and other parts of the world during his lifetime.

Although Kwee and Tse were both journalists and columnists of Chinese (respectively, Hokkien and Cantonese) ancestry in colonial settings, only separated by a generation, they were distinctly different in character, beliefs, forms of social engagement, and historical circumstance. For example, Kwee experienced the Japanese occupation and violent revolution of the Dutch Indies, whereas Japan occupied Hong Kong in 1941 after Tse had died. Kwee's literary work perfected language switches, for instance, between Indonesian, Javanese, Hokkien, Dutch, English, and Japanese, while Tse mainly excelled in his stylistically sophisticated English, on occasion interspersed with carefully chosen Chinese names and phrases written in characters. Colonial cosmopolitans like Tse and Kwee internalized and challenged contrasting purposes and norms of their times.

They refracted political purposes in ways hard to stereotype into convenient categories.

Kwee and Tse are today largely undervalued. Anderson recounted the hard task he had to track down Kwee's works. Many of Tse's works seem idiosyncratic and difficult to connect with, not offering ready-made visions and templates for twenty-first-century movements and identity politics. Even so, Tse may find some new resonance through his "Proclamation of Independence" (1902) and his national anthem (1912) in juxtaposition with other anthems of Hong Kong.

It is indicative that China's official histories under Nationalist and Communist Party auspices credit Tse with his "contributions" to Sun Yat-sen's revolutionary attempts in South China and rebut him for withdrawing from the revolution to become a "comprador capitalist". Party historians write into a tradition of historical determinism which evaluates individual agency in terms of how it furthers the "objective" progress of the forces and modes of production; obviously, in this narrative, Tse's "class consciousness" was "reactionary", while Sun, within the "historical limitations" of the time, was "progressive". In any case, both parties, in order to claim Sun's legacy for themselves, retrospectively claim that Sun reflected "historical necessity", while Tse's rejection of Sun relegates Sun to an ancillary role, in their view going against the grain of history. Even so, the PRC and ROC still think Tse is a legitimate object of study because Tse did contribute to the "anticolonial" and "anti-feudal forces", albeit only for a period, before falling prey to his "class constraint". Historical sources at hand, however, tell a different story, one of political visions, individual ambitions, and moral values contending in the public sphere, with Tse as an important participant. The relative oblivion that befell Kwee and Tse among others indicates the degree to which cosmopolitanism, be it colonial or not, sits awkwardly with political claims for national and ethnic purity.

In essence, my approach is to discern the diverse meanings associated with Chinese nationalism, Han Chinese supremacy, and sino-centrism which both Tse and Sun shared up to a certain point, and the ways in which these ideas were realized in political movements, revolutions, and state building between the 1890s and 1937. As we shall see, Tse represented an open-ended aspiration for China's future that increasingly diverged from Sun Yat-sen's and Chiang Kai-shek's visions. The China coast contingencies of foreign power competition, wars, reform movements, uprisings, and railway concessions between the 1890s and 1911 – just to mention some well-known episodes – were driven by contention of foreign powers, Chinese (Han, the Manchus, and many others) officials and military men, the Qing court, Chinese insurrectionists and activists in mainland China, British Hong Kong, and in the diaspora. In this context, countervailing registers of personal integrity, culture, ethnicity, nationhood, and cosmopolitanism were utilitarianized situationally and opportunistically to make sense of existing realities and visions of the future.

Beyond the contending interests of myriad actors, the dynamics of the two decades were particularly manifested by technological progress, Hong Kong's breathless expansion, rapid industrialization, and growth of transport, media, and telecommunication that constantly shifted power relations, all reflecting a global rather than national thrust of development.

Therefore, Tse's story provides excellent material to critique Chinese Communist Party (CCP) and Kuomintang (KMT) Chinese national history accounts of Sun's "progressive" and Tse's "retrograde" roles in the Chinese revolution and the struggle of the colonized against the colonizers. Using Benedict Anderson's formulation, this book will go beyond Tse's entrepreneurial, political, and cultural activities in their own right, and rather explore their "interlocked relationship" in order "to reimagine the 'colonial cosmopolitanism' of that era, created by a huge wave of urbanization, capitalist expansion, new means of communication, and rapidly expanding education (including self-education)" (Anderson, 2018, p. 177).

Hong Kong as a cosmopolitan city was the backdrop of Tse's Han Chinese nationalism and he never turned against British colonialism. He related Chinese identity to world-spanning Christianity: "Proving" the Chinese to be God's "chosen people", in a curious way both superseded and confirmed the existing order. He consistently promoted the "brotherhood of mankind", while at the same time, as we shall see, arguing for the rightful place of the Chinese in the world with reference to the Bible, universal moral judgment, and scientific knowledge. For example, he alluded that the Chinese ranked higher than Europeans in the biblical bloodline from Adam and Eve, that the Garden of Eden had in reality been in what was in his time called Chinese Turkestan, that the Europeans sinned badly when starting World War I in 1914, and that Chinese art throughout history had belonged among the most civilized in the world.

The cosmopolitan, universal frame of reference characterized Tse's expressive style of English writing, the result of his Australian schooling and training for the Hong Kong civil service. It is factual and, with the force of frequent biblical references, plays to straightforward, commonsense reasoning. Tse stylistically juxtaposed, on the one hand, common sense, facts, proofs, and truth (biblical and scientific) and, on the other, misconceptions, lack of knowledge, and "theory" (to his mind meaning "unproven facts", hence falsity). Apart from his three books, his entire oeuvre consists of lengthy "letters to the editor" (i.e. unsolicited manuscripts) published in English language newspapers in East Asia, which provided a set format of polite confrontation – pointed courtesy, combined with indirectly stated acerbic contempt for the opponent's ignorance or low motives, created a frame for promoting his contrasting ideas as true and representing the most advanced learning.

Each age and context probably have their fitting stylistic subterfuge. Where European Renaissance thinkers resorted to the format of "symposiums" to contrast opposing views without being open to accusations of heresy, or where today's social media content must be brief and stir simple moral sentiments in order to have the broadest possible influence, so colonial cosmopolitanism demanded the invocation of common sense, scientific discourse, civility, and basic Christian faith, whereas personal attacks and themes openly provoking racial, nationalistic, and sectarian discord were generally considered uncomfortable, morally base, and prone to be censured by the editor.

Tse's education and life environment in Australia and Hong Kong gave him ability, capacity, and freedom that the Qing dynasty would never have offered him, including to oppose the Qing from what in essence was a Han supremacist stance. That being said, Tse's perception of the (Han-)Chinese was ambiguous when it came to visions of statehood. Did he embrace a united China? If so, why did he oppose Sun Yat-sen and Chiang Kai-shek? In any case, Tse's identity story invites students of conventional scholarship on Hong Kong and diasporic Chinese to unpack Han Chinese nationalism and sino-centrism (Mullaney, 2011).[4] Today, political assumptions about overseas Chinese including in Taiwan, Hong Kong, and Macau, not to speak of the diversity of populations in the PRC, are still open for debate as evidenced in ongoing efforts that have been made to decrease their political, cultural, and linguistic diversity, increase their clientelist subordination, and to extirpate their rich history in favor of simplistic ideological narratives.

Learning objectives and discussion topics

Tse Tsan Tai's life spanned Hoiping (Kaiping) in Guangdong, Sydney and Grafton in Australia, and Hong Kong. However, Canton (Guangzhou) was also a key place for him. Place is important for bounding historical narratives as points of material resources, social interaction, meanings, as well as symbolism and references that their users (inhabitants) draw on. That place is always *meaningful* we know because even any white spot on the map, any no-man's-land (terra nullius), any *non-lieu* ("non-place" in the sense of Marc Augé) is designated and used as such by somebody for some reason or with some intention that we can explore and explain in a historical narrative. What we are interested in here is the intersecting and contending interests and imaginings of different groups and individuals in relation to the places that bore on Tse's identity.

For each of the above places, the point of view differs: Kaiping – to tease out how Tse decided to refer to his ancestral background and capitalize on family history; Grafton and Sydney – to discuss the overseas Chinese identities in relation to Australian situations and Christianity and how they provided resources for Tse's life course; Hong Kong – to identify Tse's cosmopolitan colonialism and role in Hong Kong's synarchy; Canton – to cover the place as Tse's remote site of rebellion and danger.

While discussing Tse and the 1911 Revolution, we aim to make sense of how Tse changed his racist views of nationalism over time, the shifts in the geopolitical environment, and British policies toward the Qing Empire in relation to Kang Youwei's and Sun Yat-sen's secretive political activities. How can one evaluate the moral judgments, preferences, strategizing, and power games that Tse Tsan Tai, Sun Yat-sen, and Kang Youwei wrapped their nationalism around?

In Tse's quest for the Garden of Eden, he claimed that the Chinese ranked higher in the Christian hierarchies than the Europeans. Consider to what extent Tse's reading of the Bible lifted his argument into a universalist claim for peace and brotherhood of all humans. What is the significance of the scientific discourse of the Deluge?

Tse Tsan Tai joined together art connoisseurship and business operation as fields of complementary interaction within the wider frame of Hong Kong synarchy and colonial cosmopolitanism, which bound elites across ethnic boundaries. How did his notion of national heritage tally with his trade in works of art? More importantly, how is it possible to argue that Tse was part of a public sphere? If so, how did this public sphere relate to ethnic nationalism and independent thinking? How did this public sphere differ from the personal communications that went along with his correspondence on art with Sir James Lockhart?

1
"A native of Sydney"

The son of a Guangdong immigrant from Kaiping, Tse was, as the *Town and Country Journal* in Australia put it in 1915, a native of Sydney (Tse, flyer, 1915b). As a teenager, he followed his parents who elected to relocate to British Hong Kong, where at the time the border with Qing China's Guangdong Province was open. The colonial environments in Sydney and Grafton, Australia and Hong Kong conduced to creativity among young migrants such as Tse. The following three aspects contributed to Tse's achievements and influence in the British Crown Colony of Hong Kong.

Australia and Chinese Australians

Tse's writings and correspondence hardly bore any traces of bitterness against the white Australian policy and British colonialism and imperialism, but they were very China-centered with support especially from overseas Chinese and his American, Australian, and British progressive colleagues and friends. Notions of racial purity/oneness/unity as devotion to God prevalent in the Australian federation[5] were toward the end of Qing China (1644–1912) matched, by many Chinese radicals, in the form of racial pronouncements that singled the Manchus out as the "other" race who "usurped" a "pure" Chinese dynasty, the Ming (1368–1644). Racism of this sort held the Manchus solely culpable for China's modern backwardness, and therefore it aimed to annihilate them in an effort to restore "pristine" China. This version of racial purity is as clearly expressed in Sun Yat-sen's revolutionary slogan "expel the Tartars [Manchus] and restore China" as it was in Tse's 1924 account of the 1911 Revolution.

In countering the Australian form of racism, John Fitzgerald argues that: "Even a cursory examination of what Chinese Australians were saying and doing reveals that they were no less committed to freedom, equality and fraternal solidarity than were other Australians"[6] (Fitzgerald, 2007, viii). Embracing egalitarian ideals upon their arrival in Australia in the mid-nineteenth century, many Cantonese Australians became devout Christians, more than as a form of accommodation, who "derived comfort from their conviction that Christian values transcended national ones" (Austin, 2004; Fitzgerald, 2007, ix).

Between 1840 and 1940, about 20 million Chinese emigrated across the world, and less than 1% of them went to Australia. Tse's silence on the Australian issue of anti-Chinese racism was conspicuous in that many of the Chinese Australians to this day "do not appear to have considered themselves victims of local racism or special targets of high policy and immigration quotas. They lived out their lives as though the challenge of being Chinese and Australian was a relatively trivial one when compared with the other problems that life presented" (Fitzgerald, 2007, xii–xiii).

The fortuitous combination of an expanding and ethnically composite community under British colonial rule with emerging civic institutions centered on local chambers of commerce, Masonic lodges, philanthropic societies, political parties, and Christian churches, in addition to hometown bonds, provided

Australian Chinese entrepreneurs with particularly favorable growth opportunities. John Fitzgerald notes that "the complex of civic institutions that developed in Sydney was commensurable with the complex that emerged independently in Hong Kong", whereby to manage "local community affairs and mount claims through the press and to the government for equality of treatment in Australia" were a prominent function (Fitzgerald, 2007, pp. 177–180).

Tse Tsan Tai's affection for his hometown of Grafton in Australia was and is still reciprocated. Tse was praised by John Harvey Crothers Sleeman (1880–1946)[7] – an Australian journalist and publicist – as "the greatest Australian-born Chinese" in 1933 (Sleeman, 1933, p. 137; Noonan, 2008, p. 113). Grafton is a small town on the Clarence River in northeast New South Wales between Brisbane and Sydney. Historian John Fitzgerald has pieced together from scattered sources captivating details on Tse's young years (Fitzgerald, 2007, pp. 14–16). The Tses, known as the Ah See family, had a general store next to a local newspaper, the *Clarence and Richmond Examiner*. In 1932, Henry Benjamin Waterhouse (1861–1945) of the *Grafton Daily Examiner* reminisced about how a local journalist remembered the Tses well. In July 1876, the district was visited by a disastrous flood, and the newspaper was a heavy loser: "The printing office was submerged to the extent of about eight feet, covering all the machinery, destroying the composition rollers, filling the cases of type that were on lower frames with mud, while all stationery stocks were destroyed. In those days the mechanical staff were mostly young men and juveniles, who were boarded on the premises" (Waterhouse, 1932).

The newspaper office staff noticed the "plight of the Chinese family next door, and we immediately took steps to ensure their safety. There was Ah See, his wife, and several young kiddies, including a baby in arms. ... By some means we became possessed of a rope, and we improvised a sling at one end of it, lowered it over the balcony and swung it over toward the front door of the Chinaman's shop next door. There it was caught by John See, and one by one his family and himself were drawn to safety on the balcony of the 'Examiner' office. ... They [Tse's family] had to remain with us several days until the water subsided sufficiently to allow them to again enter their store ..." People caught in the bad floods ran out of food. "John See came to the rescue. He handed over the keys of his shop and told us lads that we could get whatever we liked from the shelves in the way of tinned goods – in fact, anything eatable at all". People survived on the tinned foodstuff in Tse's shop by using Waterhouse's ivory-handled razors to open the tins[8] (Waterhouse, 1932).

In the mid- to late-nineteenth century, Grafton was a center of the underground secret triad Yee Hing led by the legendary Loong Hung Pung (1849–1878) on the goldfields of western New South Wales. Many of its members and families were prosecuted back in China in the failed Taiping Uprising of 1851–1864 against the Qing government (Wang, 2021). Loong's heirs and successors built up the network's links with secret revolutionary cells inside and outside their native places of Guangdong and Hong Kong to bring down the Qing Empire[9] (Fitzgerald, 2007, pp. 14–15).

Scholars have pointed out that equally significant were "the founders and members of the NSW (New South Wales) Chinese Chamber of Commerce, the oldest Chinese chamber in the world after that in Hong Kong, and the Ma, Gock, Lee, Liew and Choy families, who built China's finest and grandest department stores in Shanghai on the model of Anthony Hordern's in Sydney" (Fitzgerald, 2007, p. 16). "Chinese clubs and societies in the Australian colonies were unabashedly modern and international in their style and orientation", and "Chinese in Australia wanted to be modern and cosmopolitan rather than being an Australian subject of the British empire" (Fitzgerald 2007, pp. 224–225).

Australia's impact on Tse's formation was manifest: His official biography told us that Tse was "baptized by his Godfather, the Rt. Rev. Bishop C. C. Greenway, of the Grafton (New South Wales) Church of England" (Duncan, 1917; Tse, 1924, p. 6), so colonial empire was not a destination but a conduit. Baptism not only made him a parish member, but of the Kingdom of God, while his education at Grafton High School and at Queen's College in Hong Kong equipped him with knowledge and social skills to suit, beyond national and racial bounds.

Even so, Tse also seemed to have represented anti-Qing insurrectionism; his biography, written by Chesney Duncan in 1917, explicitly included the following: "Tse in 1909 argued that north Australia was discovered by the Ming Chinese, asking the Chinese government to have it investigated" (Duncan, 1917) and Tse stated his "ambition" in the *The Chinese Republic. Secret History of the Revolution* as:

> My father was a leader of the Chinese Independence Party of Australia, and when I was about twelve years of age he told me the story of the cruel conquest of China by the Manchu Tartars, and I promised him that when I grew up, I would return to China and do my

best to help in driving the usurping Manchu Tartars out of China. I have kept my promise, and this accounts for my past activities in connection with the movement for Reform and Independence in China.

(Tse 1924, p. 7)

To what extent was Tse a hidebound millenarian rebel? On balance, he probably was not, for his *ex post facto* claim to have fulfilled his childhood pledge to his father seems more a bivalent narrative trope, both suggestive of redemption and of filial piety, than a statement about deep-seated and exclusive political motives and ideals.

Was his idea that the Ming could have beaten the West to discover northern Australia an indication that he harbored Chinese nationalist dreams of a Ming restoration? Chesney Duncan's summary from 1917 cited above, when compared to Tse's original words as published in *China Mail* (Tse, 1909), reveals that Tse, based on a news story about German scientists on the search for a pre-historic land bridge in South East Asia, exhorted the scientists to examine still existing Chinese settlements in Timor founded during the Ming Dynasty and speculated that early Chinese expansion, which might even have reached norther parts of Australia, had neither been promoted nor recorded by the rulers. Stylistically, that article suggested scientific dispassion, used the words "colony" and "colonize" apolitically to mean "settlement" and "settle" (rather than "dominion" and "rule"), and in doing so gently challenged conventional European perceptions of discovery and colonization, abstaining from simplistic nationalist finger-pointing. In the 1909 publication, the ironical slur on the "Chinese Government" is nowhere to be found. We can only infer why it was added in 1917.

Canton – a caged tiger? "A rebellion center and mother of revolution"

In modern history, the conurbation of Hong Kong, Macau, Canton (Guangzhou), and other places in the Pearl River Delta was the most important channel for local, national, and international trade in China. Traditionally, river and sea channels in this part of South China, forming an A-shaped gulf/bay forty miles long, linked Canton to the former British Crown Colony Hong Kong (1842–1997) at its right foot and the former Portuguese colony (circa 1557–1999) of Macau at its left. Besides trade, Canton and the Pearl River Delta were closely tied in history to huge migration waves from North China that since the sixth century peopled South China and spilled into Southeast Asia, resulting in a complex ethnic and linguistic patchwork in the area. During the Qing, the speech form in Canton, generally known as Cantonese, became the regional administrative and trading language of the Pearl River Delta, including Macau and Hong Kong, while the related but mutually incomprehensible Toysanese dialects in See Yap ("four counties") west and north of Macau, and the unrelated Hakka dialects spoken in northern Guangdong and in widely dispersed communities across the delta, indicated deep-seated divisions in the population. Tse Tsan Tai's ancestral home county of Kaiping belonged to See Yap, from which significant emigration to Hong Kong, Southeast Asia, Australia, and the Americas continued to take place.

Canton was the center of the Canton trade from about the sixteenth century to 1844 officially. It was later viewed, along with other Southeast Asian cities, as a "staging area" for Christian missions in China (Wang, 2007, ch. 1). It was the main site of the Sino–British clash during the Opium Wars (1840–1842, 1856–1860) that led to the concession by the defeated Qing regime of the Island of Hong Kong and the Kowloon Peninsula to Britain. It was the center of revolutionary activity in Guangdong from c.1895 to 1911, the site of the fledgling Chinese Communist Party's and the Nationalist Party's unsuccessful attempts to construct a cohesive modern nation-state through mobilizing workers and peasants between 1922 and 1927, and the only window through which the outside world could view China between "liberation" in 1949 and the beginning of "reform and opening" in 1979. Since 1957 the annual China Import and Export Fair has also been held there.

Alongside Chinese diasporas in Australia, Europe, the North and South Americas, Hong Kong, Hawaii, Japan, Vietnam, Myanmar, Indonesia, Malaysia, South Africa, and North and South Americas, Canton played a key role in the Chinese revolutions of the twentieth century. After the demise of the Qing government in 1912, the city became the headquarters of the Nationalist Party (Kuomintang, KMT; Guomindang, GMD) and the base, shared by both the KMT and the Chinese Communist Party (CCP), of the violent anti-warlord and anti-imperialist Nationalist Revolution.

With instrumental financial, public opinion, organizational, moral, and human support from overseas Chinese, the 1911 Revolution brought about the Republic of China (1912 until now, albeit since 1949 exiled to Taiwan), thus replacing the last imperial rule of

Qing China. War correspondent Frederick McCormick commented over a century ago: "if this is a Cantonese-made rebellion and revolution, as some claim it is, then it is a monument to the laundrymen, truck-growers, section-hands, miners, servants, and shopkeepers of the United States, as well as to the Cantonese merchants, manufacturers, and shippers of the East Indies and Oceania" (McCormick, 1913, p. 228).

Tse Tsan Tai's story alerts us to the complex making and unmaking of Chineseness, anti-Qing, anti-anti-Qing, and nationalisms.[10] Canton also linked China's domestic and global dimensions of nationalist and revolutionary activism: It was the transit point for Chinese migrants and gave name to the shared language of overseas Chinese and people in the Pearl River Delta, including in British Hong Kong.

One Hong Kong, two colonizers

A general understanding holds that Tse Tsan Tai's activities were bound up with Hong Kong as a place (Cheung, 1997, p. 8), but really one needs to see it as a place in between places. In Hong Kong's history, two Indo-Pacific colonial powers, Britain and China, intersected and rapidly transformed a makeshift trade entrepôt on a "barren island" to a unique metropolis of world significance with a seven and a half million strong population. Bernard Luk claims that "[f]rom the beginning, Hong Kong was a Chinese as well as a British colony". Where the former's strength rested upon its ethnic demographic hailing from neighboring counties in South China, originally as outcasts of the Chinese Empire, the latter held military, political, economic, and administrative sway over the territory through contractual agreements with the former

(Luk, 1991, p. 653). Luk does not distinguish between the two main meanings of "colony" (settler community versus dominion of an empire), for his argument is cultural and educational, examining the dual orientation of Hong Kong's ethnic Chinese populace toward the British and Chinese empires and its effect on educational and cultural institutions, policies, and practices. In that sense Hong Kong was "firmly … a periphery of two centers", even if Hong Kong in long periods "served as the safe haven for the full spectrum of Chinese opinion" (ibid).

Luk's pragmatic understanding of "colonialism" highlights a fundamental problem of colonial empire that Benedict Anderson famously pointed out in his book on *Imagined Communities* – the complexity of nascent nationalism, or rather the nations that communities of colonial subjects imagined and struggled for, as exemplified in the Dutch Indies and French Indochina (Anderson, 1991). If we transpose Anderson's notions to the situation in Hong Kong, it is true that both Hong Kong's Chinese settler communities and, following the inclusion of the New Territories at the 1898 "Convention for the Extension of Hong Kong Territory", their "indigenous inhabitants" were predominantly South Chinese, that is, speakers of Cantonese and Hakka dialects. However, the Chinese nationalist ferment seamlessly linked to the international Chinese diaspora; the ancestral lineage (clan) links were basic elements of the Chinese Empire; while literati culture and the written language centered on Chinese classics. As a result, the Chinese in Hong Kong tended to imagine their nation beyond the Hong Kong Chinese vernaculars and local communities. The imagined nation, accordingly, affirmed China's territorial expanse even when that imagined nation habitually rejected its actual political rulers

Luk describes how in the mid-1920s the "British in Hong Kong felt greatly threatened and adopted a cultural policy that deeply affected the Chinese culture component of the [school] curriculum". Hong Kong's Governor, Sir Cecil Clementi, promised Hong Kong government support for a Chinese Department to be established at Hong Kong University; he promised, moreover, to establish a new government secondary school, whose teaching would be in Chinese, alongside the existing government and missionary schools in which classes were taught in English. This school would include a normal section to train teachers of Chinese for other schools (Luk, 1991, p. 659).

Clementi's cultural politics proposed "an idea of Chineseness that emphasized cultural heritage over statehood and citizenship", was "a bastion of cultural conservatism amid political and intellectual upheavals" (p. 659), and aimed to bolster stability in the Chinese population. In teaching and social communication, Cantonese prevailed over Modern Standard Chinese (Putonghua), even though it was not until 1974 that t became, next to English, the official language of the Crown Colony (Lee and Leung, 2012, p. 1). In other words, the pragmatic British approach ensured that the "Chinese colonization" of Hong Kong was cultural only, that Cantonese made it linguistically distinct from the rest of China, and that it remained a sanctum for Chinese dissidents and activists.

In the early twentieth century, foreign countries, colonies, and foreign settlements, and Christian churches were used by overseas Chinese revolutionaries as a shelter to escape from the Qing government (McCormick, 1913, pp. 401–402). John Carroll identified the need for a history of Hong Kong as a "special place" and the active role of China's Hongkongers throughout history, who aligned their own distinct position with "Hong Kong's historic mission to open China" and to promote a "more cordial co-operation … and close intercourse" between China and Britain (Carroll, 2006, pp. 521–522). The story of Tse Tsan Tai supports Carroll's point that Chinese elites in Hong Kong at the turn of the twentieth century drew heavily on foreigners in British Hong Kong to secure Hong Kong Cantonese/Chinese interests – vindicating the power of the "colonized" (Mark, 2018). Ambrose King observed that emerging socioeconomic elites in Hong Kong were or are "order-prosperity minded and come from a very narrow sector of the population" (King, 1975, p. 426).

During British colonial rule, increased Chinese participation in the two small governing councils of Hong Kong (Legislative and Executive Councils) steadily grew after World War II. The Chinese unofficial members were less than 50% from 1945–1950, 62.5% from 1960–1963, 70% from 1964–1967, 77% from 1968–1969, and 84% from 1970. This was a "reflection of the growing strength and vitality of the Chinese community on the one hand, and the sensitive responsive capability of the government to absorb the socio-economic leaders on the other. The British are not attempting to create a mass-consensual community: they are, however, attempting to create an elite-consensual polity" (King, 1975).

From Tse Tsan Tai's time to 1997, "Hong Kong's real and day-to-day governing power [lay] in the civil service, headed by the Colonial Secretary who, under the direction of the Governor, [carried] on the general administration". By 1972, "one in every fifty of the total population was employed within the civil service. Because of this very fact, the bureaucracy has contributed a great deal to the stability of Hong Kong by serving as a mechanism for assimilating the potential 'discontented' into the governing machinery" (King, 1975, pp. 428–429). Hong Kong's civil service grew more and more open to Cantonese Chinese like Tse by the end of the nineteenth century, as part of the formal and informal, direct and indirect, synarchy emerging under British rule, that is, "a joint administration shared by both the British rulers and non-British, predominantly Chinese, leaders. The kernel of synarchy is a form of elite consensual government: it is a grass-tops approach to the problem of political integration" (King, 1975, p. 425).

By the standards of the 1930s, Tse Tsan Tai was an early example of "the willingness and ability of the British to change and enlarge the elite circle by co-opting emerging leadership groups in which the masses are primarily not sensitive to political rights and participation" (King, 1975, p. 430). The energy of the rising young generation was absorbed and channeled into non-political activities; and, above all, social stability has been enhanced through various official and unofficial schemes.

By the 1880s, Hong Kong was governed through an elite-consensus or integration, but with an elite-mass gap that was narrowed although still a problem. John Carroll notes that even during the 1920s and 1930s, "Chinese in Hong Kong collaborated with the British colonial government … where the rise of Chinese nationalism threatened Western imperialism in China" (Carroll, 2006, p. 542). "The ingenuity of the British governing elites lies in their sophisticated response in timely enlarging and modifying the structure of ruling bodies by co-opting or assimilating emerging non-British socio-economic elites into 'we' groups at critical periods. Consequently, any strong counter-elite groups are prevented" (King, 1975).

It may therefore seem counterintuitive that to Tse Tsan Tai, British Hong Kong was a haven and hideout for revolutionaries. Did Tse break the master narrative? Perhaps an answer is that he waited until 1924 before publishing his account of the 1911 Revolution.

Taking our cue from acute contemporary observers, we find that southern Chinese revolutionaries gained initial momentum during the Taiping Uprising of the mid-nineteenth century and constituted a large pushing force that toppled the Manchu court, thus facilitating the founding of the Chinese Republic in 1912 (McCormick, 1913, p. 228). They were driven by the hope to restore the Ming Dynasty (1368–1644) whom they imagined as "pure" Chinese, although the Mings had in reality been a succession of brutal autocrats. The revolutionaries reinvented the Ming as a model of ideal Han Chinese governance and used their name in a race-driven rebellion against the alien and "savage" "Manchu bandits" ruling the Qing Empire (Cantlie and Jones, 1912, pp. 127–133). Thus Nanjing (Nanking), which had been the capital of first the Ming Dynasty and then the Taiping Uprising in addition to being the site of some Ming emperors' tombs, was loaded with new meanings by Sun Yat-sen (who was also entombed there a few years after his death in 1925 when Nanjing was declared the capital of the Republic of China) and his followers in their tribute to the Ming autocratic rulers: "The spiritual influences of your grave [Ming emperors] at Nanking have come once more into their own. The dragon crouches in majesty as of old, and the tiger surveys his domain and his ancient capital. … Your people have come here to-day to inform Your Majesty [Ming emperors] of the final victory" (Cantlie and Jones, 1912, pp. 127–133).

After the 1911 Revolution that brought about the abdication of the boy emperor Puyi, ending the Qing dynasty (1644–1912), Tse came out openly as a revolutionary of thirty years (1882–1912), who had "devoted his life to the work of freeing the Chinese from Manchu rule" (Tse, September 9, 1912).[11]

Sonia Lightfoot describes Tse's role as a perceived danger to the colony:

> Tse, his father and his brother were politically involved in the republican revolution, which at the time of Sun Yat-Sen's revolutionary activities came too close to the governor of Weihaiwi for comfort. The commissioner [former Governor of Hong Kong, Sir James Lockhart] was certainly not in favour of this method of bringing China to democracy by revolutionary means.
>
> (Lightfoot, 2008, p. 22)

> Tse, in his revolutionary zeal, had finally become embroiled in the chaos in China: he had cast his net too wide. The many changes in his employment, his association with the Tong Meng Hui [factually wrong; *my comment*] and his high profile in newspaper circles had made him something of an embarrassment. As with his association with JHSL and the German Ambassador, he was running with the hare and hunting with the hounds, a dangerous thing to do.
>
> (Lightfoot, 2008, p. 42)

As already mentioned, Tse, in his own narrative, shouldered a huge familial obligation to redress "the cruel conquest of China by the Manchu Tartars" and promote the "cause of Chinese independence".

It is true that violent insurrections or militant plots against the Qing Chinese government ran counter to the stated British policy in Hong Kong, although the British government at the turn of the twentieth century encouraged the Qing regime to reform and protected political refugees and dissidents such as Kang Youwei (Kang Yu-wei) and Sun Yat-sen (1866–1925) on British soil from extradition to the Qing and assassination by Qing agents, in defense of British sovereignty:

> While this government will perform its duty in preventing the Colony [Hong Kong] from being made the base of operation against Canton [Qing China], the result of which would be injurious to our trade which must suffer from any serious disturbance, the assassination of persons in Hong Kong who may be obnoxious to the Chinese Government is intolerable.[12]
>
> (TNA FO 17/1718, p. 521)

Indeed, an inordinate amount of time was spent by senior British Foreign Office and Colonial Office staff all the way up to the relevant ministers (Secretaries of State) tracing anti-Qing revolutionaries and preventing them from being caught or killed by the Qing.

Tse had, upon graduation from Queen's College (Hong Kong, HK) in 1890 at the age of 18, worked as an official under Sir Osbert Chadwick at the Public Works Department of the HK colonial authority. Meanwhile, he was actively networking with young students in Hong Kong and important British and Australian figures through letters to local newspapers and the Chinese Patriotic Mutual Improvement Association founded in Hong Kong in 1890 with Yeung Ku Wai, his classmate and soon-to-be young revolutionary martyr, as president and himself as secretary in order to organize anti-Qing military uprisings and public education and opinion. In 1900, Tse left the Hong Kong colonial civil service for good to take up the compradorship at Boyd, Kaye & Company.

Tse flourished in the relatively free world of British Hong Kong. In July 1896, at the age of 24, he designed a military sun helmet and presented it to the British government through Lord Wolseley. Known as the "Wolseley Sun-helmet", it became a lasting icon of British presence in the colonies. As a civil servant, author, and writer, he also proposed aerial navigation by dirigible cigar-shaped airships built of aluminum and propelled by motor-driven fan propellers in 1899. He sent drawings and full particulars of his airship named "China" to London to the famous inventor of Maxim guns and flying machines, Sir Hiram S. Maxim, with a request that Maxim make the necessary test experiments as Tse "could not afford to go to such a great expense".[13] Tse claimed that in time of war "the cigar-shaped balloon can be enclosed in an aluminum shell to protect it from the missiles of the enemy" (*The Far Eastern Review*, January 1908, p. 245).

Tse was actively involved in initiatives for constructing railways and opening mines, suppressing the Indian opium trade, founding a society against foot-binding in China, the anti-opium society of South China, the Chinese club and free library in Hong

Kong, suppressing slavery, founding international and national societies for the protection of ancient historical relics (1904 and 1908), educating poor boys of the Hoiping District of China, sending sons of rich families to Europe and the United States for education, terminating the anti-American boycott in China, conserving the Canton River, building a New City, condemning the Canton Bay reclamation works, negotiating the cancellation of the 1904 Canton-Macau Railway Convention, developing Manchurian mineral resources by natives of Guangdong and Fujian provinces, forging closer understanding between the United States and China on the future control of the Pacific (1910), promoting universal peace and brotherhood, condemning a secret understanding for the partitioning of the Qing Empire, and forging an alliance between China and Japan for world peace. These many civil society activities and contributions, if anything, belied Sonia Lightfoot's impression that Tse caused discomfort and embarrassment. To the contrary, he helped sustain a crucial civic sphere that the colonial government could not do without and abstained from activities that could seriously jeopardize the protection of Chinese/Cantonese Hongkongers. After all, even in a nondemocratic "synarchy", a liberal civil society can achieve outcomes that no autocratic government can attain.

In 1924, witnessing how Sun Yat-sen's Sovietized separatist party-state (KMT-CCP) in nearby Canton was powered by violent nationalism that separated South China from the internationally recognized, albeit weak, Northern Beijing Government (1912–1928), Tse decided to publicize his eyewitness account of the 1911 Revolution. In it, he pointed out the ongoing betrayal of original ideals for a democratic China and challenged the dominance of the KMT/CCP and narratives, in particularly their idolization of Sun Yat-sen.

Hong Kong's colonial government perceived the Canton KMT-CCP military government as a problem, perhaps even a threat. Tse Tsan Tai at the same time regarded it as autocratic, short of what he and many others had fought for.

2
The 1911 revolution

A Christianized democratic China?[14]

Often considered an unfinished revolution with Sun Yat-sen (1866–1925) as its canonized hero (Kayloe, 2018; Bergère, 1998), the 1911 Revolution led to the demise of the Qing dynasty, the last imperial dynastic rule in China. The event has occupied a prominent place in historical narratives ever since. How come? What did Tse Tsan Tai's influential but often forgotten account of the Revolution tell us about his ideals of a republic? Why did Tse, a core participant and eyewitness, elect to publish a "secret history" of the revolution in 1924 more than a decade after the event? How does it differ from the mainstream knowledge of his time and ours? For a moment in the early twentieth century, a *genuine* parliamentary form of democracy with free and open elections by its peoples seemed within reach in China, a possibility that now, one century on, still reigns on paper and in the realm of dreams.[15]

Tse's terse history of the 1911 Revolution is a valuable primary source written by a firsthand eyewitness, although he admitted that a fuller history was needed which "will consist of about six or more large volumes, and will contain photographs of the leaders of the Revolution and their foreign friends and sympathizers, besides reproductions of important historical documents and letters, and much highly interesting correspondence and descriptive notes and interviews, between the years 1892 to 1912" (Tse, 1924, conclusion).

Tse's early recourse to a racist war against China's Manchus – the imagined enemy of the equally imagined monolithic and "pure" Chinese – admixed with the sustained fight for a just and democratic China. The atrocities committed in the seventeenth century during the Manchu conquest of the China Proper south of the Great Wall must thus, in his view, be matched by a violent, vengeful revolution of the early twentieth century to rid China of the "Manchu usurper" and to "restore China" (光復中華) – Tse envisioned China as a *nation*. This begs the question as to how the abstract idea of nation is translated to individuals and societies (Anderson, 1991; 2018, x); nations do, in essence, not just exist because people imagine them, but because they yearn for inclusion in and recognition by a community – nation is both hope and promise. Taking Anderson's idea about nation a step further, how can a nation constitute itself without lapsing into arrogant and unprincipled claims vis-à-vis other nations? And how can nationalism prevail without understanding itself as part of an *inter*national community?

Tse's account of the 1911 Revolution was initially published as a serial installment in the columns of the *South China Morning Post* in 1924 under the title of *The Chinese Republic. A Short History of the Revolution*. Also, *the Secret History of the Revolution*, followed almost immediately by a reprint as a small book. The bulk of Tse's 1911 history later appeared in the magazine *United China*

Magazine, the Journal of Chinese Revolutionary Progress in October 1933, pp. 475–489. Its much-abridged edition in Chinese was not published until 1937.

Tse's history of the 1911 Revolution carefully documented activities, contacts among revolutionaries, and his and others' evaluations, while we lack comprehensive expositions of how he thought the new Republic should be constituted. In other words, the connection between citizen and polity as envisaged by Tse remains obscure. Polemicists could, if they wished, point out that he never really revealed how it ought to have been done to prevent the failure brought about by Sun Yat-sen.

Tse's short book in lieu of a preface reprinted a letter to him from his good friend and biographer, editor, and newsman, Chesney Duncan, dated December 14, 1924, from seaside Penang in what is today Malaysia. Using letters from friends and well-wishers was a ploy that Tse often resorted to, imputing the authority of an outside gaze into his own to suggest objectivity and to reinforce his own standing.

He styled his account a *secret history*, a genre that had come to refer to "forgotten" historical evidence that revised orthodox narratives and was considered faithful to history: *Revisionism* was on his mind. He emphasized the 1911 Revolution's Taiping heritage and sharpened the Manchu-Han ethnic and racial division lines (Leow, 2022) so as to engender a sense of nation.

Tse documented events, revolts, and global preparations leading up to the Revolution. He sought to influence public opinion and solicit support from foreign governments including Britain, the United States, Japan, and Russia – after all, he addressed his public in English. Casting the Manchus as a race of "usurpers", by implication he advanced the idea that the Chinese nation was racially "pure", a point that helped bring together the visions of *Ming restoration* with contemporary casual social-Darwinist classifications of *race* in European and American political and geographical discourses (exemplified in Curzon, 1901; Huntington, 1907 and 1915), and with the evolving meanings of *nation* signifying emotionally shared culture, language, history, or destiny. This was an idea gaining momentum after the Napoleonic wars and, for example, giving substance to the movements that led to the unification of Germany in 1871. Elevating the anti-Qing struggle from backward-looking millenarian insurrections to the fight of a "pure" race against its usurpers seemed at the time more progressive and palatable to an international audience and legitimated anti-Manchu genocide as a just cause. To Tse, the overthrow of the Qing Empire and the ousting of the Manchus was an important accomplishment, yet, at the same time, a source of dismay, as the newly established republic did not meet his hopes.

It was not until the time when the Nationalist (KMT) and Communist (CCP) parties established their "united front" government in Canton (Guangzhou) that Tse Tsan Tai decided to tell his side of the story. Of course, the proximity of this military government to Hong Kong was a concern, but it was confounded by a powerful new configuration of the *nation* as a concept in the wake of World War I. The Russian revolutionary leader Vladimir Lenin (1870–1924) had taken an interest in the "national question" and in particular "national self-determination" since 1903, thus adding it to the canon of the communist ideology (Knudsen, 2020) as well as to the Russian Socialist Party Programme (Lenin, 1914, ch. 9).[16] Lenin realized in December 1917 that "national self-determination" backfired during the Brest-Litovsk peace negotiations between Russia and Germany when Poland, Lithuania, and Courland (Kurland) demanded and gained independence from Soviet Russia with reference to national self-determination.

According to Knudsen, US President Woodrow Wilson (1856–1924) propelled national self-determination center stage of international politics within the context of the Versailles Peace Treaty and the founding of the League of Nations. National self-determination was practiced when determining some border issues following World War I, but initially met strong resistance from colonial powers. It remained in the toolbox of America's international politics that appealed equally to the so-called interventionist and isolationist politicians, and after World War II it became an important element of the United Nations institutions in 1945.

Although Tse Tsan Tai, to my knowledge, did not use the term, national self-determination made the politics of the Chinese nation a pressing issue in new ways that must have alarmed him. There was a perceived realpolitik threat to the British empire of Wilsonian ideals for and Japanese designs on China, which upset the Far Eastern power balance, not to speak of the existential threat to Hong Kong's many Chinese and foreign residents from what they regarded as nondemocratic forces building up huge military potential with strong Soviet support in Canton just 125 km away as the crow flies – what started as a fledgling military government under Nationalist leader Sun Yat-sen's control in

1917, by 1923 had become a Soviet-funded, officially declared base for the Nationalist Party's effort to gain military control of all of China and was in 1924 replenished, under the guidance of Soviet Russia, with the Communist Party joining the Nationalist Party as individual members (Fitzgerald, 1996, pp. 120–121, 367).

At the time, Canton's United Front government and state-sponsored nationalism aimed to impose one indiscriminate China upon many diverse peoples across China who were then looked down upon by both KMT and CCP Leninist party elites. It was incumbent on Tse to clarify his position, on the one hand explaining his early dedication to and sacrifice for the 1911 Revolution, and on the other distancing himself from its aftermath. Thus, Tse Tsan Tai wrote about his direct experience of the 1911 Revolution, which affirmed the kind of synarchy emerging in British Hong Kong that served the well-being of its ethnic Chinese population.

Tse's racism and nationalism

Contrasting Chinese historical suffering at the hands of foreigners, Anne-Marie Brady points out how little weight China's historical accounts gave and still give to "the violence of Chinese against Chinese in the turbulent history of the last 150 years – the Taiping Rebellion, the Nationalist government and assorted warlords, and the actions of the Chinese Communist Party itself in its struggle to gain power and then maintain it" (Brady, 2003, p. 28).

Indeed, anti-Manchu ethnic cleansing during the 1911 Revolution was crucial for rallying a racially "pure" Han Chinese nation for revolutionaries. This was documented by American journalist, Frederick McCormick, through his travels in then China (McCormick, 1913; Rhoads, 2000). As time went by, anti-Manchu racism slowly faced as other types of utilitarian imagining of the Chinese nation gained political importance in China.

Ambiguous definitions of the Han/Chinese versus Manchus abounded as sino-centrism arose in modern history and in the China study field. Both ethnicities were constructed as if they were "pure" races, even though they both sprang from synthetic groups of a mainly Eurasian scope and reach who had successively peopled China's dynamic agrarian empires The last of these, the Qing Empire, saw the royal Aisin Gioro, Nara Hala, and other Manchu clans of the Jurchen, as well as tribes and peoples of Tungusic, Mongolian, and other origins tied into the banner troops who generally hailed from Manchuria and other places outside the Great Wall. These highly composite groups conquered Ming China in 1644, superimposing their power on a population that in its own origins was also highly intermixed.

Tse illustrated the perceptions of who the Chinese were, citing a letter dated December 22, 1911 (Tse, 1924, pp. 26–27, "Dr Yung Wing's Advice"). In the letter, Yung Wing,[17] the proposed president of a new democratic and Christian republic of China, who at the time was in the United States, championed an ethnically pure Chinese government:

> A new China should be in the hands of pure Chinese, and not in the hands of trimmers and traitors with European predators to intermeddle in our civil and domestic affairs; if foreigners are employed, Americans are far preferable. We can have them under contract, on the basis of retention or dismissal, as we think best.

> Such an important question should be calmly discussed and firmly decided upon in National Convention, by delegates to meet in a central city.

Nationalism and racial self-consciousness were awakened naturally and through mass politics against the Manchus. American war correspondent Frederick McCormick recorded wholesale massacres of the Manchus as they took place, numbering 8,000 and 15,000 in Xi'an alone, and many more in other places (McCormick, 1913, pp. 62, 175, 116–117, 125–126, 130). But the Manchu court and international diplomatic corps in Beijing did nothing to "move the Manchus above the blame of the Chinese revolutionaries" and to refute the revolutionists' "delusion" or imagination to blame the Manchus, for they thought the Manchus deserved the perdition (McCormick, 1913, pp. 422–423, 225, 236, 246).

Anti-Manchu racism during the 1911 Revolution and until well after the founding of the Republic of China in 1912 was evident in the emotionally charged writings of Han Chinese martyr radicals such as Zou Rong (鄒容, 1885–1905), Ning Tiaoyuan (寧調元, alias 林士逸, 1883–1913), Chen Tianhua (陳天華, 1875–1905), and many others, who, reflecting each their place of origin, in different ways vilified the Manchus as social pariahs, "tartars" (韃子, 胡兒), "Manchu dogs" (滿狗), who "escaped" the knives (漏刀的) – as Monica Chang Kin-ian verbally presented at a scholarly conference held in summer 2022. Eventually, this racist storm subsided as the Chinese Republic gradually took shape. Foreign "sea powers," China's revolutionary leaders, and emerging republican power holders agreed that Chinese territory must remain intact lest Japan and Russia took possession of Manchuria and Chinese Turkestan

(Lattimore, 1962, pp. 79–102). Manchus, alongside Muslims (Hui), Mongolians, Tibetans, and Han Chinese were, on their home soil, officially declared part of the new Republic.

Tse Tsan Tai's racist perceptions extended to Black people too. Though they belonged to what he thought of as the Brotherhood of Man, "[t]he existence of the Black race, with its frizzled hair and calf-less legs is one of the inscrutable mysteries of God. … Most of the black *races* … are still savages and of poor mentality, and it does not appear likely that they will ever become the equals of their Shemitic and Japhetic brethren in intelligence and learning" (Tse, 1922, p. 3). By contrast, Tse argued that it was a fallacy to consider the Chinese as the yellow race because "[i]n North China to-day many Chinese quite as white and with classical features equal to those of any European. The color of the Chinese varies from white to different shades of brown, but is never *yellow* [sic]". Although he advocated racial blending, he excluded Black people:

> In the interests of Universal Peace and the Brotherhood of Man, I think we should encourage this mixing and blending of the different races, as it is the only way to solve the difficult and distressing race and colour problems, which confront us today. … But I do not mean indiscriminate mixing, or that a highly cultured white should marry an ignorant and savage black.
>
> (Tse, 1922, p. 2)

Needless to say, Tse balanced his own colonial cosmopolitanism and social position in relation to universalist norms, Christian narratives of the 'descendants of Noah and his three sons Shem, Ham, and Japhet", and the perceptions of race, eugenics, civilization, and primitivity that dominated ethnographic sciences of his age.

Nation versus government

Determined to bring down the Qing imperial government at all costs, Tse Tsan Tai made a distinction between his beloved country, China, and its ruling regime and "enemy" race, the Manchus. This differentiation was shared by many revolutionaries most of whom were in exile around the world in the early twentieth century but were in close contact with Tse and others of kindred spirit in British Hong Kong.

Nationalists, reformers, and revolutionaries actively relied on overseas Chinese, foreign governments, settlements, and colonies as financiers, ideologues, weapon suppliers, shelters, and covers. Japan, for example, hosted 20,000 Chinese reformers by the early 1910s (McCormick, 1913, p. 302). Sun Yat-sen and many others were, on the one hand, hosted in and sought support from Japan and, on the other hand, condemned Japan for it. Sun seemed hypocritical – his ideas suggested democracy and welfare, yet his actions indicated that power was being concentrated into his own hands. But Tse's disdain for Sun's character was kept on the quiet, even if it chimed in with divided opinions among reformers, revolutionary insurrectionists, and their corresponding foreign supporters. Only in late 1924, on the eve of Sun's death and at the urging of his "Chinese and European friends", did Tse decide to unmask Sun Yat-sen:

> Now that Dr Sun Yat-sen has been condemned and execrated by his countrymen at home and abroad,

and fallen from the lofty pedestal upon which we all helped to place him, and whilst some of the leading participants in the great revolutionary drama are still alive, I think I am now quite free to publish, in the interests of historical accuracy, the secret history of the Great Revolution, without being charged with the guilt of belittling or discrediting Dr Sun Yat-sen in the eyes of his countrymen and the world.

(Tse, 1924)

Yet, the rifts among most Chinese elites and militarists were matched by a burning desire to turn the riven country into a union, commonwealth, or a United States of China. In 1912, McCormick wrote of the Republic of China's self-made problems, anti-Manchuism, and anti-imperialism:

As I retrace my steps across Manchuria the problem of the 'Flowery Republic' [China, ROC] impresses me as one which its leaders and its people have yet to grasp. China has completely digested and assimilated the Manchus, and is now supremely the undisguised and ungoverned 'Chinese Question.' Any revolution for her regeneration must henceforth be a revolution of the Chinese people. They have been steadied within and held together by the Manchus, whose place has been taken by the Powers who now hold China together from without.

(Mccormick, 1913, p. 444)

Was and is China too large for unification without suppressing others?

Since the founding of the Republic of China in 1912, it took Taiwan seven decades to democratize in 1987 with the end of the KMT party-state's martial law. In the twenty-first century, Taiwan is widely seen as a global beacon of democracy, ranking, according to the Economist Intelligence Unit's 2021 Democracy Index, as the eighth strongest democracy in the world (Hale, 2022). During the last two centuries, diverse polities in China have been stuck with unaccomplishable unification, despite civil wars.

In 1915, American professor of law Frank Goodnow, who was adviser to the first President of the Chinese Republic Yuan Shih-kai on constitutional matters, was not ebullient about the prospects for democracy in China. He found it expedient to establish "in the central government a legislature and in the provincial and other local governments provincial and local councils which shall represent the most important classes, such as the merchants, the literary class and the larger property owners" (Goodnow, 1915, p. 220).

According to Goodnow, this effort should be linked to "a serious effort" at once:

> to offer to the classes of the people which are conscious of common interests and have intelligent aspirations the opportunity to participate more widely and influentially in the government of the country than they have up to the present time enjoyed … Otherwise the country will continue to be under the blight of absolutism and … will possess probably the worst form of government which has yet been devised – namely a military dictatorship.
>
> (Goodnow, 1915, p. 220)

In 1930, Arthur N. Holcombe (1884–1977, Harvard faculty 1910–1955) shared his observations from a nearly two-year field trip:

> I became convinced that, if the Chinese possess the political capacity to organize and operate a modern government, capable of meeting the obligations which fall upon governments under the strenuous conditions of the modern world, the outlook for peace in the Far East is bright, but that if they lack such capacity, which I found to be a widespread opinion among foreigners, both in China and elsewhere in the Far East at the time of my visit, the prospect for domestic tranquility in China is poor without foreign intervention. The chances of successful foreign intervention without embroiling the Powers with one another also seemed poor.
>
> (Holcombe, 1930, preface)

Britain, Hong Kong, and Qing China's power game

Tse Tsan Tai's history of the 1911 Revolution uncovers two aspects of British Hong Kong that are usually understated, if not hidden, in ideologically driven history writing which tends to focus on national humiliation. First, the Qing government systematically violated British sovereignty in pursuit of its own interests. Cross-reading Tse's account against the British records, a picture of aggressive and shrewd Qing officials emerges, who took full advantage of international law to further China's advantage by hiring many skilled foreigners like Halliday Macartney (1833–1906) who was in Qing China's diplomatic service from 1877 to 1907, including as councillor and secretary to the Chinese Legation in London."[18]

Second, the Crown Colony of Hong Kong, while selectively cooperating with the Qing regime on certain matters, protected and facilitated a public sphere for Chinese critical activism and debate directed toward changing China.

When read against Tse Tsan Tai's accounts, British Foreign Office archives (TNA FO 17/1718 [08 & 09]) disclose fascinating details such as protecting Kang Youwei (Kang Yu-wei) from assassination attempts, freeing Sun Yat-sen from kidnapping by the Chinese legation in London, and dealing with the murder by Chinese agents of insurrectionist Yeung Ku-wan in 1901.

Following the failed plot to seize Canton and launch an uprising in Guangdong Province in 1895 – to which Tse Tsan Tsai had directly supplied money and arms – the Viceroy of Guangdong "applied" to the British Governor of Hong Kong "for a surrender of 5 leaders" – he demanded that they be extradited, including Sun Yat-sen who was known to be the leading conspirator. "The [British Hong Kong] Governor refused on the ground that the offense was a political one, he however issued a decree of banishment against Sun". But if any of the anti-Qing leaders "had rendered themselves liable to prosecution under the Foreign Enlistment Act, 1870, proceedings should at once be instituted against them" (TNA FO 17/1718, nos. 107–108, April 29, 1896). In other words, they could not be extradited to China, but if they had recruited people in Hong Kong for military schemes outside Hong Kong, they could be tried at a British court. Sun was, however, banned from staying in Hong Kong.

A year after the Canton uprising, on October 1, 1896. the now exiled Sun Yat-sen turned up in London. Ten days later, he entered (not being forced by) the Chinese legation in London, was disappeared, and held as prisoner there until the British intervened and had him released on October 24. He was "locked up in a room with barred windows by Sir H. Macartney's order … The door was constantly guarded by two men" (TNA FO 17/1718, nos. 112–123). Sun managed to get a porter, George Cole, at the Chinese legation to deliver a letter to his friend Sir James Cantlie (1851–1926) whom Sun knew from his studies at the College of Medicine in Hong Kong where Cantlie had been dean. At the time, in 1896, Cantlie was home in London at Portland Place, near the Chinese legation, due to poor health. Cantlie immediately resorted to legal recourse while leaking the news out to newspapers to get Sun freed from the Chinese confinement (Cantlie and Jones, 1912; Sun, 1897).

Sun noted that upon entering the Chinese legation, Sir Macartney said to him that "you are in China now. Here is China". The interpreter who had lured Sun into the legation told him that the Qing Chinese government wanted Sun to be captured at any price, dead or alive The Qing Chinese regime fiercely argued for their rights "on their soil" at their embassy to jail and extradite Sun back to China for execution (TNA FO 17/1718, nos. 80–82).

Calling it a flagrant violation of international law, on November 18, 1896, Lord Salisbury handwrote: "We must protest to prevent any modification in our international rights … against us by interference from our default [i.e. we must protest so that they cannot interpret our inaction to mean that we accept a change in Britain's international rights]. But otherwise the matter affects our interests very little" (TNA FO 17/1718, no. 126). The British authorities "demanded the release of the prisoner [Sun], Lord Salisbury stated that the man's detention against his will in the Chinese legation was, in the opinion of Her Majesty's Government an infraction of English Law which was not covered by and was an abuse of, the diplomatic privileges accorded to a foreign representative" (TNA FO 17/1718, no. 133, December 1, 1896).

Condemning the "novel extension of principle" that the Qing Chinese embassy in London attempted to effect: "The case of Sun Yat Sen, who thanks to Lord Salisbury's prompt intervention, was yesterday released from his imprisonment in the Chinese Embassy, has naturally drawn attention to the whole question of the immunities which Ambassadors and their Suites [sic] enjoyed under the aegis of International Law. … The persons and the dwelling-places of Ambassadors and their followers may still be deemed as sacred; but we cannot permit Embassy-houses to be turned into prisons for the incarceration of men who have committed no offence against the laws of the country" (*The Standard*, October 24, 1896; TNA FO 17/1718, no. 34).

In June 1898, Lord Salisbury (1830–1903, prime minister 1895–1902) commented on Qing China: "If I am asked what our policy on China is, my answer is very simple: It is to maintain the Chinese Empire, to prevent it from falling into ruins, to invite it into paths of reform, and to give it every assistance which we are able to give it, to perfect its defense to increase its commercial prosperity. By so doing, we shall be aiding its cause and our own" (Cameron, 1989 pp. 362–363).

China's story of national humiliation (*guochi*) was invented mainly through the exploitation, by different historical agents, of the emotional and political connotations involving a series of legal documents signed between China and foreign countries that are considered unfair during the "treaty century" of 1842–1943/1949 and beyond. Many of those treaties were signed under duress, which is not uncommon in world history, but the rhetoric of unequal treaties as the source of "national humiliation" has formed a distinct Chinese nationalist discourse up till this day (Wang, 2005). Its invention and reinvention by the Nationalist Party (Guomindang, Kuomintang, GMD/KMT) and the Chinese Communist Party (CCP) weaponized shame for use in their revolutionary and nationalistic polemic, defining Chinese in contrast to foreign, thereby equating nation with sovereign statehood. If we unpick the circuitous logic, the nation is humiliated by other states, claims self-determination, and acquires sovereignty; because it is a sovereign state, defined in opposition to other states, we can draw the conclusion that it is a nation. This false syllogism requires the myth of national victimhood to be kept alive.

In historiography, emphasis on British public moral outrage (Schiffrin, 1968) overshadows the narrative of how Sun Yat-sen's life was saved because the British government defended civil liberty and domestic and international law in the face of the Qing authorities' infringement of British sovereignty under international law. Lord Chamberlain, Secretary of State for the Colonies (June 1895–September 1903), seemed less concerned about Sun the man than about the principle. The spectacular case, of course, also figured in the House of Commons. Hansard records:

> Sir Edward Gourley (Sunderland): I beg to ask the Under Secretary of State for Foreign Affairs [George Nathaniel Curzon, 1895–1898] (1) if he will be good enough to inform the House when he first heard of the alleged kidnapping of Sun Yat Sen, and what measures he adopted for the purpose of obtaining his release; (2) whether his capture and detention at the Chinese Embassy was contrary to International Law; if so, what representations has he caused to be made to the Chinese Government; and (3) whether Sir Halliday Macartney, as a British subject, is to be held responsible for the capture and detention?

Mr Curzon responded:

> In answer to the first paragraph, the first intimation of the subject was received at the Foreign Office on Sunday, the 18th of October. Steps were immediately taken to ascertain the facts of the case, and as soon as trustworthy evidence was received a note was addressed by Lord Salisbury to the Chinese Minister [ambassador] pointing out that Sun Yat Sen's detention was an abuse of the diplomatic privilege enjoyed by the Chinese Legation, and requesting his immediate release. This request was complied with on the 23rd October. In answer to the second paragraph, Sun's detention was certainly not warranted by International Law, and was regarded as a serious abuse of the privileges and immunities which are granted to foreign representatives, and the Chinese Government were so informed through her Majesty's Minister at Peking and requested to give strict instructions to their Minister

in London to abstain carefully for the future from any acts of the kind. In reply to the third paragraph of the Question, the act was that of the Chinese Minister, and he must be responsible for it.

(Hansard HC Deb, February 15, 1897)[19]

In July 1897, Sun left London for western Canada. His charisma and high-profile collection of funds from overseas Chinese in Vancouver, Victoria, and other places were watched carefully by different governments. "In the eyes of the world, the Manchu regime represented evil, duplicity, and as Sun liked to call it, 'Tartar' cruelty, while Sun Yat-sen carried the twin banners of enlightenment and Christianity" (Schiffrin, 1968, p 129).

In March 1896 the British Hong Kong government banished Sun from entering Hong Kong for five years, and Chinese embassies and consulates around the world continued to play the power game and optimized their interests while expressing gratitude to the British authorities. From June to September 1898, reform efforts at the Manchu court in Beijing reached a peak with the Hundred Days' reform. The young Guangxu emperor encouraged Kang and his disciple Liang Qichao to make reform proposals. During the one hundred days from June 11 to September 21, 1898, the Emperor, with the assistance of Kang, Liang, and Tan Sitong, issued 40 reform edicts. He called for changes/modernization in administration, education, technology, economy, law, military, and police systems. The reforms ended abruptly in disaster. Empress Dowager staged a coup and forced the emperor into seclusion. She ordered the arrest and execution of leading reformers on the grounds that they had been plotting a coup.

On September 21, 1898, Kang Youwei, now the most wanted man in China, escaped from Tianjin on board the P&O Royal Mail Steamer "Ballarat" lying at the Wusong harbor (Shanghai). On the advice of the influential Welsh missionary, Timothy Richard (1845–1919), Kang solicited British support by referring to the Anglo-Russian conflict in central Asia and the Indo-Pacific:[20] "The emperor [Guangxu] is really well informed, very clever, and very hard-working. Two hundred British troops (!) [sic] would be sufficient to re-instate him, for which he and the whole of China would be very grateful to England. The Emperor is for England, and the Empress [Dowager] is for Russia" (TNA FO 17/1718, nos. 183–191).[21]

A high-born prodigy, a Chinese Renaissance and Enlightenment figure, political ideologue and activist, Kang was instrumental in shaping modern Chinese taste for antiquities and geoculture. Yet he was best known as a radical reformist, a Confucian fundamentalist, an evolutionist, and a cosmopolitan Qing loyalist – indeed, a host of oxymora can be applied to him (Wang, 2020a).

The British consulate in Shanghai reported: "The day before he [Kang] arrived in Shanghai most urgent telegraphic orders for his arrest were received, and a very large reward was offered for his capture. Fortunately, … the man, who must now be styled a political refugee, was transferred to a Peninsular and Oriental Company's steamer at Woosung, bound for Hongkong. … As soon as the Chinese authorities were aware that the man had eluded them, they became very pressing in their demands for his arrest and surrender, but without success" (TNA FO 17/1718, nos. 176–178, 195–196[22]; Kang, 1899, pp. 60–61).

Kang took refuge in Hong Kong before moving on to Singapore as soon as Viceroy Li Hongzhang (Li Hungchang) came to Canton in 1900 (Tse, 1924). The Chinese embassy in London did not stop pressuring: "… I have received a telegram from my Government instructing me to call the attention of Her Majesty's Government to the fact, that a man of the name of Kang Yu Wei, a Member of a Society of disaffected Chinese Subjects who are endeavouring to excite troubles in the South of China, is now residing at Hongkong and to request that, as an act of international comity, he may be expelled the Colony" (TNA FO 17/1718, nos. 199–201).[23]

In March 1900, the British commissioner (Resident-General of the Federated Malay States) in Penang, Sir Frank Athelstane Swettenham (1850–1946), reported on their effort to protect Kang from assassins dispatched by the Qing: Kang's "quarters have been changed more than once in order to baffle the assassins who have arrived to earn the reward for his [Kang] head offered by the Empress-dowager, the Viceroy and others"[24] (TNA FO 17/1718).

Sun Yat-sen (1866–1925)

By 1923, Sun Yat-sen's Chinese revolutionary politics, under the influence of Soviet agents and Chinese betting on all horses, turned against foreign imperialists, colonizers, and Chinese warlords, and blamed China's problems on the former's oppression and the latter's collusion. This was such a contrast to the different Sun in 1911/1912 when he wrote a letter, about his presidency in the newly formed Republic of China in Nanjing, to his British "imperialist" physician, James Cantlie. In 1896 Cantlie saved Sun's life in London and portrayed Sun in glowing terms as "a truly noble character" in 1912. Cantlie praised that Sun "has induced the Powers, through their representatives, to hold their hands whilst China worked out her own salvation"[25] (Cantlie and Jones, 1912, foreword).

In 1911–1912, Frederick McCormick's reports on Sun are more reserved: "He [Sun] is a mystery. He is vaguely known as a human shuttle that has moved for some years from colony to colony among those Western nations who have sheltered and encouraged their borrowed Chinese citizens and subjects" (McCormick, 1913 p. 257).

Early 1912 was a messy moment when no foreign countries recognized the new Republic of China in Nanjing of South China, and when the last emperor of Qing, China's legal sovereign, abdicated in Beijing of North China. McCormick sensed that "there was something about China's situation that President Sun Yat-sen and the Government at Nanking [Nanjing] were unwilling to tell". One day Sun's top government member pressed for foreign support, leaking to McCormick that: "Japan wants to make with us an offensive and defense alliance. … We do not know how long we can resist without recognition. We must have recognition from others than Japan before we can answer her. … We cannot afford to offend Japan, she has been our friend" (McCormick, 1913, pp. 290–291).

In the end, McCormick praised Sun as "a prophet honoured in his own country". Sun had no large organization in China, but he united the reformers on the one side and the conspirators on the other (McCormick, 1913, pp. 304, 342–343). However, Sun was unable to stand his ground, making a radical turn to Soviet Bolshevism that cast doubt on his loyalty to his original ideal for a representative government by the people through peaceful means.

Our main protagonist Tse Tsan Tai was highly critical of Sun, and so were some of Sun's colleagues as documented in Marie-Claire Bergère's biography published in 1994. Was it mainly because of Sun's personality and high-handed shift toward the Leninist world revolution dictated by one single party-state? Certainly, Sun was taking every opportunity to secure his leadership position through foreign funding and alliances with all Chinese and foreign forces of different stripes, including bandits and secret societies. In early 1900, for example, Sun secretly maneuvered to involve Henry Blake, Hong Kong's governor, and Ho Kai (He Qi), a well-respected Chinese barrister in Hong Kong, to persuade Viceroy Li Hongzhang to declare independence of Guangdong, but to no avail (Wang, 2022; TNA FO 17/1718).[26]

In July 1900, the Singaporean police, entrusted with watching over the safety of Kang Youwei, picked up that Kang "had received by letter and telegram from abroad advice bidding him beware of a party of three Japanese recently sent [by Sun Yat-sen] on a mission to Singapore for his destruction". The police in Singapore pursued this lead and found out that this group was trying to find out where Kang was staying. While warrants and charges for banishment were prepared by the British Singaporean authority, a Japanese interpreter working for the police leaked the information to the three Japanese.

One of them, Ryōhei Uchida, left suddenly for Hong Kong, whereas the remaining two, Torazō Miyazaki, Sun's close ally who introduced many influential Japanese senior officials to Sun, and Kōshichirō Kiyofuji, wrote a letter to Kang that they had come with friendly intentions, that Miyazaki was an adherent of Count Okima and Count Itayaki, and that their party was very strong in Japan (TNA FO 17/1718, nos. 341–349).[27] On the following night, the Singapore police arrested Miyazaki and Kiyofuji and found two swords, a dagger, and over $27,000 in Hong Kong and Shanghai bank notes. These two men were also sending and receiving telegrams by cipher. On July 11, the Executive Council of Singapore decided to banish the two Japanese for five years and they were sent away at once for Hong Kong. Both men had made false statements about their identity and said that they had come to Singapore to see Kang, who was well-known in Japan, to hear what he thought about current affairs in China.

A couple of days later five people arrived by ship from Saigon, comprising of Sun Yat-sen and four Japanese, including Kang Youwei's invitee, Nako Nisi Ju Taro [sic]. Singapore authorities denied Sun access to Kang. Interviewed by Singapore British officers, Sun said that the money Miyazaki and Kiyofuji had carried belonged to him, and that he intended to engage Kang and Kang's supporters to support Sun's party and rebellions in China, especially in Canton.

The British authorities in Singapore knew that Sun intended to buy arms and ammunition in Hong Kong, Saigon, and probably Singapore. "Probably at Singapore Mr Sun-Yat-Sen did desire to arrange for joint action with Kang-Yu-Wei [Kang Youwei], and possibly Miyasaki's and Kiofuji's [sic] object was to obtain Kang-Yu-Wei's head (and the reward therefore [100,000 taels, about $120,000!]) if he failed to join Mr Sun Yat Sen's party with all his influence".[28]

In 1896–1897 during his eight months' stay in London, while reading diligently at the British Museum Library, Sun Yat-sen made personal contacts, including some among Russian political exiles including Felix Volkhovsky (1846–1914), editor of *Free Russia*, who endured imprisonment and solitary confinement in Russia and escaped to Canada and later settled in London in 1890. Both met in London no later than March 1897; Volkhovsky inspired Sun to pursue a hazardous revolutionary career and wage violent revolution in China (Wilbur, 1976). Together with his own reading, Sun became:

> convinced that revolution, in some form or another, was a universal process. His first week in London had impressed him with the immensity of Europe's accomplishment, but when he left nine months later he realized that the industrial revolution had not been beneficial to all segments of Western society. … The signs of the coming turmoil and class strife were all around him: Socialists and Fabians in Britain, Populists and Single-taxers in American – all were protesting against the unjust distribution of wealth.
>
> (Schiffrin, 1968, pp. 136–137)

Attempts to simultaneously solve the problems of socialism, nationalism, and democracy have not been successful in China during the last one and a half centuries. The Declaration of the Guomindang (KMT) First National Congress made by Sun Yat-sen on January 31, 1924, denounced foreign treaty rights in China:

> All Unequal Treaties (*yiqie bupingdeng tiaoyue*), including foreign concessions, consular jurisdiction, foreign management of customs services, and all

foreign political rights exercised on China's soil, are detrimental to China's sovereignty. They all ought to be abolished so as to leave the way open for new treaties based on the spirit of bilateral equality and mutual respect for sovereignty.

(Wang, 2005, ch. 2)

In an interview with a Japanese journalist in November 1924, Sun urged Japan to assist China in its efforts to abolish the unfair treaties and national humiliation:

Since the 1911 Revolution, China has been in chaos. China's disintegration is not the fault of the Chinese, but, instead, is caused exclusively by foreigners. Why? The answer lies in the 'Unequal Treaties' between China and foreign countries … In recent years, Westerners in China have gone even beyond the 'Unequal Treaties' to abuse their treaty rights … At present, China's abrogating of those treaties is dependent upon the sympathy of the Japanese people.[29]

The "oppressors" before 1912 had in Sun Yat-sen's own words been the "Manchu bandits" (Cantlie and Jones, 1912), in 1923–1924 they were "foreigners", and Sun solicited support from Japan, a major beneficiary of the unequal treaties, to have them abolished. According to Sun's political autobiography published in English in 1897, the original essence of the anti-Qing political movement was "the establishment of a form of constitutional government to supplement the old-fashioned, corrupt, and worn-out system under which China is groaning". "The idea was to bring about a peaceful reformation, and we hoped, by forwarding modest schemes of reform to the Throne, to initiate a form of government more consistent with modern requirements" (Sun, 1897, p. 131).

In late 1896/1897, while in London, devoid of anti-Manchu racial terms, Sun publicized his deep appreciation to Britain, its people, and free press in newspapers in English for saving his life:

> Sir, will you kindly express through your columns my keen appreciation of the action of the British Government in effecting my release from the Chinese Legation? I have also to thank the Press generally for their timely help and sympathy. If anything were needed to convince me of the generous public spirit which pervades Great Britain, and the love of justice which distinguishes its people, the recent acts of the last few days have conclusively done so. ... Knowing and feeling more keenly than ever what a constitutional Government and an enlightened people mean, I am prompted still more actively to pursue the cause of advancement, education, and civilization in my own well-beloved but oppressed country.
>
> (Sun, 1897, pp. 133–134)

Sun had "little talent for finding the bayonets", in Arthur N. Holcombe's words in 1930. It was "Bolshevists from Russia who showed his followers how to transform his idea into a revolution which could take the field in force and rout its enemies" (Holcombe, 1930, p. 156). Commencing in summer 1920, the Soviet Government reoriented its focus to spread Communism on East Asia where "the imperialist Powers were more exposed to attack and less capable of defending themselves". Great Britain became the first target of Bolshevism in China because it had greater interest than any other country. The successful revolution in Outer Mongolia, the ensuing founding of the Mongolian Soviet Republic, and the incorporation of Siberia into the Russian Soviet system in 1921 cleared the way for a more aggressive infiltration of Soviet agents in the disintegrated China.

Adolf Joffe, Soviet Russian diplomat, and Michael Borodin/Grusenberg/Berg, an experienced Russian revolutionary agitator, met and worked on Sun Yat-sen in 1922–1923 who was at perhaps the lowest point of his political life, short of money, and just expelled from Canton by the military operations led by Guangdong Governor, Cheng Jiongming (1875–1933). Unlike Sun, Chen was in favor of the US-style federal government in China, rather than a highly centralized, unified China. Under the guidance of Borodin and with the closest attention from the Communist International and the Soviet Government, Sun permitted the fledgling Chinese Communist Part (CCP) to join his own party Kuomintang (KMT) to agitate the masses, launch workers' strikes, peasant uprisings, propaganda training, and military campaigns. A new militant party-state order was thus created in Canton, modeled on the Soviet Russia's dictatorship. It was one state, one party, and one voice, in a word (Fitzgerald, 1996, ch. 5).

Soviet Russia, along with the Third International – the Comintern – not only laid down the basic revolutionary strategies for the CCP, but also provided the GMD with a modern party ideology. The emergence of new political groupings and expressions, including imperialism, warlordism, colonialism, semi-colonialism, and semi-feudalism, had direct links with the Russian Bolshevik theory of world revolution. To Sun, Lenin's theories of a worldwide revolution, nationalist movement, and united front provided sound explanations of and political solutions to the problems facing China. In his eulogy of the Russian leader, Sun called Lenin a "National Friend and People's Mentor".[30]

But Sun's transformation to "governing the state through the party" (yidang zhiguo 以黨治國) "against the republic and democracy" (Qin, 1989, vol. 2, p. 130; Luo, 1954, p. 81) also had its origins in his stubborn pursuit of national unity and his suppression of different voices within his own Nationalist Party (KMT, banned in 1913 by Yuan Shikai in the North). As part of the reorganization, in July 1914, Sun Yat-sen formed a new party in Tokyo, Japan, Zhonghua Gemingdang (Chinese Revolutionary Party), that lasted until October 10, 1919, when it was regrouped into the KMT in Shanghai's French Concession. The Chinese Revolutionary Party's membership required a signed written oath of allegiance to the party. Sun stated that it was "a secret society, not a political party. All those overseas could still use the KMT name, but with changed content and organization" (ibid).

Structurally, as the sole premier of the new party, Sun placed this recast organization's political, financial, general, military, and party affairs branches directly under himself and *above* the Examination, Monitoring, Executive, Judicial, and Legislative Councils of the Nationalist state. The construction of a new party was "especially enforcing compliance of the party head ... All members must pledge that they are willing to sacrifice their own life and individual free rights. They must obey orders" (Luo, 1954, p. 2).[31] Sun also demanded that all Hongmen (Masonic secret societies) in Singapore must obey him, the party chief, as "the only condition of the Zhonghua Gemingdang" (Luo, 1954, Sun, 1914, pp. 16–17).

Highly critical of Sun's character and his alignment with Soviet Russian Bolshevism as well as the Chinese Communist Party (Tse, 1924; Tse, 1937), Tse in the Chinese version of his terse secret history of the 1911 Revolution toned down his disapproval of Sun's "rash" disposition and highlighted their divergent ideals – "Tse Tsan Tai and Sun Yat-sent were in good relations, but regrettably their mission objectives were different. Sun was pro-Russian Bolshevism and aligned with the Communist Party to achieve world revolutions. In contract, Tse insisted to emulate the U.S.-French type of united people's republican government to advance the realm of humans and peace and happiness for the realization of one world" (Tse, 1937a, p. 4; Figure 2, Tse spelled out he and Sun Yat-sen's main differences).

In 1914, Tse Tsan Tai took pride in presenting a very different worldview, a religious and ethnic promotion of peace and one world, while Sun embarked on a path of one party, one state, and one voice that has been swirling mainland China into autocratic and unsustainable futures to this day.

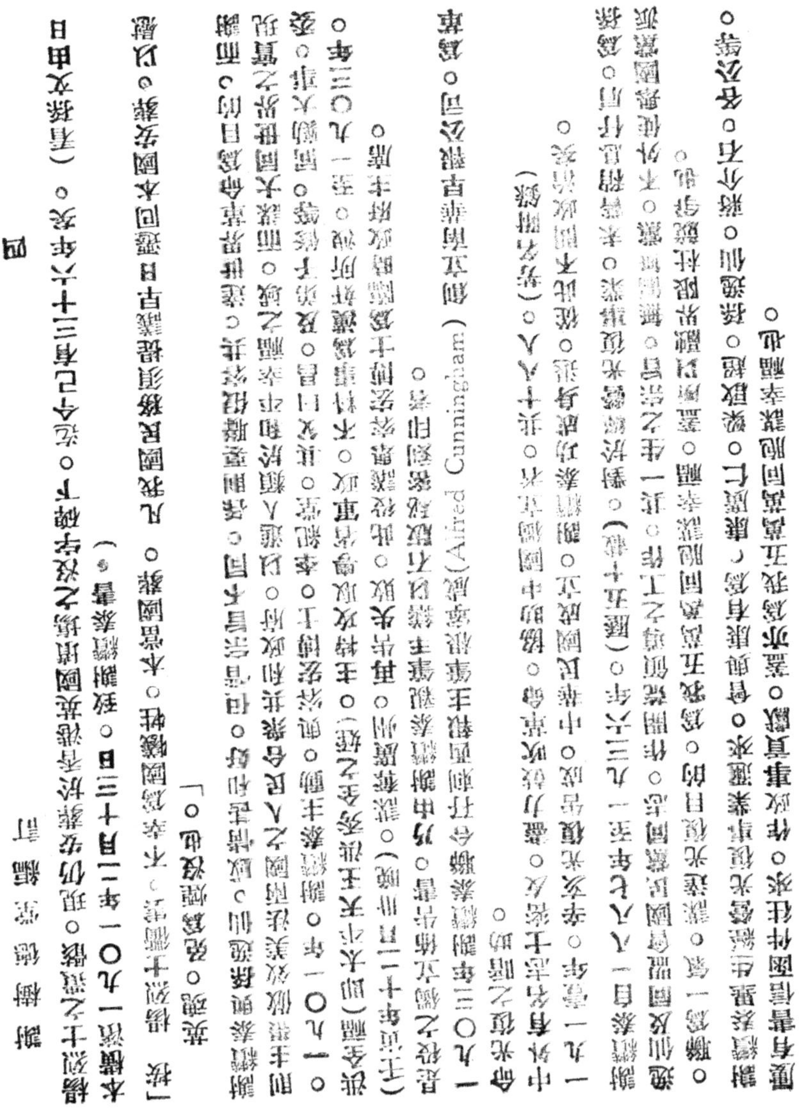

Figure 2 Tse Tsan Tai's and Sun Yat-sen's divergent political ideals in 1937. Source: Tse, 1937a, p. 4.

3
"The world's great problem solved"[32]

The Ancient translators and commentators of Genesis wrongfully located "Eden" in Armenia and Mesopotamia, because they were ignorant of the geography of the World, and the existence of China and other vast continents. ... The Ancients in their ignorance imagined that Mesopotamia and Asia Minor was the whole world.

---Tse, 1920b

This war in Europe ... is so ghastly and so calamitous, that men will desire rest not only for a century but perhaps till the end of the world. ... The pendulum of the world's thought has swung far over to the other side that of international conciliation and universal brotherhood of a few years ago.

– Reid, April & October 1915 (Reid, 1921, p. 289, p. 291)

Mr Frank N. Meyers, of the Bureau of Plant Industry, Department of Agriculture, Washington, D.C., who recently made explorations in the Kansu [Gansu] Province of China, reports the discovery three of what he believes to be the original home of the

> apple, plum, apricot, etc. This discovery, if confirmed, will afford further evidence of the great antiquity of China's people and civilization, and support the theory that mankind originated in Chinese Turkestan, as set forth in Mr Tse Tsan Tai's recent book, "The Creation: The Real Situation of Eden, and the origin [sic] of the Chinese".
>
> – Hongkong Daily Press, March 26, 1915

In November 1914 when Tse Tsan Tai finished his *The Creation* essay in seven days and seven nights, he wrote to his art collection client Sir James Lockhart, enthusiastically relating his "scientific" discovery of the location of the Garden of Eden, which was "the death blow to the Darwinian [sic] theory of the origin of species and the Ascent of Man" (Tse, November 24, 1914, letter 81).

Since antiquity, the real site of that paradise has been intriguing people to look for. St Augustine did it, and so did medieval monks, John Calvin, Christopher Columbus, Mesopotamian archaeologists, German Baptist ministers, British irrigation engineers, and the first president of Boston University (Wilensky-Lanford, 2011). All started with the same brief Biblical verses, but each ended up, respectively, in Berlin (Germany), California, Chinese Turkestan, Ethiopia, Florida, Iraq, Israel, Missouri, the North Pole, Ohio, Somalia, Sri Lanka, Syria, and more (Wilensky-Lanford, 2011). The relevant scripture verses are in Chapter 2 of Genesis:

> And the Lord God planted a garden in Eden, in the east, and there he put the man whom he had formed. ... A river flowed out of Eden to water the garden, and there it divided and became four rivers.
>
> (Bible, Genesis 2:8 and 2:10)

Tse believed Eden was a real place, but it was in a spurt of divine inspiration in late 1914 that it dawned upon him that Eden was in Chinese Turkistan, today's Xinjiang. On October 28, in British Hong Kong, he sat up all night and finished the draft of his very short book of forty-seven pages, *The Creation*, mapping the Book of Genesis as thunders bolted, and as World War I raged in Europe. The revision and rewriting took him seven days and seven nights – "without God's inspiration and help it would have been impossible for me to write this book as I have done". After all, God created the world in six days and rested for one day.

On March 10, 1915, the *Town and Country Journal* in Sydney, Australia also introduced Tse's influential work *The Creation. The Real Situation of Eden and the Origin of the Chinese*:

> In a little book published in Hongkong an attempt is made to prove that the Garden of Eden was situated in Chinese Turkestan, and not in the Euphrates Valley, as archaeologists hold. … The book is written by Tse Tsan Tai, otherwise James See, who is a native of Sydney.
>
> (Tse, flyer, 1915b)

Five historical situations

How can we explain Tse's work on the Garden of Eden and the origins of humans? Tse's *The Creation* of 1914 is an interesting historical source that yields insights arising from five historical situations.

First, human origins emerged as an important scientific and religious question during Tse's day. The rise of archaeology in the late nineteenth century placed the human self at the apex of evolution and kindled an iconoclastic inclination to destroy false traditional interpretations in search of the authentic, universal truth about oneself and others (Wang, 2020a).

The rational, secular, empirical, and dispassionate gaze on the world bore in it immense technological opportunities and virtually unlimited ability to expand human knowledge. In 1894 Tse Tsan Tai invented a dirigible airship and named it "China" (Tse, 1937c). An active participant in the intellectual pursuit of his age, Tse kept abreast of innumerable sciences, and believed that all "men have the right to think independently, and to use their own brains instead of being bound hard and fast by the opinions of others, no matter how great they may be in the world of Geology and Science" (Tse, 1917b).

Second, the turn of the twentieth century witnessed the ever-growing fascination with Central Asia, including Chinese Turkestan (Xinjiang), in the rise of new disciplines like geopolitics and Asian studies, and a determination to explore them through Asian historical sources. Geopolitics came of age as a field of study in 1904 when Halford John Mackinder (1861–1947), a British academic and politician, read his influential polemic, "The Geographical Pivot of History", to the Royal Geographical Society. Mackinder presented two major themes of world history in a pithy formulation: First, during the post-Columbian age, "every explosion of social forces … will be sharply re-echoed from the far side of the globe". Second, he stressed the central importance of what he regarded as the global heartland, the core expanse of Eurasia, in the "life of world organism" (Wang, 2020a, ch. 2, pp. 100–103). But most importantly, Mackinder laid bare dynamics that eerily portended Japan's victory over Russia later in the same year, and opened up new debates on power relationships both in Eurasia, Central Asia, and East Asia.

These developments also influenced Tse's way of looking at those regions; for him, the crux was to understand the Chinese nation in this context. It felt natural for Tse to examine the world order in terms of national origins, following patterns described well by scholars – "Archaeology has been conscripted frequently to validate cultural borders and ancestry, often in the service of dangerous nationalist mythologies…Given that ethnicity and nationalism are such powerful forces n modern Europe, it is crucial for anthropologists to understand the historical processes through which identities are constructed and transformed by competing the ways in which the distant past is marshaled as a symbolic resource authenticity and continuity" (Dietler, 1994, p. 585). In Tse's words, "I have been working to reconcile Science and Religion for the past 25 years – all for the honour of God and the Holy Bible" (Tse, 1937a). He was keen to bring together visions of power, the science of human origins, and the Chinese nation into one universal truth that transcends individual and partisan interest.

Third, Tse reconciled his Christian faith with patriotic love for China and its antiquities – on the one hand, applying scientific and rational inquiry to underpin Christianity through innovative reading of the Bible and, on the other, by associating notions of civilization and savageness, as well as contemporary ethnography's scientific categories of race with proximity to God, for example, being the "chosen people", relative rank in the descent from Adam or Noah, by baptism and faith, or, in my view most importantly, in terms of sin and redemption. He argued that Europe had sinned against "universal peace" and the "brotherhood of man". Revealing the geographical location of Eden, together with relative closeness to God, proven with archaeology, geology, and all other modern sciences was essential for defining a nation's real claim to greatness. Lifting the argument out of human strife with reference to incontrovertible scientific fact and to the scripture to reach "universal peace" and a true "brotherhood of man" was a most important driver for Tse.

In many ways, Tse echoed a trend toward universalism and spirituality that had gained momentum among global elites in the American Gilded Age and Europe's Belle Époque in the last decades of the nineteenth century and lasted until World War I. Tse, in fact, added a further layer of complexity, for his colonial cosmopolitanism and Chinese nationalism made him at once both civilized and universal; his contribution to colonial synarchy was indispensable, yet he refocused, at least rhetorically, the morals of the West, moved the geographical origins of humanity closer to China and claimed that the Chinese by birthright were closer to the Biblical patriarch Noah, and by implication Adam, than the Europeans.

Fourth, Tse's book drew on people's desperation for hope at a time when war and peace weighed heavily on their minds.[33] He provided solace and rational explanations for free-spirited Christian minds across the world. Christians like Tse Tsan Tai in British Hong Kong and American missionary reformer Gilbert Reid (1857–1927) in the then young Republic of China (1912–present) were drawn to offer biblical solutions to the "unparalleled" war for "its worldwide catastrophe" through emphasizing common humanity and severing the Christian faith from militarism. "The war spirit, like electricity, has encircled the globe.... The weapons of death are unsurpassed for ferocity and horror" (Reid, 1921, p. 278; Martin, 1896).

As Austria, Russia, Germany, Britain, Belgium, and France entered the Great War with each other, many wondered why Christianity and the Great War seemed "to be boon companions, when they ought to be foes" (Reid, 1921, p. 281). Reid argued it was a fallacy to call European civilizations Christian, although a large part of the former has "come from Christianity, but Roman law, Greek ideas, Teutonic, Slavonic, and other characteristics, many other influences, have all entered in to form what is known as European or Western civilization". All the nations at war did so "without regard to Christianity" because national interests rather than the behests of religion compelled them to act. War was "the work of diplomats and the outcome of militarists" (Reid, 1921, pp. 281–282).

Reid again stressed the importance to discriminate the conflict between the spirit of the age, militarism, and armaments and the spirit of Christ, patience, forbearance, meekness, gentleness, long-suffering, compassion, love, and forgiveness. Distinction should be made between "national prosperity imbued with Christian principles from that which follows the teachings of the great Powers of the world" and "Christianity organized as the Christian Church and Christianity as a teaching of truth" (Reid, 1921, pp. 284–286). In other words, governments in Europe should be blamed for war crimes, according to Reid. "Peace amongst the nations might never come, if only man was in the problem. But God reigns, and his breath breathed into human lives will vivify the hopeless cause. We look for the return of Christ, not perhaps as the ascended Nazarene, but as a Spirit of Power and Love, and He will change the course of history. ... If China wants to learn, let her learn not the form of Christianity now being displayed in the European war, but the form lived by 'the meek and lowly Jesus,' whose personal character stands forth blameless" (Reid, 1921, p. 289).

Tse's claim that God was punishing Europe in World War I, echoed the above wider perception in the Christian church, but his attitude toward African Americans was racial and racist in today's world. By denouncing European war crimes, he divided the world into the civilized and savages along new lines: "And, instead of killing and exterminating them (the savages of the World) in wars of conquest, and robbing them of their possessions – eventually leading to fratricidal wars amongst themselves – it is their (the Christian nations of Europe) duty to educate and civilize them, as the ... Southern States of The United States have been educated and civilized, and to place them on the same plane as themselves" (Tse, 1914).

Inverting the then popular perceptions of civilization and savagery, he opened the way for divine recognition as the "chosen". His location of the Garden of Eden at Lop Nur (in Chinese Turkestan) was based on matching geographical and geological features with a few verses in the Bible. Superficial similarity between names (Shinar versus China, Noah versus Nüwa) in the Bible and in Chinese ancient texts provided evidence, while incongruities often resulted in misunderstandings.[34]

Fifth, criticism of Tse's *The Creation* by his contemporaries was abundant, to which Tse responded in self-defense but attempted to palliate the bitter disputes by "humbly" asking for the "indulgence of all scientists and geologists … owing to the tone of the language which he has been obliged to adopt in replying to the attacks of hostile critics" (Tse, 1915b). He repeatedly explained that his conclusions were not definitive and remained open for further proof. The trappings of dispassionate academic discourse, that is, the consistent reference to "facts" and other evidence, and reference to higher principles in scholarship and religion, which he presumed to be common knowledge, in general gave him an advantage in newspaper debates.

Tse's works and ways of publicizing them came close to James Leibold's observation about Chinese discourses at the time: "The Republican-era's rich intellectual milieu included a wide variety of strategies for obtaining modernity: some were co-opted by the Chinese state(s) and others were marginalized … While many of these narratives crossed political divides, the competitive nature of state power forced different actors to modify and differentiate their approaches, reorganizing the heterogeneity of the nation to ultimately arrive at the same unified national imaginary. What was different about early twentieth-century China was not the use of tradition to create different typologies of human variation, but rather the use of new technologies of scientific classification to reorder and historicize humans within the finite and geographically bounded communities that formed the basis of the modern nation-state system" (Leibold, 2007, p. 115).

In the case of Tse's 1914 work, these disciplines helped legitimate the transformation of the formerly peripheral region into an integral component of a unitary geographical polity. Yet Tse did more than invent such a history of the Han Chinese as a modern nation on the basis of a unified *modern* template of nationhood, for he asserted its universal moral and religious primacy above and in contrast with other nations.

How did Chinese empires survive? Or rather, how was it possible for a geographical entity the size of the Qing to morph into a nation? Leibold suggests that "[a]mong the large agrarian empires of the 19th century, China alone survived the transition from empire to nation-state with its territory largely intact, resisting the spatial fracturing experienced by the Austro-Hungarian, Ottoman, Prussian and Russian empires. It did this by successfully stretching, in the words of Benedict Anderson, 'the short, tight skin of the nation over the gigantic body of the empire'" (Leibold, 2016). As an idea, an imagined community it did, and Tse certainly contributed significantly to this complex nation-state–building process, despite the chaos in the aftermath of the 1911 Revolution, including Outer Mongolia's secession and later demand for national self-determination, and the fracturing of political control in the first half of the twentieth-century China.

Creation myths, nationalism, and sino-centrism

Paralleling biblical and Chinese mythologies in *The Creation* as Tse did is not a claim for similarity, but a claim for identity. The Chinese myth is described as an *equally valid* transmission of the very same origin event that the Bible narrates. The Chinese heritage, by implication, is of equal authenticity and has equal authority, so it complements the biblical account. Nations (民族), etymologically referring to ancestral descent, conventionally need origin myths for their legitimization, to serve as a starting point for their histories. As nationhood merges with statecraft, history becomes a guide for political action, where previous societies may have relied on divination and belief in fate. The nation's need for history as a record of continuity and a mirror for rulers arises because rulers legitimate their actions in an unpredictable world riddled with contingencies confounding the need to maintain stability, fight enemies, recognize established rights, and modify equitably social relations. At the core of any nation is a history against which to gauge and legitimize the present. To paraphrase historian Timothy D. Snyder, the predicament of the present provides an occasion to go back to history and see what the situations were (Snyder, 2022). At the very juncture posing itself with the new Republic in 1912, Tse's instinct was to *internationalize* the national origin myth and to make a moral claim beyond warfare and against powers relying on military conquest.

The biblical patriarchs Abraham, Isaac, and Jacob, who embodied God's designation of the Jews as the "Chosen People" and formed their descent line, were in themselves of little help to Tse's argument, so he identified three ancestors from the Chinese myth and superimposed them onto the biblical figures – Adam (Tianhuang), Cain (Dihuang), and Seth (Renhuang), from whose lines five patriarchs of the Chinese nation descended: Henoch (Fuxi Taihao), Noah (Nüwa), Shem (Shennong), Arphaxad (Huangdi), and Reu (Yao). In Tse's formulation, the Chinese, and so Tse, descended from Shem, Noah's oldest son, as the Jews, God's chosen people, did (Tse, 1914, pp. 24, 31). "The Modern European nations, whose ancestors did not become thoroughly civilized, until the advent of Jesus Christ", by contrast, descended from Japhet, Noah's youngest son. Tse argued that Christians were therefore later, after the crucifixion of Jesus, at Pentecost, when the disciples were chosen by God to bring the gospel to all peoples of the world[35] (Tse, 1914, pp. 22, 26, 39ff).

A Christian dreamer of one humanity with Chinese nationalistic bent, Tse in his study of Genesis and the Chinese creation mythology brought China's early civilization to a prime position. Primacy involves the moral duty of universality, that is, universal peace and the brotherhood of man. "And, when the nations and governments of the World have reached a state fit to be Federated, I hope and pray that China will take the lead in turning the 'Garden of Eden,' i.e. 'Chinese Turkestan, into an 'International State,' and that the Parliament of Nations will be established there (in China)" (Tse, 1914, pp. 34–35, 32ff). Thus, Tse intervened with a biblically and historically inspired moral mission for the emerging Chinese national identity. This point has not been given due attention in our contemporary discourse yet (Zarrow, 2012, ch. 5).

In his work on the Garden of Eden, Tse Tsan Tai obviously rejected secularization and atheism and elevated Christianity as the fountain of mind. In many ways Tse went further than the national foundation myths that began to take shape in eighteenth- and nineteenth-century Europe.

As in other places of the world, in Europe, root-seeking scholars and poets had trawled old sagas, chronicles, eposes, and ballads to, on the model of Rome's Romulus and Remus myth, construct a shared imaginary past for their own people. From high culture expressions of the nation like the Ring des Nibelungen and the Kalevala to kids' bedside stories about King Arthur or Barbarossa, nations used what was needed to distinguish themselves from each other and in their relations with church and Christianity. Of course, the core of the Old Testament links two myths, the cosmological creation myth (Genesis) and the foundation myth of the Jewish people (the Books of Moses), in potential yet unspoken conflict with nationalism – national myths largely emerged as marks of uniqueness within Christianity.

What happened when the need for distinct nationhood moved beyond Europe? In Japan, popular interest in, for example, the *Kojiki* written in 712 (古事記 Records of Ancient Matters) and the *Nihon Shoki* (日本書紀 Chronicles of Japan) written in 720 was rekindled and fulfilled the need for national narratives in the late nineteenth century. In China, a multitude of ancient myths, like the one on Pan Gu (盤古) which Tse was to focus on, were widely popularized as distinctive national treasures (Wang, 2020b). However, the nationalist ferment in China in the 1880s and 1890s had begun to instrumentalize religion for its political project. According to Peter Zarrow, Huang Zunxian (1848–1905, Qing Chinese minister to Japan 1898) believed that "Christianity in essence and, in all, about 70% of Western learning were derived from [the sage of Chinese antiquity] Mozi". Chen Huanzhang (1880–1933), who founded the Confucius Academy in 1930, ranked Confucianism "as a spiritual system on a par with Christianity and other world religions" (Zarrow, 2012, pp. 21, 252).

Tse Tsan Tai undertook to explain in detail the Chinese origin myths as essentially identical to the Jewish and Christian Genesis. He comprehensively integrated creation, genealogy, national origin, cataclysmic events, geographic location, historicity, and scientific truth in the form of a "revelation" aimed both at a Chinese and a global audience.

First, he believed that the Garden of Eden was in "Chinese Turkestan" and mapped the biblical description to the features of the Tarim Basin, near Lop Nur. But he showed no awareness that similarities between Christian Genesis and Chinese myth might have had parallels of a similar nature elsewhere.

Take the symbol of the wolf and the creation legends linked to Türkiye, the city of Rome, and the Roman Kingdom as an example – the Ergenekon or Bozkurt (Gray Wolf) legend was connected to the founding of the Turkish Republic in 1923. A similar fantasy can be found in Roman mythology – the Capitoline Wolf (La Lupa Capitolina) and the suckling twin founders of Rome, Romulus and Remus.

Second, according to Tse, the descent of the first ancestors Adam, Cain, and Seth led on to Noah (Nüwa 女媧) and his sons Shem (神農炎帝 Shennong Yandi), Ham, and Japher. After the Deluge, for which he referred to the floods of Chinese legends and geological seabed sediments at great altitude in China's northwest, humanity divided into three branches. The Chinese, alongside, for instance, the Assyrians, Persians, Babylonians, Hebrews, Manchus, Japanese, and the "races of Northern India" descended from Shem. The "Hindoo," Arabian, "and other kindred nations" descended from Ham. The descendants of Noah's third son Japhet "established the Modern European nations, whose ancestors did not become thoroughly civilized until the advent of Jesus Christ" (Tse, 1914, p. 22). "What I seek to prove is that mankind has originated from the same source, and that the Chinese, and likewise the Jews, are of Shemitic or Semitic stock, and that both came from the district south of the Yellow River Bend", the heartland of the Chinese civilization (Tse, 1915b, p. 5).

The fusion of the myths established a new genealogy of civilization, by which the Chinese nation ranked high, alongside the Jewish, eclipsing, so to say, European civilization and by implication Western powers' claim to Christianity. Did the claim to civilization arise from military might, from higher moral principles and piety, or from closeness, by descent, to God? Tse's claims were in line with debates at the time. He rallied "scientific evidence" in ways that already irked missionaries and other clergy of all denominations, whose recourse to catechisms and church dogma floundered, and were not uncommon in the rich mixture of professional and amateur scholarship as well as charlatanism that filled the scope between, on the one hand, general and special relativity and, on the other, pyramidology with hopes of a unified scientific explanation of the universe. Tse wove his biblical and scientific evidence into fluent reasoning, where beliefs and assumptions seamlessly morphed into scientific truths, which he defended to the hilt in polemic battles (Tse, 1915b, 1917, 1918, 1919, 1920, 1922, and 1923).

Tse's Christianity and nationalism boldly asserted the Chinese nation's primogeniture to the Christian dominion, its moral supremacy over sinful Europe that had just, in 1914, descended into fratricidal war, and its territorial claim to Christianity's place of origin. The little book in which he reclaimed the Garden of Eden for China was dedicated to "all who are working for Universal Peace and the Brotherhood of Man" (Tse, 1914, p. v).

Unlike many other creation stories such as the biblical narrative in Old Testament that originally belongs to the Jewish tradition, no Chinese creation myth or epic recounted ancient folk migrations. In Chinese mythology, "the cosmos was accepted as a given, requiring no explanation" (Hucker, 1975, p. 22). It did reveal early agricultural, technological development, and cultural sages who brought coherence to the construction of Chinese nationalism in later times. By contrast, the Japanese counterpart, as seen in *Kojiki* (Records of ancient matters) written in 712 CE, portrayed a polytheist mythic world that helped establish the unique character of the Yamato clan who founded the early Japanese state (Wang, 2020b).

Tse Tsan Tai's effort to unify Christian and Chinese imaginings of cosmological, human, and national origins drew its content out of universal narratives reaching millennia back into prehistory. Tropes found in Greek myths are also manifest in Beowulf and Gilgamesh. Early Christianity absorbed aspects of Mithras and Sol Invictus rites, while it is impossible to clearly distinguish the origins of shamanism and the many mutually inspired faiths cohabiting the Eurasian continent. Many a national storyteller rummaged through humanity's shared baggage of tales to assemble the unique origins of their national descent from well-worn clichés. Those involved did not see the irony of nations gaining their one and only beginning by donning the universal cloak of nationalism. If anything, by imagining the overlaps between myths, Tse was ultimately able to rally the rich font of incredibly old stories to forge a vision of a Chinese civilization that was "more" worthy and established than others, a civilization perhaps not about to realize that it was in reality the mainstay of Christianity, but which he imagined as having a high moral mission to make the world peaceful and turn it into a "brotherhood of man".

4
Where business, culture, politics, and advocacy converged

In 1983, on the eightieth anniversary of the *South China Morning Post* (SCMP) as the oldest surviving paper in Hong Kong, Robin Hutcheon, SCMP editor in chief from 1967 to 1986, honored its cofounder Tse Tsan Tai in praise of his all-round talents:

> Tse's ambitions were boundless, and his ability fully matched them. Though reforms in China was his chief interest, he had the makings of a Chinese Galileo. … he befriended the most prominent men of his times, both Chinese and Europeans … He was an advocate of so many causes that a list assumes almost encyclopedic proportions … He also developed a keen business acumen and made a sufficiently large income to support his wife, five sons and six daughters in a town residence in Queen's Road East with a country estate in the New Territories.
>
> (Hutcheon, 1983, pp. 11–12)

Along the above lines, this chapter looks further into the intersection of politics and social advocacy as exhibited by Tse in British Hong Kong.

In China at the turn of the twentieth century, foreign works in Japanese, English, Russian, French, German, and other languages carried the authority of modernity: "They were relevant to Chinese interests; they circulated via modern media enabled by new print technologies; and, they reached far beyond the treaty ports through newly developing distribution networks" (Wagner, 2012). Tse Tsan Tai belonged to such networks of modern men and women whose interests often converged in unexpected ways.

Around 1900, after ten years in the British Hong Kong government, Tse switched to private business and met British journalist Alfred Cunningham (1870–1918), who shared the same passion for reforms in China. In 1903, both men founded the *South China Morning Post* (SCMP) Ltd, a joint stock company, with Cunningham as the general manager and Tse as its comprador, an important commercial intermediary. The initial three-person board of directors comprised influential businessmen – Arthur G. Ward of the Victoria Lithographic Company, G. W. Playfair, chief manager of the National Bank of China established in 1891, and Creasy Evens, a solicitor (King and Clarke, 1965, pp. 72–73; Hutcheon, 1983, p. 12). In 1913, ten years after its founding, the SCMP for the first time declared a profit of over $11,000 (Hutcheon, 1983, p. 42).

To Tse, the power of the press was all too apparent. Tse knew and corresponded with almost all distinguished journalists and publicists of the day, among whom were George Ernest Morrison (1862–1920), *The Times* of London correspondent, "sage adviser" to Yuan Shikai, first president of the ROC, and opinion shaper on China at the turn of the twentieth century (Lo, 1976); Dr Timothy Richard, a British missionary, deeply involved in Chinese politics and modernization effort; D. Warres Smith of the *Hongkong Daily Press*; Alfred Cunningham; B. A. Hale, editor of the *China Mail*; Thomas Petrie; and Chesney Duncan (1854–1935), editor of the *Hongkong Telegraph* (1895–1899) and *Strait Echo* (Penang, 1903, 1905), correspondent of the *London Globe*, *Japan Gazette*, *Shanghai Mercury*, and the *China Times*.

Who was talking to whom, and how did they perceive themselves and each other through self-identification? What was their common and different point of reference?

Collector, dealer, and promoter of antiquities protection[36]

Among many identities, Tse Tsan Tai was also a principal art collecting agent and dealer for Sir James Stewart Lockhart (1858–1937), a successful British colonial officer in Hong Kong, Guangdong, and Weihaiwei (today's Weihai, Shandong Province) for over forty years. From 1895 to 1902, Lockhart held a senior post in charge of the administration in Hong Kong as Colonial Secretary and was posted as commissioner to British-leased territory, Weihaiwei, from 1902 to 1927. In Sir Lockhart's papers on his Chinese painting collection, Tse stood out conspicuously as Lockhart's early agent and main consultant. Lockhart found Tse's taste of art "excellent" and "reliable" (Lockhart's letter to Tse, June 18, 1912, letter 47 draft; Lightfoot, 2008, p. 149).

Both men corresponded regularly from 1910 to 1917 about Chinese art collecting. Tse was introduced to Sir Lockhart, then Registrar General of Hong Kong in 1887, shortly after he at the age of sixteen had arrived in Hong Kong from Sydney, together with his mother and five siblings. Tse recalled: "My father's old friends welcomed us all ashore, and we quickly found ourselves at home in a strange city with strange surroundings". He was well received by Sir Lockhart who "advised me to enter Queen's College preparatory to joining the Hongkong Government service" (Tse, 1924, Biographical Sketch).[37]

With classical and sinological training, Lockhart took a serious interest in collecting Chinese paintings, ink rubbings, and decorative art, and in 1910 appreciated receiving an album with views of Mount Tai (the sacred mountain in Shandong) and Confucian birthplace nearby, which Tse's brother, on Tse Tsan Tai's suggestion, had sent him, inviting Lockhart to preface a print publication of the collection. Tse agreed to help Lockhart find some cartoons for his collection. "Since the publication of my Political Cartoon (1899) I have not repeated the exploit! … I intend[ed] to publish another some years ago, but knowing that it would create great offence in Chinese Official links, I schematically suppressed it". Tse explicitly blamed the Qing Chinese government's lack of free speech and civil liberty: "The Comical political papers of Europe and America could not live in China, as they would be suppressed in no time" (Tse, February 19, 1910, letter 1; Lightfoot, 2008, appendix 1).[38]

After the Republic of China was established in 1912 and no sustainable peace between North and South China was in sight, Tse again mentioned China's despotism when he sent Lockhart some thirty or so cartoons and caricatures from magazines that were out of print: "Some of the authors [of those cartoons] have already suffered the death penalty! Such is the path of the caricaturist in China! It appears that all such magazines have now been suppressed" (Tse, June 11, 1915a, letter 86; ibid).

On other occasions, Tse's advocacy of heritage preservation surfaced naturally: "Something must be done to prevent priceless 'masterpieces' from leaving the country, and to raise Chinese art from the low level to which it has fallen. … You may rest assured that I will continue to help you, privately, to add to your collection" (Tse, December 5, 1910, letter 19; ibid).

Several weeks later, Tse kept his promise by mailing some newspaper cartoons from Hong Kong to Lockhart in Weihaiwei. As a collector himself, Tse asked Lockhart whether he collected Chinese works of art because of their newly discovered value on international markets: "They are the rage now in England and on the Continent, and fetch very high prices. Some are really worth thousands of pounds each. Their real value will only be appreciated when China possesses her National Art Gallery" (Tse, April 11, 1910, letter 2; ibid).

Tse sometimes went beyond Chinese ethnonationalism and othered both China and the Chinese while touching upon his involvement in global cultural preservation: "I am really sorry for China and the Chinese, as *they* [my emphasis] do not realise the immense value of the paintings … which they are losing from year to year. … I have already advocated the formation of a Society for the protection of China's Historical relics (monuments, paintings … but the Chinese appear to be asleep)" (ibid). "My hobby has always been books and works of art," Tse wrote. And he intended to present his collection of paintings to China when "the people are ready and prepared to take proper care of them" (ibid).

Foreign democratic guardianship of Chinese art was favored: "In my opinion Chinese 'masterpieces' will not be safe until China has a Parliament and possesses an Art Gallery based upon the National Art Galleries of Europe. ... At present there is no genuine movement in China connected with Chinese art and the purchase and presentation of Chinese 'masterpieces'" (Tse, May 31, 1910, letter 4; ibid). But at other times Tse reversed such a position and resorted to Chinese patriotism. According to him, he refused to sell some of his own collected items: "They [the visiting German consul of Hong Kong alongside other dignitaries] made anxious enquiries about Chinese pictures, and even asked if I was willing to part with some of mine! ... 'They are for the Nation,' I said. I could not do anything for them" (Tse, January 27, 1912, letter 41; ibid).

As an art lover since his boyhood, Tse stepped into character in his letters to Lockhart, showing how politics and art differed. More importantly, his skills, energy, and engagement in local business and community culture were part of the British Hong Kong elite activities. Tse, with a bit of awkward candidness and sometimes humor, greatly appreciated recognition. "The German Consul D. G. Voretzsch [Dr Jur. Ernest Arthur Voretzsch, 1868–1965] invited me to his home, and showed me his pictures ... but only 2 or 3 caught my eye. ... His pictures cannot compare with yours [Lockhart's], but he says his best pictures are at home in Germany. ... But how is it possible to get really good things unless a fair price is paid for them?" (Tse, July 31, 1911, letter 28; ibid). In early 1912, Tse was happy to host a visit from Voretzsch who brought Owen Stumbel, German foreign minister, and Stumbel's sister, Fran Koch, wife of "the famous Dr Koch of Berlin" to see his pictures: "My collection is getting famous(!), but it is so troublesome to show pictures to people" (Tse, January 27, 1912, letter 41; Lightfoot, 2008, appendix 1; Duncan, 1917, p. 8).[39]

Tse was indeed personable with Lockhart, sending the latter photos of his sons and daughters. Sometimes, Tse also passed on his political judgment of British administrators in Hong Kong, such as Sir Francis Henry May (1860–1922) as "one of the best Administrators Hong Kong has ever had" (Tse, January 25, 1911, letter 23; Lightfoot, 2008, appendix 1). Tse was also proud to tell Lockhart that his daughter Po Young obtained first prize and Po Ching second prize again in February 1912, distributed by H. S. Sir F. A. Leyrid at Queens' College in Hong Kong, Tse's alma mater.

Tse joked about a slump in business: "My brothers Tom & Sam are in Hankow (Wuhan) and Shanghai, both are doing well. ... Unfortunately, none of us are millionaires yet! ... However, I think a man should be content with good health and sufficient to keep him clear of the bill-collectors – and also a hobby of – say pictures!!!" (Tse, February 11, 1914, letter 72a; ibid). We know that as of 1933, Tom (Tse Tsi-shau, Thomas A. See) had the Man Ning Patent Medicine Co. Ltd in Shanghai, with skin ointment sold through Wing On Co. Ltd, the first department store in Hong Kong and Shanghai, opened by three Australian-Cantonese brothers in 1908 and 1916 respectively.

Tse also deferred to his contemporary art historians: "I have seen Binyon and Giles' books on Chinese art but not Friedrich Huiths which is considered to be the best book places? [sic]" (Lightfoot, 2008, p. 120). Authenticity, quality, and pricing (usually $100–$500 for each piece)[40] in European and Japanese markets were the chief elements of collectability involving paintings from China's

Tang (618–907), Song (960–1279), Yuan (1271–1368), and Ming (1368–1644) dynasties that he discussed with Lockhart. Lockhart made remissions to Tse by wire or draft through the Hongkong and Shanghai Bank. The shipping of Lockhart's purchases as parcels from Tse was made by Captain Mooney on his *Chipshing*, a Jardine Company's steamer running between Hong Kong and Weihaiwei. "Please keep this business private as we cannot get *bargains* if people know what they may be worth in Europe and China at a further date that I cannot say".

Tse shared his appraisal of color quality and painting techniques: "Brush-work is wonderful – difficult to equal and impossible to excel. Each line and stroke possess spirit and form, and the magic touch of the true born genius. … The beauty of Chinese paintings is that there is no retracing, daubing, or retouching. … Each line can be traced and admired in these compositions of harmonious poetry. The ancients painted dreams! They painted the soul of nature, such as it is understood by aesthetics and poets. Even when they attempted to copy nature in figures (human), animals and birds, they never departed from the rules governing the rhythm and force of contours, lines, strokes, and dots, all requiring to be calculated to a nicety before being executed on silk or paper" (Tse, June 20, 1910, letter 5; Lightfoot, 2008, appendix 1).

In the early twentieth century, China and other places in the world drew a great deal of interest as a luscious field for archaeologists. And Tse stayed up-to-date on it: "Finds, hidden in the ground, may yet be found which will enlighten the world as to the origin, etc and of the Chinese Race" (Tse, August 9, 1910, letter 11; ibid).

In early November 1911, when the news of the fall of Beijing reached Hong Kong, Tse slowly started to imply or disclose to Lockhart his deep ties to the 1911 Revolution: "the Chinese almost went mad with excitement. The Colony [Hong Kong] was one roar (crackers and shouts) from 9 p.m. up till midnight! Never in the history of this Colony has there been such a demonstration by the Chinese". But Hong Kong suffered great financial losses due to the "stoppage of monies at Hankow [Wuhan] and Shanghai" (Tse, November 9, 1911, letter 33; ibid). In the following month, Tse revealed that he may not be able to help Lockhart with collecting because his friends "were vying me to join the Republican Government of China. … Rest assured that England will always be next my heart" (Tse, December 8, 1911, letter 34). But two weeks later on Christmas, Tse informed Lockhart that he had decided not to join the Republican Government neither in Nanjing nor in Canton, although he did not yet disclose to Lockhart his many ties to the 1911 Revolution as well as his dislike for party politics and Sun Yat-sen (Tse, December 25, 1911, letter 36; ibid).

Then, on February 15, 1912, Tse finally broke his silence with circumspect, purposely revealing his true anti-Qing revolutionary identity of 25 years, now that his political goal of a republican China was attained. Tse also reaffirmed his retirement from politics due to health which "has been undermined with anxiety and worry" (Tse, February 15, 1912, letter 42a; ibid).

Tse made this revelation to Lockhart obviously after he had learned that Sun Yat-sen voluntarily stepped down as the provisional president of the Republic of China (ROC) in Nanjing in South China, paving the way for Yuan Shikai in Beijing in North

China, the candidate preferred by Britain, to become the first official ROC president, whom Sun hoped would bring the divided South and North together. Tse must have been well-informed of current affairs and favored a peaceful transition to a united Chinese republic. The day before, he had met Hu Han-min and Sir Boshan Wei Yuk (1849–1921)[41] – "Mr Wei dresses in foreign style [without the Manchu pigtail and robe], do you know he played an important part in bringing about the bloodless independence [from Qing China in Beijing] of Kwang Tung [Guangdong]?" (Tse, February 15, 1912, letter 42a; ibid).

Tse's voluntary disclosure must have confirmed to Lockhart and other leading British civil servants in Hong Kong and China the latent risk of divided loyalties among their own Chinese civil servants and the potential pull of Chinese politics. Together with other considerations, this must have reinforced Britain's resolution to grant their Chinese civil servants the benefits and freedom to keep their majority "natives" onboard in British Hong Kong.

To Tse, Chinese nationalism and conscious and unconscious sinocentrism were necessary aspects of elite inclusion in Hong Kong. He claimed that "China's Art is indigenous", emphasizing the excellence of China's *own* ancient civilization while championing universal understanding of the East "to enable the World to properly appreciate Chinese Art" alongside the best of art in other continents:

> I hope it will be possible in the not far distant future to see the great paintings of Europe represented by the side of the great paintings of India, Persia, Japan and China. ... To quote Sir Charles J. Holmes, Director of the National Art Gallery: "Only by exhibiting the

> great painters of the East in juxtaposition with the great painters of Europe could we properly estimate, proclaim and emphasize the place of the East in the vital artistic achievement of the World".
>
> (Tse, 1928, conclusion, p. 18)

By 1917, a combination of at least two factors put an end to the Tse-Lockhart art collecting relationship: The raging "World War is still spilling the blood of the world's strongest", which affected Tse's source of procurement of art objects. The other factor was that in 1913–1914, joint foreign and Chinese efforts by, among others, Frederick McCormick, Kang Youwei, and Tse Tsan Tai himself, had moved President Yuan Shikai to repeat an existing, yet ineffectual, ban on antiquities export and private art dealings between Chinese and foreigners.

In the first three decades of the twentieth century, foreign possession and trading of Chinese antiquities highlighted the intertwined role foreigners, their Chinese associates, and foreign legal regimes played in the complex history. Most of the art protection advocates were both saviors and sinners by default, simultaneously being active Chinese art collectors and dealers, as in the case of Tse Tsan Tai and Sir James Lockhart. Both were fully aware of the situation, and several times Tse suggested collecting modern art, which was easier to obtain. Such an irony is a repeated theme in Tse's letters to Lockhart: "It is strange when the Museum … was opened at Peking on the 10th October last, China had no ancient masterpieces in exhibition. Where have they all gone to? Such a great country, and nothing to show!" Tse blamed the Chinese for "China's pitiable plight" – "It is most disgraceful, but, what can be done, if the people do not know how to value and treasure them?" (Tse, November 24, 1914, letter 81; ibid).

The territorialization of artifacts warranted government ownership. The early Chinese legal regime of cultural relics commenced in 1906 and continued through the 1930s. The profusion of illegal and legal Chinese antique markets only tapered off in the late 1940s after World War II and the founding of the People's Republic of China (PRC) (Wang, 2020a, ch. 6).

Businessman and industrialist

Tse was a resourceful entrepreneur, engaged in a great variety of business ventures. His business career was in constant change. His pre-1912 profitable business activities, including the *South China Morning Post* (SCMP), financially supported the anti-Qing political and militant mission (Tse, February 11, 1914, letter 72a; Tse, 1937). Prior to his cofounding the SCMP in 1903 together with Alfred Cunningham, he had been a partner of C. L. King & Co. (Florida Water, etc. 雙龍公司), comprador and assistant comprador of the American firm, Shewan Tome's & Co. (1900, 1915)[42] and Boyd Kaye & Company after quitting the Hong Kong civil service in 1900, partner of Quan Wah & Co. (Masons & Contractors 崑華建造公司), director of Chung Kwok Po Co. (the *China* newspaper 中國日報) to financially and politically "aid Chinese reform and revolution" and of Man U Tong Co. Ltd (printers & publishers), all in 1901 (Tse, 1937a).[43]

In 1907, Tse left the SCMP to negotiate the cancellation of the 1904 Canton-Macau Railway Convention while working as assistant manager of Wing Kee & Co. (stevedores & shipping agents 同記公司), but, as SCMP's earliest comprador, he remained influential to the newspaper's advertising, broader business, and publishing decision-making, a legacy that persisted even after his death (Zou, 2014; Hutcheon, p. 100).

Tse's highly varied business career kept him at pace with developments in science and technology, situated him at the core of information dissemination, and with influential human circles in Hong Kong, mainland China, Southeast, Central, and East Asia, Africa, North America, Europe, and the Oceania. In 1905 he started an experimental farm on his estate and summer retreat, Seeton in Tsuen Wan (in the New Territories of Hong Kong), where he carried out mixed farming "on the most modern lines to the great benefit of the district".[44]

Although the exact role that Tse played to promote the cancellation and later revival of the 1904 Canton-Macau Railway contracts between Portugal and the Qing Chinese government needs to be further researched, it is quite certain that as a member of the Canton-Macau Railway Syndicate (Duncan, 1917, p. 2), he was not only involved in the issues of railroad ownership and Chinese sovereignty, but also dealt with technical development enterprises, exploration for petroleum sources, coal mines, as well as limestone, marble, and precious stone quarries and mines – all at the time politically sensitive.

On the Canton-Macau Railway, Qing Chinese-Portuguese negotiations took place from 1901 to 1904, chiefly between José de Azevedo Castelo Branco (1852–1923), Portuguese minister to China and governor of Macau (1901–1904), and Qing minister of commerce Lü Haihuan and merchant Sheng Xuanhuai in Shanghai. The agreement stipulated equal share ownership by private Chinese and Portuguese merchants through subscriptions and a railway company/foreign syndicate. The railway would eventually belong to the Qing Chinese state after fifty years, but both governments were not responsible for any financial losses.

In the end, the Portuguese government disapproved the agreement, and no money was raised on the Portuguese side, because it deemed it limiting to its sovereignty to allow the Qing government to set up a custom house at Macau to collect tariffs on imports and exports through Macau. The Chinese side argued that the railway constituted an expansion of Portugal into Chinese sovereignty. As part of gathering countrywide storms over foreign ownership of mines and railway lines in China, in September 1907 Cantonese merchants petitioned to the Qing government to cancel the Sino-Portuguese agreements to allow Chinese merchants to take over. Chinese merchant Leung Wan Kwai (梁雲逵) lobbied businesses in Hong Kong, Canton, Tianjin, Shanghai, and other places to raise large funds for railway construction between Canton and Zhuhai (just north of Macau in history), but the plan did not come to fruition.[45] In 1909 the Qing foreign ministry informed their Portuguese counterpart that their bilateral convention was annulled. In 1910 the Qing government was said to sanction Leung's proposal that the railway be constructed by capital supplied by Chinese merchants, and the Qing state was to construct it (*The Straits Times*, September 17, 1907, p. 6; January 2, 1909, p. 6; April 18, 1910; Rockhill Papers, November 11, 1904). Even so, the railway was never built.[46]

In 1909, Tse worked as assistant manager of Hamburg Tung Kee (shipping agents), and later as a managing partner at Quong Yick Co. Tse allegedly helped to equip and train insurgents, using his yacht to send revolutionaries to Red Tower, owned by prominent businessman Li Ki-tong, in Tuen Mun in the New Territories of Hong Kong for military drills (Chueng, November 6, 2013, p. S7).⁴⁷ In 1911, when the Revolution broke out in Wuhan, Tse worked for Wing Kee & Co., the famous coal merchants, shipping agents, and ship chandlers in Hong Kong (Duncan, 1917, p. 2; Tse to Lockhart, November 9, 1911, letter 33). Two years later, Tse informed Lockhart of his resignation, working in copartnership with H.E. Chang Pat Sz (1814–1916, Zhang Bishi 張弼士, Qing official and Indonesian Chinese known as China's Rockefeller) for a mining concession, Yunnan Petroleum Co. in Yunnan Province (Tse, 1937a, p. 8).

At the end of 1910, Tse shared with Lockhart that business had not been good: "We have just succeeded in floating the International Petroleum Company Ltd. With a Capital of $1,500,000 for working petroleum Concessions in the […] [sic] of Timor (Portuguese)". His nephew, F. Ki Yat, was chairman of the board of directors, and Tse himself was a chief promoter of the company, appointed as adviser to its Chinese board (Tse, December 15, 1910, letter 19; Lightfoot, 2008, appendix 1; Tse, 1937a, p. 8). In 1913, Tse also partnered with Sir Po Shan, Wei Yuk at Kuk Kong Coal Mining Co.

World War I (1914–1918) affected Hong Kong businesses. Tse reported to Lockhart in 1915 that: "Business is very dull, and I suppose it will remain so until this terrible War is ended". "This War is hitting everybody, and disturbance is becoming general. My only regret is that I am not in a position, at present, to contribute to the difficult War funds as others have done, as I have experienced several very lean years, and besides I have a large family to support". His brothers, Tom and Sam, had to wind up their business in Hankow and Shanghai too (Tse, June

11, 1915, letter 86; December 6, 1915, letter 87; Lightfoot, 2008, appendix 1).

In the turbulent 1920s, Tse engaged also in a ferry business at Yaumati Steam Launch Co. Ltd, was managing partner of Hong Lim Mining Co. (N. T. Limestone & Marble), and owned Tai Hing Mining, Tai Hing Salt, and Yat Chong Mining companies. In his authorization letter to Miss Clara B. Mitchell, dated September 1, 1937, Tse's main business address was still The Tai Hing Mining Company at No. 239 Hennessy Road in Hong Kong (Tse, 1937b). The waxing and waning of business, however, was balanced by a sustained web of human relations especially in the opinion making world that Tse forged and valued over a long period of time.

Constellations of friends and associates

Tse Tsan Tai's network was extensive, and he followed a habit of listing and mentioning them publicly. His constellations of friends and associations encompassed foreign dignitaries of different political, national, cultural, and religious stripes. He took particular pride when his short books and pamphlets were in the holdings of leading libraries and "other famous Scientific Institutions" (Tse, undated flyer) in the transatlantic world, such as Oxford's Bodleian Library, the Vatican Library of Rome, the New York Academy of Sciences, and the Smithsonian Institution.

He communicated, as we have seen, mainly through "letters to the editor", pamphlets, and short books in a style sailing close to academic discourse, which gave him the opportunity to address and debate with many scientists and opinion makers, promoting his "discoveries, which are all supported by geological and scientific facts" (Tse, 1920b, original emphasis). He made it known that his "discoveries have upset the erroneous theories and conclusions of some of the greatest geologists and scientists of the world, and given tradition a rude shock!" (Tse, ibid).

Tse made known the comments on *The Creation* book made by Timothy Richard (1845–1919), a famous Welsh Baptist missionary and general secretary of Christian Literature Society for China in Shanghai: "I should be glad if every Missionary [sic] would purchase a copy of your book" (Richard, 1915a).

> Forty years ago the promising pioneer of American Presbyterian Mission work in Shantung [Shandong], the Rev. Mr McIlwaine, endeavored to reconcile the Chinese history of the Creation of the World and the Deluge with Bible History. We now turn with great pleasure to another attempt to solve the same problem made by an earnest Chinese student of fairly wide reading.
>
> (Richard, 1915b)

How did Tse and his constellations of friends and associates respond to themselves and each other? In his 1917 biography, "Tse Tsan Tai: His Political & Journalistic Career", Chesney Duncan projected an upright, outstanding, multitalented citizen of the modern world:

> The career of Mr. Tse Tsan Tai has been more remarkable than that of the vast majority of his fellow Chinese citizens. Famed as a social and political reformer, scholar, and patriot, he has also won renown as a

> capable business man, philanthropist, journalist, author, inventor of dirigibles, historian, Art Collector and connoisseur of ancient Chinese Art (paintings). Further, he is a staunch teetotaler and non-smoker.
>
> (Duncan, 1917, p. 1)

Duncan also praised Tse highly for being a member of "no Political Party in China", for having been "among the first to give to the World ideas, which have led to far-reaching developments" for a serviceable dirigible in 1894 when "little was thought of aircraft" (Duncan, 1917, p. 2, 8). On matters of science and religion, Tse corresponded with his friend Sir Hiram S. Maxim (1840–1916), who firmly believed in the aeroplane to conquer the air rather than through airship dirigibles. In 1896, Tse invented a new style military sun helmet, which the British authorities acknowledged.

Sir Maxim was an expert on firearms, an American-British inventor, holding over 25 patents in the United States and Britain, best known for his invention of the world's first automatic machine gun, the Maxim gun, flying machines, and others, and shared the same like as Tse for engineering. Maxim, an atheist, had been in communication with Tse since 1899 (Tse, 1916). Tse attributed his sustained friendship with Maxim to mutual appreciation: "It seems that the attraction … must have been mutual, and he [Maxim] always kept me informed of his inventions and thoughts; and whenever he waxed enthusiastic his letters would reach the surprising volume of twenty-three pages!" (Tse, 1916).[48]

Maxim's fearless, independent thinking inspired Tse, although Tse disagreed on but tolerated the former's attacks on Christianity and missionaries:

> Sir Hiram was a man who had the courage of his opinions, and he feared nobody. When he published his latest book "Li Hung Chang's Scrap Book," he was, quite prepared for the hornets' nest which it was certain to stir up. In attacking the Roman Catholic Church, and Missionary effort in China, I must say that he went a little too far: but his admiration and respect for the Chinese was always genuine, and the book contains much food for serious thought and reflection.
>
> (Tse, 1916)

What was Tse Tsan Tai's contribution to the formation of a cosmopolitan public sphere in British Hong Kong at a time when the English and Chinese press were subject to a wide range of influences, for example, revolutionary agitation, political partisanship, nationalism, and an international outlook? How was his place among China coast opinion makers and geopolitical influencers? Did he represent a particular political ideology? What were Tse's personal and professional networks like? Two points can be made:

First, Tse was a colonial cosmopolitan with a composite identity, who by and large pursued independent knowledge, "free of biases and partisanship". Second, through his devotion and ability to speak and write English, Tse cultivated generations of Sinophiles and pro-China foreign publicists and sympathizers in the news media world in the face of the rising Japan and complicated international politics in China.

In his *The Chinese Republic. A Secret History of the Revolution*, he revealed some of his network of foreign friends and supporters, which he shared earlier in 1912 with Sir Lockhart:

> In this brief history I shall recount without fear or favour the parts played by myself and my chivalrous English and Chinese friends and colleagues – Dr G. E. Morrison, Dr Timothy Richard, LL.D., Dr Yung Wing, LL.D., Sir Kai Ho Kai, Kt., CM.G., Warres-Smith, Alfred Cunningham, Thomas H. Reid, T. Cowen, Chesney Duncan, Mrs Archibald Little, B. A. Hale, Thomas Petrie, Sir Hiram S. Maxim, and Colin McD. Smart – from the year 1890 to the year 1912, when the Manchus were ousted from China and the Republic of China firmly established, and when I retired from the political arena.

Between the lines was Tse's sadness at the preceding thirteen years lost in civil war and bloodshed between Zhili and Fengtian military cliques with the participation of Sun Yat-sen and "those militarists" (Tse, 1924). As neighboring Guangdong Province and, in fact, the rest of China were engulfed in the Nationalist Revolution, violent Chinese nationalism was expressed in anti-Christian, anti-imperialist hatred leveled especially at Britain, which held the most business and geopolitical interests in China. However, labor and peasant unions' strikes and unrests that were organized mainly by CCP and some KMT radicals failed to translate their political agenda into full-scale anticolonialism in Hong Kong.

Very different from the situation in India, Tse Tsan Tai, like many Hong Kongers, "remained loyal to the colonial government, and Canton politics were too divided and volatile to create and sustain any serious anticolonial feelings" (Carroll, 2006, pp. 105–106; Wang, 2007). Violent illiberalism in neighboring Canton, Guangdong and mainland China strengthened many Hong Kongers' appreciation for the colony's absorption of local elites into governance, the rule of law, political and economic stability, as well as their pride in traditional Chinese antiquities. All of these ultimately helped with the Hong Kong people's othering of China, reaffirming their sense of belonging and commitment to British Hong Kong.

In the early 1930s, when Japan invaded China, Tse's political agenda was briefly revived, but did not last long. Both the Nationalist Party (KMT) and CCP actively infiltrated British Hong Kong for fundraising, public opinion-shaping, and other purposes. It is said that Chiang Kai-shek, Sun Yat-sen's successor as leader of the Nationalist Party and Government in Nanjing, sent his personal representative Chen Qiyou (陳其尤,1892–1970) to contact Tse in Hong Kong and that Tse urged Chiang to unite all political forces in China to resist Japan.[49] This might explain Tse's 1937 abridged version of the 1911 secret history, which was distributed to all Nationalist Government offices, associations, newspapers, and all compatriots. In it, Tse toned down his personal grudges against Sun, but clarified that they both went on a different path – Sun converted to Bolshevik Communism whereas, for Tse, civic independence, nonpartisanship, and British American type of constitutional democracy was a more optimal way to move forward (Tse, 1937a).

In the early 1930s Tse renewed his efforts, alongside a new generation of journalists who were coming of age, to challenge the official narratives of the 1911 Revolution and the ruling KMT dictatorship in their fight to demythologize Sun Yat-sen to honor the contribution of earlier Australian Chinese to the Revolution. One young passionate journalist, with a similar upbringing to Tse, made a difference.

United China?

The late 1920s and early 1930s saw an end to major political and military divisions as the Nationalist Party, now with Chiang Kai-shek's leadership, "unified" China under the Nanjing Government. The new "central" government not only legitimatized itself with a new constitution, shed its united front with the CCP, and imposed a nationalization campaign aimed at bringing culture, education, research, infrastructure, and other core institutions into Chinese – as opposed to foreign – hands, but also laid the foundations for national myths, monuments, and ceremonies. This new force toward nationhood sought to supplant or intrude upon the public sphere as Tse had known it since his adulthood and posed a vociferous challenge to colonial institutions and personal networks that had so far sustained Tse's worldviews and activities.

Under these circumstances, Tse went back to basics and found soulmates and supporters among others who had also journeyed through cosmopolitan-colonialist experiences and felt equally dismayed at Chiang Kai-shek's brand of nationalism.

Vivian Yung Chow (1906–1941, 周成貴) was a lay Anglican church preacher of Cantonese ancestry (from today's Dongguang City), born in Lismore, New South Wales, Australia. Chow's maternal grandfather Stephen King, who was in Grafton, where Tse Tsan Tai grew up, was the second Grand Master of the Yee Hing network and a founder of the Revolutionary and Independence Society of Australian Chinese. Grafton was a hub of Loong Hung Pung's Yee Hing fraternity/secret society/Hung Mun/Chinese Masonic Society/Chinese Republican Association/the Chee Kong Tong (Zhigong Tang), a radical and later deradicalized ethnic organization in charge of Chinese gold miners, laborers, merchants, and others in Australia who tended to have many different aliases (Fitzgerald, 2007, pp. 76–77, 243–244). In San Francisco in 1925, Hung Mun formed the Chinese Zhigong party headed by Chen Jiongming (1878–1933), a military and 1911 revolutionary leader.[50] With many offices in Canada, Taiwan, the United States, Southeast Asia, the PRC, and other places, Chinese Hung Mun are still in existence, although many have fallen within the CCP united front web as the Zhigong Party.

Along with his brother, Chow went to China in 1925, settled down in Shanghai and did not return home in Lismore until 1932. In the 1930s Chow was coeditor of an English magazine, *United China Magazine*, devoted to opposing Japan, the KMT Nationalist Government in Nanjing, and to uniting New China. It promoted the importance of Australian Chinese in the 1911 Revolution and the Australian Chinese devotion to free spirit, the Australian and New Zealand Army Corps (ANZAC), egalitarianism, and sportsmanship. In 1911 the Yee Hing Company in Australia went public, opening its new headquarters in Sydney as a respectable ethnic organization (Fitzgerald, 2007, p. 93).

The narrative of Tse, Chow, Australian Chinese Yee Hing, and homeland associations also advanced the legend of Loong Hung Pung (1849–1878), the pioneer ahead of Sun Yat-Sen and other revolutionaries, who organized the Chinese miners to remit funds to anti-Manchus revolutionaries in China and later directed the Australian Chinese to go back to China for military uprisings to topple their own government, the Qing. John Fitzgerald speculates that this might explain the return to China (Hong Kong) of the Tse family in 1887 and their direct involvement in uprisings in Guangdong while under cover in Hong Kong. Chow and his supporters were fired up, propagating a succession of leaders, from Loong Hung Pung (1849–1878) to Stephen King Jung Sao (1878–1904), allegedly a British trained detective and attached to Scotland Yard, and Tse Tsan Tai as the Australian Chinese founder of the Chinese Republic, "opening the way for Sun Yat-sen as father of the Chinese nation" (*United China Magazine*, October 1933, p. 448, 427).

Deeply troubled by the enshrinement of Sun's grand mausoleum on a peak of Purple Mountain in 1929 in Nanjing (Nanking), Chow challenged the "popular but untrue story" of Sun Yat-sen's fatherhood:

> [T]he fiction and of the matter is solely concerned with the 'deeds' and 'exploits' of Sun Yat Sen, the self-created martyr, the self-created 'Father of New China.' The greatest fiction in the world is the story of Sun Yat Sen's founding of the movement he requested to join. His selfish and personal wish to be buried on Purple Mountain, Nanking to rest with the Ming Emperors, clearly shows that he was entirely ego-maniacal.
>
> (United China Magazine, October 1933, p. 427)

To further discredit the KMT's idolization of Sun, Chow published "The Proclamation of Independence" (in Canton to establish a commonwealth government), drafted and written by Tse Tsan Tai and secretly lithographed on stone by Alfred Cunningham on December 26, 1902, as proof of Sun's lower starting position in the founding of the Republic of China. The Proclamation highlights that "all men among us are free and have equal rights under impartial and uniform laws. … That the laws shall be justly administered by officers who shall be paid fixed and liberal salaries as servants of the sovereign people, instead of masters over an enslaved people as heretofore…" (*United China Magazine*, October 1933, p. 431). "Similar in conception and purpose to the American Declaration of Independence", the original lithographed Proclamation was being kept in a large bank vault in 1933 to give "pride and inspiration" to generations of Chinese unborn (*United China Magazine*, October 1933, p. 432).

Through his broadcasts and printed works, Chow held Sun's policy of world revolution and pro-Russian stance responsible for the "introduction of Bolshevism in China", in contrast with Tse Tsan Tai whose "policy has always been the cementing of friendly relations, and a thorough understanding between China and Great Britain and her Colonies, and the United States of America. He has been working for a true Republic form of Government, based upon that of the United States of America"[51] (*United China Magazine*, October 1933, p. 435). Chow dared to differ, representing an inherently contradictory modern effort to create a unified China from a divided reality.

Was unification of so complex and large a China an impossible ideal? Was it worth the internal bloodshed? Buried in the Chinese Christian Cemetery in Pok Fu Lam, Tse Tsan Tai (1872–1938) had lived a busy 66-year life with a purpose, from initially organizing armed revolts, aiming to overthrow the Qing Manchu dynasty, to fully embracing civility and peace – thus manifesting the gradual fusion of local elites into British colonial governance in Hong Kong. A comprehensive examination of his manifold activities indicates that Tse went beyond narrow Chinese nationalism, or jingoism, or Chinese imperialism that muddled or equated one single political party with the country, the state, the government, and the people. Tse's contemporary, Sao-ke Alfred Sze (1877–1958), ambassador to the United States (1920–1929 and 1933–1936) and the United Kingdom (1914 and 1929), believed in the capacity of the Chinese for self-government one century ago, but defined the politics of recognition as "the patriotism which is love of something not ourselves, love of our own people and cities and our native fields, and which, being love, does not in the least insist that that which is loved is superior to other things or other people, unloved because unknown" (Sze, 1922, p. 247).

Reading Tse Tsan Tai holistically from the vantage point of the twenty-first century yields appreciation for his refusal to accept the jingoism, ultranationalism, patriotism, and the idolization and canonization of Sun Yat-sen prescribed by political parties, the KMT, and its successor, the CCP, on the mainland. "As a party of the working class the communist movement was of little consequence. Once it learnt to harness mass discontent over racism, foreign humiliation and colonial infringements on China's territory, the communist movement grew to become the most powerful political organization in the country" (Fitzgerald, 2007, p. 231). Can *people* fully embrace and defend democracy, freedom, and civil liberty for the sake of democracy, freedom, and civil liberty? Does China have a democratic future? Why does it take so long for China to realize its own people's original ideals for a constitutional liberal democracy? Which obsession among Chinese elites forces them to keep intact the Qing China territory just to subjugate it with its own brand of autocracy?

Consider the lyrics of the national anthem for the Republic composed by Tse Tsan Tai in 1912 and set to music by Pastor/Padre Jacob Lao entitled "Liberty":

> The people hear and answer Liberty's call: Freedom and Peace are attained within Thirty Days; Tyranny and Corruption have been banished forever; And the future is as superb [sublime, Tse's handwritten correction, undated] as the Ocean. Law and Justice will rule ti'l the world enjoys Universal Peace; All the World rejoices in China's glorious rebirth; And the Nations present their respectful felicitations.
>
> (Tse, 1924; United China Magazine, 1933, p. 403)

5
Conclusion: Chinas and the curse?

In 1997, at the height of renewed hopes for a democratic China that arose after being dashed during the June 4th Massacre, the influential Dutch journalist Willem van Kemenade (1943–2016), wrote: "For the foreseeable future, however, Chinese politics seem to be fixed in their Marxist-Leninist ways, which are largely irrelevant to the great majority of the people. At the same time, leading academics are reinventing and reformulating China's own pre-Communist and premodern Confucian uniqueness and 'superiority'" (Kemenade, 1998, pp. xii–xiii).

What does Tse Tsan Tai's identity story tell us? Identities and post-life identities are always fluid in the life of humans and their places, physical and imagined. Like many men and women of his age, Tse was a man of many pursuits, taking an interest in not only world, national, and local affairs, but also science and religion. For us, of our time, where everything is politicized, or rather weaponized, making sense of who Tse was, what we can learn from him, and what we can use him for may feel awkward. Why could Tse shed his youthful radicalism and still remain committed to his original ideal of a democratic Republic of China? Why did he resist the violent Soviet Bolshevism, communist autocracy, and militant anti-imperialism that beguiled so many of his contemporaries and former comrades in arms like Sun Yat-sen? What does it help us to understand the eulogized "father of the nation", idolized by both sides of the Taiwan Strait for his systematic plan for China's political governance and with a socialist economy (Bergère, 1998) as an aspirant dictator whose postmortem personality cult propped up Chiang Kai-shek's autocratic rule? How can we, today, accept the fact that Tse's adopted home place, the British Crown Colony of Hong Kong, gave him, an ethnic Chinese, a respected voice, career, wealth, personal and civic life, Christian faith, and opportunity to contribute to Chinese nationalism? The answer is that we can only weaponize heroes, saints, baddies, and demons, not real historical persons. The way to learn from history is to understand, based on all-inclusive evidence, how and why people acted as they did within their context. The less a historical person resembles a hero or baddie, the more we learn.

For students of Chinese modern history, the narratives pursued under KMT and CCP auspices are integral to their respective political legitimization and ideological frameworks. They are, moreover, built on a history writing practice inspired by Marxist-Leninist ideas of dialectical or historical materialism and historical determinism, which reduces individual agency to functions of economic development and explains them as mere exponents of class interest. Although both economic development and class in themselves can be inspiring and fruitful starting points for specific historical narratives, *historical determinism*, that is, the idea that historical development is predetermined by productive forces and a sequence of modes of production, turns history writing into a shallow ornament stuck onto preconceived political dogma, and deprives humans of their role as makers of history – if they do not abide by the ordained progressive class conscience necessary for reaching the next mode of production, they are reactionaries and deserve to perish. This applies to the past and to the present, so, bereft of free will and agency, people living in Leninist party–states are always at the mercy of autocrats.

Furthermore, the Chinese Communist Party's (CCP) ambition to alter and harness the whole world increasingly calls our attention to diasporic Chinese in Southeast Asia, South Asia, the Oceania, Africa, and Latin and South America to understand the emergence of geostrategic situations more fully. The KMT party–state, the Republic of China (ROC) – defeated in mainland China in 1949 by its archrival, the CCP, before retreating to Taiwan – held the China seat as one of the five permanent members at the United Nations Security Council from 1945 to 1971, replaced by the People's Republic of China (PRC). Thus, as Chien-Wen Kung points out: 'Far from being irrelevant to the present, the KMT's historical interventions in postcolonial Southeast Asia are antecedents of the PRC's involvement in the region in our time. We cannot study one without the other" (Kung, 2022, p. 222; Ong and Nonini, 1997).

Over one century ago, Chinese revolutionaries effectively used racist slogans such as "The Manchus must go", "All against the Manchus", and "Expel the Tartars and restore China" that paralleled various forms of racism in other parts of the world. The 1911 Revolution, however, proved that blaming the Manchus was not only false but also divisive. Ultimately, China's problem was, or is, the Chinese (McCormick, 1913, p. 283, p. 332). As the global China struggle against the reinforcement of tyranny is unfolding, Tse's identity story offers much to mull over: Does China's problem lie in its own obsession with unification of diverse aspirations and peoples throughout history? Is it China's curse to be too big and too centralized at the expense of local and individual freedom? Does Hong Kong's new generation of the twenty-first century see eye to eye with Tse Tsan Tai (1872–1938)?

6
Historical documents reading

Excerpts of Tse Tsan Tai's writings

I. *The Chinese Republic. Secret History of the Revolution* [中華民國革命秘史] 1924[52]

The last of the Mings

The last purely Chinese dynasty to rule China was the Ming, whose founder was a monk named Chu Yuan-chang (Hung Wu) [Hongwu].[53] Through weakness, decay, and misrule the dynasty hastened to its end, and the disaffected throughout the Empire seized opportunities to rebel. The rebel leader who finally succeeded in raising a following strong enough to threaten Peking was Li Tzu-cheng [Li Zicheng].

The army protecting Peking against the advancing rebel hordes of Li Tzu-cheng was commanded by General Wu San-kwei [Wu Sangui], who, fearing defeat and the loss of the Capital, opened negotiations, for the armed assistance and support of the Manchu

Tartars beyond the Great Wall, where their Chief Nurhachu (天命)[54] had been patiently organizing his armies and waiting for the opportunity to grasp the throne of China from the Mings.

The Manchu Tartar Chief Tsung Teh [Chongde] gladly accepted General Wu San-kwei's invitation, and rapidly advanced with his army into the plains of Chihli; but before he could reach Peking the rebels under Li Tzu-cheng had already seized and sacked the Capital, and the weakling Emperor Tsung Ching [Chongzhen], the last of the Mings, had strangled himself on the top of the Coal Hill, behind the Palace.

The advent of the Manchus

When General Wu San-kwei arrived at the Capital with the Manchu Tartar Chief and his army and drove out the rebels, the treacherous Tartar Chief refused to retire as previously agreed, and forcibly occupied the Palace of the Mings. His death happening shortly afterwards, his son Shun Chih [Shunzhi] mounted the Dragon Throne and was proclaimed the first Manchu Emperor of the Tai Ching (Ta Tsing) [Qing] Dynasty of China.

Thus ended the Ming Dynasty, followed by the advent of the usurping Manchu Tartars in China.

How the ferocious and barbarous Manchu Tartars completed the conquest of the Chinese Empire, after cruelly slaughtering millions of the inhabitants, and how they governed the country, since the day they usurped the Throne of the Mings, has already been recorded, and is now history. But, the following from the pen of my old friend and colleague Chesney Duncan is interesting:

As regards the part I played in the almost bloodless annihilation of one of the most degraded and monstrous despotisms that ever disfigured the annals of history, I counted it an honour to be able to assist, however feebly, in the triumph of civilization over barbarism of a particularly pernicious description. The Manchu usurpers were hampering the progress of the world and imperiling the political and commercial interests, of all really progressive states.

Movements for independence

Risings against Manchu misrule have been many and frequent, the most formidable being that of the "Taiping" under the leadership of Hung Hsiu-chuan [Hong Xiuquan], but all were ruthlessly suppressed.

The next great movement for the ousting of the usurping Manchus was the Great Revolution, culminating in the establishment of the Republic of China, the secret history of which I am now publishing to the world.

Since the failure of our first attempt to capture Canton on the 26th October 1895, the assassination of my "brother" and colleague Yeung Ku-wan [Yang Quyun], first President of the Hing Chung Whui [Xingzhong hui] Revolutionary Party in Hongkong, on the 10th January 1901, and the failure of my second attempt to capture Canton with a force under the command of Hung Chuen-Fook on the night of 28th January 1903, and establish a Commonwealth Government under a "Protector," I decided not to engender party strife by actively opposing Dr Sun Yat-sen, but allowed him and his followers a free hand.

At my first meeting with Dr Sun Yat-sen and others on the 13th of March 1895, after our two parties had joined hands, his look and speech did not favorably impress me, and I had the strange feeling that it would be wise to keep away from him. My first impressions of Dr Sun Yat-sen are recorded in the following entries in my diary.

Meetings at headquarters

Sunday, 5th May, 1895: *"Sun Yat-sen appears to be a rash and reckless fellow. He would risk his life to make a name for 'himself.' Sun proposes things that are subject to condemnation – he thinks he is able to do anything – no obstructions – 'all paper'!"*[55]

Sunday, 23rd June, 1895: *"Sun has got 'revolution' on the brain, and is so 'occupied' at times, that he speaks and acts strangely! He will grow crazy yet. I for one could not trust him with the responsibility of the leadership of the Movement. One may think little of life, but in 'acting' it is highly necessary to see that the lives of the leaders are not needlessly sacrificed. I believe Sun wishes everyone to listen to him. This is impossible, as, so far, his experience shows that it would be risky to rely solely upon him".*

Consequently, after the failure of our first attempt, to capture Canton, and well knowing Dr Sun Yat-sen's character and disposition, and having already formed my opinion of his ability and worth, I declined to join his party, but quietly laboured through the English and Chinese press for the furtherance of the cause of reform and independence. And, not wishing to participate in party strife and civil war, which I foretold in letters to my friend the late Dr G. E. Morrison (*London Times* correspondent), and which I knew would follow the assumption of the Presidency by the late Yuan Shih-kai, I retired from the political arena.

***

Appreciations

Regarding my work, the following quotations may prove of interest:

(1) Of my work in Hongkong no one is better qualified to speak on my behalf than yourself. Were we not colleagues together, and did we not use every effort in our power to promote the cause of progress in China? You know the risks – from the time the small Reform Committee met surreptitiously in the Colony you kept the flame burning at constant risk of your own freedom, your life, and of those you held dearest.

Mine was an easier part, to hammer away in the paper in the interests of Reform, and to influence the authorities. For years we worked together by means of the paper (*Hongkong Daily Press* and *South China Morning Post*) in the one cause.

(Alfred Cunningham – Editor of the *Hongkong Daily Press*, *South China Morning Post*, etc. Correspondent *Daily Mail*, *New York Sun*, etc. – May 4th, 1913.)

(2) You have at least the great satisfaction of knowing that you assisted in placing four hundred millions of your fellow-men on the road to a better and more humane life, and in initiating a movement which will go down in history as one of the most momentous in the records of the World.

(Thomas H. Reid – Editor of the Hongkong *China Mail*, 1894–1905, *Straits Times*, etc.; *London Times* correspondent for South China; Correspondent *The Standard*, *New York Herald*, etc. – November 29th, 1912).

(3) Having had the pleasure to reside fully forty years amongst you and having during that lengthy period had the honour and pleasure to help you in the efforts that were made many years ago to compass the extinction of the corrupt and despotic Manchu dynasty (as you will see from extracts from letters from one of your most able leaders of that time which I include in the appendices of this brochure) I venture to offer you advice at this critical juncture in world affairs which I verily believe must prove decidedly beneficial to you if you act upon it.

(From "The Way Out," 1919, by Chesney Duncan, Editor, *Hongkong Telegraph* (1895), *Straits Echo* (1905), *Times of Malaya* (1907), *China Republican* (1913), *Malaya Tribune* (1915). Correspondent *London Globe*, *Japan Gazette*, *Shanghai Mercury*, *China Times*, etc.).

As this is only a brief history, I have been obliged to withhold interesting details, and to exclude hundreds of important letters and minor incidents connected with the Revolution.

Introduction
Biographical sketch

Fifty three years ago on the 16th May, 1872, I was born in Sydney, New South Wales, Australia, my father Tse Yet-chong (謝日昌 death in March 1903) otherwise John See, being proprietor of the Tai Yick-firm (泰益) of Importers and Exporters, and my mother Kwok Shi (郭氏) one of the first Chinese ladies to land in the Antipodes.

My father was a native of the Hoi Ping district (開平縣) [Kaiping] of Kwang Tung Province (廣東省) [Guangdong] and according to the genealogical record of the family, he traces his descent from San Pak (申伯) of the Feud of Tse (謝) of the Chow Dynasty (周朝).

According to my baptismal certificate, I was baptised on the 1st November, 1879, by my God-father, Bishop C. C. Greenway of the Church of England of Grafton, and subsequently I carried on a lengthy correspondence with him, and I believe that my strict moral rectitude and conduct in life have been due to his influence, and the education which I received at the Grafton High School.

Although I am a Christian, I am also a staunch supporter of Confucius and his teachings, and all that is wise and good in other religions.

My father was a God-fearing and upright man, a stern disciplinarian, and a man of few words; and as for my mother, she is a good and pious soul, and will soon see her 80th birthday, if God be pleased.

My ambition

My father was a leader of the Chinese Independence Party of Australia, and when I was about twelve years of age he told me the story of the cruel conquest of China by the Manchu Tartars, and I promised him that when I grew up, I would return to China and do my best to help in driving the usurping Manchu Tartars out of China. I have kept my promise, and this accounts for my past activities in connection with the movement for Reform and Independence in China.

My ambition has always been to work for China and the Chinese, but never to become a "party" official. I have friends in all the different political parties, but not a single enemy.

Sowing the seed
Arrival in China

In the year 1887, when sixteen years of age, I left Sydney for China with my mother, two younger brothers and three sisters. What struck me on first landing in Hongkong on the 20th May, 1887, was the cramped pigeonholed houses, the narrow insanitary streets, and the total absence of shade trees.

My father's old friends welcomed us all ashore, and we quickly found ourselves at home in a strange city with strange surroundings.

Shortly after settling down, I was introduced to Hon. Mr J. H. Stewart Lockhart, now Sir J. H. Stewart Lockhart, KCMG, retired ex-Commissioner of Wei-hai-wei, who was then Registrar General of Hongkong. He received me very kindly and advised me to enter Queen's College preparatory to joining the Hongkong Government service.

During my stay at Queen's College, I made the acquaintance of a number of promising and patriotic young men inside and outside the College, and it began to dawn upon me that the time was ripe and opportune for planning and organizing a movement for the reformation of China's millions, and for the expulsion of the usurping Manchu Tartars from China.

Chief of those of my sixteen friends who were in my confidence and knew my secret were Yeung Ku-wan (楊衢雲), Chan Fun (陳芬), Chau Chiu-ngok (周朝嶽), Wong Kwok-u (黃國瑜), Lo Man-yuk (羅文玉) and Lau In-bun (Liu Yanbin 劉燕賓). The remainder were not let into the secret, as it was too dangerous to openly preach revolution at the time, and besides, the Colony of Hongkong was full of spies and secret agents of the Manchu Canton Government.

Accordingly we used to meet surreptitiously at Ping Kee shipping office, Praya Central, where Lau In-bun was chief shipping clerk, at the China Merchant's Steam Navigation Co., where Yeung Ku-wan was chief shipping clerk, at Gon Kee, the shipping office of Woo Gon-chi (胡幹芝), Comprador of Messrs. David Sassoon & Co., and at my own house, No. 11, Wing Shing Street.

Difficulties and dangers

So feared and dreaded were the Manchu Canton officials, and their spies and informers, that the people dared not talk of revolution or associate with people of revolutionary tendencies. Such was the state of public feeling during the years 1887 to 1895, when it was extremely difficult to gain recruits or even sympathizers.

We always met the taunts and ridicule of our chicken-hearted and doubting "friends" in silence. But nothing discouraged us, and we fearlessly and silently struggled on.

During all these long years of secret planning and organizing, I always used to mix up with the spies and secret agents of the

Manchu Canton Government, and pay visits to their "haunts". I was persistently putting my head in the tiger's jaws!

How I bluffed and blinded them is a long story, and cannot be told in the pages of this short history.

My English friends and colleagues were just as shrewd and careful as myself, and we managed to keep everything secret and to ourselves.

The seed germinates

On the 13th March 1892, we established our Revolutionary Headquarters on the first floor of No. 1, Pak Tze Lane (百子裡),[56] Hongkong, the second floor being occupied by Luk King-fo (陸敬科) and his friends of the "Iu Kui" Club.

Luk King-fo is, at present, an official of the Foreign Affairs Department at Canton, but was formerly a teacher of Queen's College, Hongkong.

We adopted as our motto "Ducit amor patriae",[57] and named our meeting place the "Foo Yan Man Ser" (輔仁文社), but this did not prevent it from being visited from time to time by European Police detectives, who were always welcome!

In the year 1894, Japan declared war against China, and the disgraceful defeat of China, followed by the "Boxer" rising, increased the growing discontent of the Chinese against the Manchu regime in China, and from this time onwards a new spirit was abroad in the land.

16th May, 1894. I advocated in the *Hongkong Daily Press* the suppression of the Indian opium trade, and widely distributed my pamphlets in England and in China, I took a leading part in the formation of the Anti-Opium Society of South China in the year 1898.

30th May, 1894. I protested in the *Hongkong Daily Press* against the slandering of the Chinese community; and for "dabbling in politics", whilst in the Government Service, I was reprimanded by the Colonial Secretary.

In the Spring of 1895, Yeung Ku-wan conferred with me, and we joined hands with Dr Sun Yat-sen (孫逸仙) and his friends and established the Hing Chung Whui (興中會) revolutionary party. We established our new headquarters at No. 13, Staunton Street, and named the meeting place the "Kuen Hang" (乾亨) Club. We frequently interviewed the late Sir Kai Ho Kai, Kt., CMG (何啟大壯士), and he secretly promised us his support. We also succeeded in obtaining the secret support of the Editors of the *China Mail* and *Hongkong Telegraph*.

Thomas H. Reid, Editor of the *China Mail*, and Chesney Duncan, Editor of the *Hongkong Telegraph*, were the first to openly and fearlessly champion the great cause in their newspapers, and at a time when nearly everybody ridiculed the movement.

On one occasion, Chesney Duncan was called before the Colonial Secretary, who reprimanded him for what he had published, claiming that it amounted to incitement of the Chinese to revolt against a Government with which Great Britain was on friendly terms. In spite of such warnings, I am proud to record that their faithfulness and loyalty has never swerved.

Organizing the revolution

(Abstracts from diaries and correspondence.)

12th March, 1895. Dr Ho Kai's "Reform" article published by the *China Mail*. Dr Ho Kai was a Barrister and a member of the Hongkong Legislative Council, representing the Chinese. He was a man of sound judgment and ripe experience.

13th March, 1895. Yeung Kuwan, Dr Sun Yat-sen, Wong Wingsheung, and Tse Tsan-tai confer together re organization of the movement to capture Canton. Wong Wing-sheung (黃詠商) was the second son of the late Hon. Wong Shing (黃勝), member of the Hongkong Legislative Council.

16th March, 1895. Yeung Kuwan, Dr Sun Yat-sen and Tse Tsan-tai discuss plans for an attempt to capture Canton with 3,000 picked men.

We obtain the secret support of the Japanese Government through the Japanese Consul.

We adopt as the design of our flag, *a white sun on a blue ground*.[58]

Dr Ho Kai accepts responsibility for the work of drafting proclamations, etc.

Thomas H. Reid, Editor of the *China Mail*, interviewed, and he promises us his support.

18th March, 1895. The *China Mail* publishes a lengthy article in our support.

21st March, 1895. Yeung Kuwan, Dr Sun Yat-sen, Wong Wing-sheung and Tse Tsan-tai confer with Chesney Duncan, Editor of the *Hongkong Telegraph*, at No. 13, Staunton Street. He assured us of his support.

The *Hongkong Telegraph* supports our movement.

Manifesto to Emperor Kwang Hsu

30th May, 1895. Tse Tsan-tai's "Open Letter" to the Manchu Emperor Kwang Hsu [Guangxu] published in the *China Mail*, *Hongkong Telegraph*, and other newspapers of Singapore and the Far East. This "manifesto" was broadcasted by means of the English and foreign newspapers in order to search the hearts of the Chinese at home and abroad.[59]

27th August, 1895. Plans for the capture of Canton being completed, orders were given for the closing of the "Kuen Hang" Club at No. 13, Staunton Street.

29th August, 1895. Yeung Ku-wan, Dr Sun Yat-sen, Wong Wing-sheung, Chan Siu-pak (陳少白), Dr Ho Kai, Thomas H. Reid and Tse Tsan-tai meet at Hang Fa Lau Hotel. Dr Ho Kai acted as spokesman, and we outlined the policy of the Provisional Government. Thomas H. Reid agreed to do his best to work for the sympathy and support of the British Government and the people of England.

9th October, 1895. Our proclamation to the Foreign Powers drafted by Thomas H. Reid and T. Cowen, and revised by Dr Ho Kai and Tse Tsan-tai.

President of Provisional Govt. [*sic*]

10th October, 1895. Yeung Ku-wan elected President of the "Provisional Government," preparatory to the attempt to capture Canton.

[*Note:* The election of Yeung Ku-wan as President greatly displeased Dr Sun Yat-sen, and it always rankled in his breast. On the 12th October 1896, Wong Wing-sheung (second son of Hon. Wong Shing) remarked, when strongly censuring Dr Sun Yat-sen for his incapacity: "I will have nothing to do with Sun in the future".] (*sic*)

On the 26th October, 1895, we made our first attempt to capture Canton, but owing to our plans being divulged to the Canton authorities by traitors in Hongkong, the attempt ended in failure. Numerous arrests and executions followed. Yow Lit (尤烈) and others escaped.

Dr Sun Yat-sen and Chan Siu-pak succeeded in escaping to Macao, and from thence they proceeded to Japan.

Dr Sun Yat-sen was subsequently kidnapped in London on 11th October, 1896, by the Manchu Chinese Legation officials, and rescued by his friend Dr James Cantlie, who was his old teacher in the Medical College in Hongkong.

Party split up

On the 13th November 1895, Yeung Ku-wan left Hongkong for Saigon, after returning from Macao. From Saigon Yeung Ku-wan proceeded to Singapore, Madras, Colombo, and South Africa, where he established revolutionary juntas of the "Hing Chung Whui" (興中會), as advised by me. Before Yeung Ku-wan left for the Straits Settlements and South Africa, it was agreed between us that in order to preserve secrecy all our letters should be numbered.

On his way back from South Africa, Yeung Ku-wan established revolutionary *juntas* in Singapore and the Straits Settlements, and obtained the co-operation and support of the anti-Manchu secret societies. Immediately after Yeung Ku-wan reached Japan, emissaries were dispatched to the Yangtze Valley provinces and the United States of America with copies of our "manifesto" and other revolutionary literature, and they succeeded in obtaining the co-operation and support of all the anti-Manchu "Tongs" and secret societies in these places.

It was from these sources that much of the fighting material was obtained, during the stirring days of the revolution.

During Yeung Ku-wan's absence in the Straits Settlements and South Africa, Dr Sun Yat-sen and his partisans had been busy organizing the "Tung Meng Whui" (同盟會) [Tongmeng hui] in Japan. As I know very little about the affairs of this organization, I leave Dr Sun Yat-sen and his followers to fill up the gap.

Unification of parties
Meeting between Kang Yu-wei and Tse Tsan-tai

On the 21st February, 1896, I met Kang Yu-wei's (康有為) brother Kang Kwang-jin (康廣仁) and other members of Kang Yu-wei's party at a dinner at the Bun Fong restaurant given by my friends and colleagues Chan Kam-to (Dr Chen Chin-tao) (陳錦濤), and Leung Lan-fan (Liang Lan-hsun) (梁蘭芬). Dr Chen Chin-tao was at one time Minister of Finance, and Liang Lan-hsun, Chinese Consul for Australia.

We discussed "reforms, and the importance of union and co-operation". Not being a "party" man myself, I strongly advised the union and co-operation of the different political parties working for the salvation of China, and this has always been my policy.

"Unification of parties and Unification of China" has always been my watchword.

On the 4th October, 1896, I met Kang Yu-wei at the Wai Shing Tea Hong in Queen's Road Central by arrangement. We discussed the political situation in China, and I counselled union and co-operation in the great work of reform. Kang Yu-wei outlined his scheme of reform, which is too long to be recorded in these pages. It will appear in the complete history. We agreed to unite and co-operate, after a confidential exchange of views.

Kang Yu-wei

The following pen picture of Kang Yu-wei is from my diary of this date:

> "Kang Yu-wei is 43 years of age and a native of the Nam-hoi district of Kwang Tung province. He appears to be a man of superior intelligence. He is learned and experienced, and possesses an excellent all-round knowledge. He possesses a highly retentive memory, and is a great lover of books. He is always busy investigating, and searching for knowledge, in all its branches. He is the most learned progressive 'Chinese scholar' of modern China. It is said that he remembers all that he reads. He is often styled by his disciples and pupils 'Kang Fu-tzu,' – the 'New Confucius'! The Chinese literati hate him.
> He has reviewed the works of Confucius, in many volumes, and for this he has been censured by the Throne. The publication of his works has been forbidden in China.

Kang is of middle stature. He is stout and strong, and looks healthy. His eyes are dark and brilliant, and his glance is quiet and sharp: his eyebrows are black, well-arched and high. His complexion is dark, and his forehead is high and well-formed, as also are his nose and thick pped mouth. His upper lip is surmounted by well trimmed black moustaches, and his ears are small but well formed. Some of his fingers (third and fourth of his left hand) grow long nails! His head and hands are not large, but are well formed and shaped. The expression of his face is keen, intelligent and fascinating. The glitter of his dark eye-balls was striking. His bearing is proud and independent. At a glance one can see that he is not a 'man of the common herd.'"

Meeting between Tse Tsan-tai and Kang Kwang-jin

On the 21st March, 1897, Leung Lan-fan brought Kang Yu-wei's brother Kang Kwang-jin and a follower named Ho Jeong (何章易一) to see me.

We discussed the political situation and the importance of union and co-operation. On 29th September, 1897, Kang Kwang-jin and I met by arrangement, and had a long confidential chat in the Public Gardens of Hongkong, under the big pine tree in the East corner, below the fountain. We agreed to work for union and cooperation and Kang Kwang-jin promised to discuss the matter seriously with his brother Kang Yu-wei. The following is from my diary of this date:

"Kang Kwang-jin said: 'Yes, I quite agree with you, let us unite. What is the use of a body without a leg and a hand? I shall be glad to place your views before my brother, and I am certain he will be pleased to favour them. Yes, we should get the 'superior' men of both parties together, and hold a conference. We desire to see a peaceful, revolution for the good of the Empire and its millions, but still we must be prepared to act at any moment! I do not favour 'desperate' attempts at 'reform.'

Men like Sun Yat-sen frighten me – they spoil everything. We cannot combine with such rash and reckless men. Yeung Ku-wan is a good man, and I hope to meet him yet. It is a pity we cannot get more able men to push the Movement. My brother and I are doing our best, but we are afraid we cannot accomplish much. There is an understanding between Chang Chitung (張之洞), Viceroy of the Liang Hu provinces, and us. And besides him there are many other sympathizers amongst the officials. My brother is afraid to make himself too conspicuous, and is consequently working very quietly. It would be ruinous to our party if my brother got into trouble. My brother has numerous enemies, and they would seize any opportunity to bring about his downfall. So you see we must be very shrewd. No one must be able to say that ours is an anti-dynastic or revolutionary movement! *We can save China*". [sic]

A political confession

Kang Kwang-jin confessed to me that he was not pro-Manchu, and that he and his brother were trying to bring about a "peaceful" revolution in favor of the Chinese. This confession has been verified by the Ta Tung revolutionary movement of August 1900.

Historical documents reading 119

Before separating, Kang Kwang-jin exclaimed: "What is our duty? We are born in this world to do our duty, which is all we can do for our fellowmen before we die".

Alas, my poor friend Kang Kwang-jin was one of those reformers who lost their lives during the Empress Dowager's coup d'état of 21st September, 1898. Little did he dream that his last words to me would come true so soon!

Kang Kwang-jin was honest and sincere, and a true patriot.

1st October, 1897. Kang Kwang-jin leaves Hongkong for Shanghai by s.s. "Loong Moon" to meet his brother and Liang Chi-chao (梁啟超). Liang Chi-chao is a noted Chinese scholar and politician, and the chief disciple of Kang Yu-wei.

3rd October, 1897. I communicate the result of my interview with Kang Kwang-jin to Yeung Kuwan in South Africa, he having announced to me his safe arrival in a letter dated 7th January, 1897.

20th October, 1897. I receive a letter from Yeung Ku-wan (28/8/97) informing me of the date of his departure for China, and reporting the establishment of a revolutionary junta in Johannesburg.

8th November, 1897. Kang Kwang-jin informs me by letter from Shanghai that Liang Chi-chao is in favor of union and co-operation.

25th November, 1897. Yeung Ku-wan leaves Durban, South Africa, for Colombo, the Straits Settlements, Rangoon, Hongkong and Japan.

The Hongkong Chinese Club

9th January, 1898. I founded the Hongkong Chinese Club with Cheung Tsoi (張才), Luk King-fo and Leung Lan-fan. See Hongkong newspapers of 9th January, 1898.

2nd February, 1898. I meet Dr Timothy Richard LL. D., at the London Mission House in Bonham Road. We discussed reform in China, and he promised to give the reform movement his strong support.

11th March, 1898. Yeung Ku-wan arrives in Hongkong Harbour on board the s.s. "Wakasa Maru". I meet him on board ship and inform him of the result of my interview with the brothers Kang Yu-wei and Kang Kwang-jin. I also give him advice regarding the organizing of the Revolution, and remind him of the importance of obtaining the co-operation and support of the anti-Manchu secret societies in the Straits Settlements, the Yangtze Valley provinces, and the United States. (See also my letters No. 12 of 4th March, 1898; No. 25 of 13th October, 1898; No. 26 of 22nd September, 1898, and No. 33 of 7th August, 1899.) Yeung Ku-wan sailed direct for Japan to confer with Dr Sun Yat-sen.

Anti-footbinding Society

12th March, 1898. Kang Kwang-jin writes to me from Shanghai asking me for Yeung Kuwan's address. I reply and at the same time advise the formation of a society for the suppression of footbinding in China.

21st March, 1898. Yeung Kuwan arrives in Yokohama.

25th March, 1898. I interview Thomas H. Reid, and the *China Mail* publishes a leading article in support of the reform movement.

29th March, 1898. Kang Kwang-jin writes to me from Peking expressing his anxiety to meet Yeung Ku-wan.

24th July, 1898. Kang Kwang-jin writes to me again from Peking expressing his anxiety to hear from Yeung Ku-wan, to whom I had already written conveying to him Kang Kwang-jin's friendly desires.

Empress Dowager's coup d'état

21st September, 1898. Empress Dowager's coup d'état.

Kang Yu-wei and Liang Chi-chao succeeded in escaping from Peking, but Kang Kwang-jin, Tan Sze-tung, Liu Kwang-ti, Yang Tzewei, Yang Shih-shen and Lin Shio were seized and executed without trial.

I will leave the story of the Empress Dowager's coup d'état and the events which followed to be written by my old friend Kang Yu-wei and his chief disciple Liang Chi-chao.

29th September, 1898. Kang Yu-wei arrives in Hongkong, and after a short stay leaves for Japan by s.s. "Kawachi Maru", on 19th October, 1898.

When Kang Yu-wei landed, he was befriended by my old friend Ho Tung (何東), now Sir Robert Ho Tung, Kt., who extended to him his friendly hospitality, in spite of the hostility of the Manchu Peking Government and its myrmidons at Canton.

Sir Robert has always been the friend of the reformers, and he is still unsparing in his time and energy in China's welfare.

8th October, 1898. I discuss with Dr Ho Kai the political situation and our prospects of success.

Martyrdom of Kang Kwang-jin

5th December, 1898. In reply to my enquiries of 17th October, 1898, regarding my friend Kang Kwang-jin, Dr Timothy Richard writes to me from Shanghai informing me of the safe and satisfactory disposal of Kang Kwang-jin's body, and he also deals with the question of the salvation of China as follows:

Shanghai, Dec. 15th, 1898. Tse Tsan-tai, Esq.

Dear Sir, I am in receipt of your letter of the 6th inst. making enquiries about your friend.

I did all I could through a friend in Peking and since then I have written to him (your friend) direct saying that everything has been arranged satisfactorily about his poor brother for the present.

I gave him details.

As to the other question for the salvation of China, I am doing all in my power. But the Manchus refuse *light* and will not invite the help of *friendly* foreigners. Some of the leading Chinese also have published documents in which they insult the best men of the West.

They want to learn foreign military and naval affairs: they want to open mines *in order* to have funds *to fight the foreigners and drive them all out of China*. It is this want of friendliness on the part of the Manchus and some of the leading mandarins and even *hatred of all foreigners* which makes it impossible that God should give power to them.

It is such principles which destroy China most of all. The salvation of China as well as of the whole world lies in the cultivation, not of militarism, but of friendship. Let the best people of China and of the West persevere in their good work of making *peace* and *goodwill* and *goodness* their chief aim, then prosperity will in due time follow.

But if nations only seek their *own national interests first*, then no matter how great they are, and whether they are Chinese or European nations, they cannot last long when they make righteousness a secondary aim. Be not weary in well doing.

With best wishes for yourself and your country, – I remain, Yours Sincerely,

Timothy Richard

(This letter is mentioned in Professor William E. Soothill's book "Timothy Richard of China" (Page 242). Professor W. E. Soothill is Professor of Chinese in the University of Oxford.) [*sic*]

Union and cooperation
Progress in the Yangtze Provinces

9th December, 1898. Letter No. 29, dated Yokohama, 24th November 1898, received from Yeung Kuwan informing me of the success of our plans, and the co-operation of the Hunan "reformers".

Yeung Ku-wan also informs me that there may be difficulty in uniting the two parties owing to selfishness and jealousy.

24th December, 1898. I send a letter to Kang Yu-wei in Japan outlining my policy and strongly advising union and co-operation in the movement for Freedom and Independence.

9th January, 1899. Kang Yuwei writes to me from Japan expressing his concurrence with my policy of union and co-operation in the work of "reform".

1st March, 1899. I write to Kang Yu-wei urging upon him the importance of union and co-operation and advising him to come to an understanding with Yeung Kuwan and his friends in Japan.

28th March, 1899. Liang Chi-chao writes to me from Tokio, Japan, expressing his concurrence with my policy of union and co-operation and informing me of Kang Yu-wei's departure for the United States.

17th April, 1899. I send a reply to Liang Chi-chao's letter impressing upon him the great importance of union and co-operation.

23rd April, 1899. Yeung Kuwan writes to me from Yokohama informing me that the members of Kang Yu-wei's party favor union and co-operation, and that Japanese friends and supporters have also advised the union of the two parties.

Meeting between Yeung Ku-wan and Liang Chi-chao

19th June, 1899. I received from Yeung Ku-wan letter No. 31 dated Yokohama, 6th June, 1899, informing me of a meeting between him and Liang Chi-chao in the office of Messrs. Kingsell and Co., in Yokohama.

Yeung Ku-wan writes:

"He (Liang Chi-chao) advised me to try my best to go on with the work of our party and he will try his best to go on with the work of his party. He does not like to co-operate with us yet. Hong's party are too proud and jealous of our Chinese English scholars.

They don't like to have the same rank as us; they always aspire to governing us or want us all to submit to them. They do not know what justice means, as Mr U Lai-un (胡禮垣) remarked in the 'Sun Ching Or Hang' (book), and I have heard several wise Hunan men make similar remarks concerning them.

Note. – My old friend the late U Lai-un was a great thinker and philosopher, and collaborated with the late Sir Kai Ho Kai in translating and writing many works on reform, which were read with avidity by Kang Yu-wei and his disciples.

He led the life of a recluse, and was a staunch supporter of the Cause of Reform and Independence in China.

I succeeded in bringing the 'leaders' together, and did my best to unite two parties, but their failure to bring about the much desired union of the two parties is most regrettable. It has all been a game of selfish political chess and scheming to become top dog!"

A political cartoon

19th July, 1899. I design and publish a political cartoon – "The Situation in the Far East" – which appeared in many foreign illustrated newspapers. This cartoon was designed to arouse the Chinese nation, and to warn the people of the impending danger of the partitioning of the Empire by the Foreign Powers.[60]

I allowed Yeung Ku-wan to publish in Japan a colored travesty of my cartoon, which led to my being questioned by the Colonial Secretary of Hongkong.

3rd August, 1899. I receive letter No. 32, dated Yokohama, 27th July, 1899, from Yeung Ku-wan enclosing copies of revolutionary propaganda, which have been circulated broadcast exhorting the people of China to rise and rebel against the Manchu usurpers.

31st August, 1899. I receive letter No. 33, dated Yokohama, 19th August, 1899, from Yeung Ku-wan informing me that revolutionary "exhortations" have been sent to partisans in America, Honolulu, Australia, the Straits Settlements, Bangkok, Saigon, and Canada, in the name of the Republican Party ("Chung Kwok Hop Chung Ching Fu Ser Whui") (中國合眾政府社會) of China.

The "Po Wang Whui" Society

4th November, 1899. I write to Kang Yu-wei severely denouncing his "Protect the Emperor" (Po Wang Whui) Society (保皇會).

6th November, 1899. Letter No. 34, dated Yokohama 28/10/99, received from Yeung Ku-wan enclosing printed copies of revolutionary manifesto and circular letters, and reporting the successful progress of the work of partisans in the Yangtze provinces, and other parts of the world. Kang Yu-wei's "Po Wang Whui" (Protect the Emperor Society) is also denounced and exposed by Yeung Ku-wan.

19th November, 1899. Hung Chun-fui (洪春魁), alias Hung Wo (洪和), alias Hung Chuen-fook (洪全福) calls to see my father and I make his acquaintance, my father having previously spoken to me about him. Hung Chun-fui was a nephew of Hung Hsiu-chuan, the "Tai Ping" king. He had traveled rather extensively, and possessed a thorough knowledge of men and world affairs.

(*Note:* Later on, I sounded Hung Chuen-fook, and he agreed to join me and undertake the task of organizing a force for the capture of Canton City.)

21st December. 1899. Imperial Edict issued for the arrest of Kang Yu-wei and Liang Chi-chao.

Second attempt to capture Canton
A commonwealth government

On making Hung Chuen-fook's acquaintance on the 19th November, 1899, and discovering he had had considerable military training and experience in the armies of his uncle Hung Hsiu-chuan (洪秀全; [Hong Xiuquan], the "Tai Ping" king, I decided to plan and organize another attempt to capture Canton and establish Commonwealth Government under a "Protector", as I was of the opinion that the "Republican" form of government was too advanced for China and the Chinese. Accordingly, I consulted my father, and he approved of my decision to entrust Hung Chuen-fook with the task of organizing the revolutionary army.

The sinews of war were supplied by Li Pak (李北) alias Li Ki-tong (李紀堂) who had already sacrificed a fortune in the revolutionary cause. Li Pak was one of the greatest financial supporters of the Revolution, a fact which it is my pleasing duty to record

24th January, 1900. Yeung Ku-wan arrives in Hongkong from Japan per s.s. "Kamakura Maru". He informed me that the Hunanese members of the revolutionary party were actively organizing in Hunan and Hupeh [Hubei] provinces in the disguise of monks, and that many Japanese were also supporting us.

Yeung Ku-wan surprised me by telling me that Dr Sun Yat-sen had demanded that he should resign the leadership of the party in his favor. He said: "We were dangerously near being split up into two parties some time ago. Dr Sun Yat-sen informed me one day that the 'Ko Lao Whui' (哥老會) party of the Yangtze provinces had appointed him 'President' and hinted that as there could not be two Presidents, it would be obligatory for me to work independently, if I would not recognize him in his new position. I confessed to Sun Yat-sen that I was quite pleased to resign my position, and advised him not to encourage separation. I also informed him that I was always willing to sacrifice my life, let alone my position, for the good of the cause. We must obey the people's will, I said. I also told him that I was not particular who was appointed President so long as the movement progressed successfully under his leadership. Dr Sun has requested me to ask if you are in favor of this change and recognize his appointment". [*sic*] (See my diary.)

In order to prevent party strife, I advised Yeung Ku-wan to resign the Presidency in favor of Dr Sun Yat-sen.

6th February, 1900. Yeung Ku-wan invited me to join the new Revolutionary Party – "Tung Meng Whui" (同盟會), which had been organized by Dr Sun Yat-sen and his partisans in Japan. Owing to the usurpation of Yeung Ku-wan's position by Dr Sun Yat sen, I declined this invitation to join his new party. And disapproving of Dr Sun Yat-sen's high-handed behavior, I decided to act independently.

9th February, 1900. I broadcasted my letter "Liberty, Freedom and Reform" from Canton, in anticipation of the success of the second attempt to capture Canton City, and in order to "blaze the trail" and "clear the way". Those were the days, when things had to be accomplished in round-about ways!

The rescue of King Lien-Shan
Tse Tsan-tai meets Mrs Archibald Little

26th February, 1900. I meet Mrs Archibald Little at the Chinese Club (Hongkong), where she lectured on the evils of foot-binding. Mrs. Little appointed my wife [Zeng Guihua 曾桂華] local Secretary of the Anti-Footbinding Society.[61] Mrs Little helped me to obtain the release of the reformer King Lien-shan (經蓮山) from "Monte Forte" Prison, Macao, by influencing H.E. Sir Henry Blake and Lady Blake to send friendly representations to the Governor of Macao.[62] My friends D. Warres Smith and Alfred Cunningham, Editors of the *Hongkong Daily Press*, and Thomas H. Reid, Editor of the *China Mail*, also interested themselves in the case, and published strong leading articles in their newspapers advocating the early liberation of the prisoner.

King Lien-shan was Manager of the Imperial Chinese Telegraph Administration at Shanghai, and was arrested in Macao by the Portuguese authorities on the false charge of embezzling the funds of the Administration which was made by the Chinese authorities. King Lien-shan was the man who sent the telegram from Shanghai urging the Empress Dowager not to depose the Emperor Kwang Hsu. This telegram was signed by "King Lien-shan and 1,231 others".

The news of King Lien-shan's arrest and imprisonment was brought to me by my old friend Tsu Sien-ting (徐善亭) who was a staunch supporter of the cause of Reform and Independence.

The following letters from Mrs Archibald Little and Mr D. Warres Smith are interesting:

Hongkong Daily Press Office, Hongkong, 3rd March, 1900

Tse Tsan-tai Esq.,

Dear Sir, – I am afraid that there is not a ghost of a chance of anything any or all of the foreign papers may say, having the most distant effect, direct or indirect, but we will do our best.

I hardly think the Macao Government will defy both European and Chinese public opinion by giving up Mr King Lien-shan. I am going to endeavour to send a reporter to the trial in Macao. We happen to have no suitable man on our staff, but will write to Macao to-day to see if I can get a man there to do it. – Yours truly,

D. Warres Smith

28th February, 1900. My father, Yeung Ku-wan and I hold a conference, and we discuss the political situation in China, and the cure for China's ills.

5th March, 1900. Li Pak calls to see me, and we discuss the political situation.

31st March, 1900. I meet Dr Yung Wing, LL.D. (容閎博士) at Thomas's Hotel, and we discuss the political situation.

2nd April, 1900. Dr Yung Wing and I have a long confidential talk. Dr Yung Wing agrees with my policy of union and co-operation under able Christian leadership.

Dr Yung Wing said: "I have not met Dr Sun Yat-sen yet. What is his age? I don't think much of Sun as he is too rash".

Dr Yung Wing, LL.D., was a graduate of Yale University, and was a true lover of his people. He was the man who brought one of the first relays of Chinese students to the United States to be educated, amongst them being the well-known statesman and politician Tang Shao-yi (唐紹儀) and it was mainly through his influence that the famous Educational Mission was sent to the United States in 1870. This may be considered the great work of Dr Yung Wing's life. In 1864 he prepared the way for the foundation of the Kiang Nan Arsenal, and the China Merchants Steamship Co. (1870). In 1876 he was appointed Associate Chinese Minister together with Chin Lan-pin to Washington, USA.

3rd April, 1900. I arrange a confidential meeting between Dr Yung Wing and Yeung Ku-wan with the object of hastening union and co-operation.

4th April, 1900. Dr Yung Wing leaves for the United States by the s.s. "Empress of China". I write to Dr Sun Yat-sen advising him to meet Dr Yung Wing in Japan.

11th April, 1900. Dr Ho Kai and I discuss the political situation, and the prospects of the success of the revolutionary movement.

The Wei Chow Movement

18th April, 1900. Yung Ku-wan calls to see me. In order to prevent selfish rivalry and jealousy between the leaders of the different parties, I strongly advised that Dr Yung Wing, LL.D., be elected President of the United Reform Parties. Yeung Ku-wan informs me that the work of organizing the Wei Chow movement is progressing rapidly and smoothly.

22nd April, 1900. Li Pak joins the revolutionary party.

26th April, 1900. Yeung Ku-wan leaves for Japan by s.s. "Awa Maru," to confer with Dr Sun Yatsen.

6th May, 1900. Chan Siu-pak, Li Pak and I confer re the Wei Chow movement.

6th June, 1900. Letter dated Yokohama 26/5/1900 received from Yeung Ku-wan informing me of his decision to visit Australia and the United States.

17th June, 1900. Yeung Ku-wan and Dr Sun Yat-sen arrive in Hongkong from Japan by the s.s. "Indus",[63] and are accompanied by a party of Japanese friends and supporters. Yeung Ku-wan, Dr Sun Yat-sen, Chan Siu-pak, Cheung Sau-por (張壽波), Hiriyama (平山) and I meet in a sampan alongside the s.s. "Indus" and hold a one hour's conference.

Yeung Ku-wan and Dr Sun Yatsen assured us of the support of the Japanese Government.

It was decided to start active operations without delay. Yeung Ku-Van landed in Hongkong, and Dr Sun Yat-sen proceeded to the Straits Settlements.

Li Hung Chang's trap

On the day of their arrival in Hongkong, Li Hung-chang (李鴻章), Viceroy of Canton, laid a trap for the kidnapping of Yeung Ku-wan and Dr Sun Yat-sen.[64]

They were invited to a "conference" on board the Canton gunboat "On Lan", but were warned in time by their Japanese friends, who frustrated the attempt to kidnap them.

25th June, 1900. Colin McD. Smart of the *China Mail* editorial staff called to see me. He assured me of his support, saying that he would follow in Thomas H. Reid's footsteps.

1st July, 1900. Yeung Ku-wan and I meet our Japanese friends and supporters, M. Fukumoto, Macamoto Ntoo, Y. Osaki, Capt. S. Hara,

M. Itoh, and H. Iwasaki at the Hongkong Hotel. We discussed the political situation in China.

M. Fukumoto assured us of the support of himself and his friends and said, "We are prepared to shed our blood for your cause".

2nd July, 1900. M. Fukumoto and his friends leave for Saigon by the s.s. "Laos" to meet Dr Sun Yat-sen.

17th July, 1900. Dr Sun Yat-sen and his friends arrive in Hongkong by the s.s. "Sado Maru", but he is forbidden to land by the Hongkong Government.

20th July, 1900. Dr Sun Yat-sen leaves for Japan by s.s. "Sado Maru".

21st July, 1900. Dr Ho Kai reports that Sir Henry A. Blake is in favor of a Southern Republic for China.

1st August, 1900. Dr Ho Kai's article based on the terms of our political programme is published by the *China Mail*.

2nd. August, 1900. Dr Ho Kai and I discuss the terms of our Programme and Appeal to the Foreign Powers.

21st August, 1900. I advocate religious toleration and the establishment of an independent Christian Church for China. See letters to Rt. Rev. Bishop Hoare, D.D., Dr Timothy Richard, LL.D., and Pastor Kranz.

22nd August, 1900. Dr Ho Kai's "Open Letter" signed "Sinensis" appears in the *China Mail*.

The Ta Tung Movement

26th August, 1900. Kang Yuwei and his followers unsuccessfully planned a revolutionary movement at Ta Tung (大通) in Anhui province and Hankow in Hupeh province. Dr Yung Wing LL. D. (容

宏博士) and his nephew Yung Sing-kiu (容星橋) were connected with this movement, and narrowly escaped with their lives.

11th September, 1900. Owing to the failure of the Ta Tung movement Dr Yung Wing flees from Shanghai, and arrives in Hongkong by s.s. "Empress of Japan".

Tang Tsai-chang (唐才常), the leader, and others were captured and beheaded.

5th October, 1900. Flag of Independence unfurled at Wei Chow by General Cheng Put-san (鄭弼臣).

The movement is supported by the *Chine Mail*, *Hongkong Telegraph*, and *Hongkong Daily Press*.

28th October, 1900. Sze Kin-yu (史堅如) attempts to blow up Viceroy Tak Sau's (德壽) yamen at Canton, and is arrested and executed.

7th November, 1900. The Wei Chow movement collapses through shortage of ammunition and men.

28th November, 1900. Viceroy Tak Sau issues a proclamation, denouncing Yeung Ku-wan and other reformers.

Assassination of Yeung Ku-wan

10th January, 1901. Yeung Ku-wan is assassinated in his schoolroom at No. 52, Gage Street, Hongkong. The assassins escaped to Canton.

Yeung Ku-wan was a noble-minded man, and was heart and soul a devoted adherent of the Cause. It may be truthfully said of him that he was one of the noblest of China's patriots, who suffered martyrdom in the cause of Freedom and Independence.

Yeung Ku-wan's body has been buried in the Protestant Cemetery at Hongkong, and the story of his life and work has still to be written.

1st March, 1901. I receive a letter from Dr Sun Yat-sen dated Yokohama, 13/2/1901, deeply regretting the assassination of Yeung Ku-wan, and forwarding obituary notices for distribution.

25th May, 1901. I have a confidential talk with Alfred Cunningham, Editor of the *Hongkong Daily Press*, regarding the movement for Freedom and Independence.

23rd September, 1901. King Lien-shan calls personally to see me, and to tender thanks to all those who interested themselves in his case, and helped to obtain his release from Monte Forte prison, Macao.

Second attempt to capture Canton

26th September, 1901. I confer with Li Pak, who expresses his willingness to join me in organizing another attempt to capture Canton City and establish a Provisional Government with Dr Yung Wing LL.D. as President.

We decide to place the task of recruiting and organizing the fighting forces in the hands of Hung Chuen-fook.

3rd October, 1901. Ng Lo-sam (吳老三) alias Ng Sui-sang (吳瑞生) is banished from Hongkong for being connected with the assassination of Yeung Ku-wan.

7th October, 1901. I discuss with Hung Chuen-fook the plans for capturing Canton.

13th October, 1901 I discuss with my father the organization of the movement for the capture of Canton.

25th October, 1901. I discuss with Dr Ho Kai the organization of the movement for Freedom and Independence.

30th October, 1901. Hung Chuen-fook, Li Pak and I meet to discuss plans for the capture of Canton and the establishing of a provisional government.

Interview with Dr G. E. Morrison

22nd November, 1901. I meet Dr G. E. Morrison, *London Times* correspondent, at the Hongkong Hotel.

We discuss the movement of Freedom and Independence and he assured me of his friendly sympathy and support. He said: "I am quite willing to help you and shall do my best to further and support the movement. My support means the support of the *Times*, and the support of the *Times* means the support of the British people. My policy is the *Times* policy".

Dr Morrison advocated in strong terms the removal of the old Empress Dowager. He told me of his friend J. O. P. Bland's timely rescue of Kang Yu-wei at Woosung.

The following is my pen picture of Dr G. E. Morrison:

"Dr Morrison is a man who commands attention by his distinguished appearance and fine presence. He is tall and close-shaven, with a bold, broad and commanding brow, large eyes with a piercing look, straight eye-brows, long nose, and firm mouth with thin lips.

His hair is light, and he is a fine looking type of Australian manhood.

I found him polished, genial and affable, and a man possessing great common-sense and decision of character".

26th December, 1901. Dr Yung Wing LL.D. arrives in Hongkong bound for the United States. I send him confidential instructions through Li Pak.

16th January, 1902. I receive a letter from D. Warres Smith, dated London 13th December 1901, acknowledging receipt of King Lien-shan's letter of thanks and gratitude.

18th January, 1902. I receive a letter from Dr Timothy Richard, dated Shanghai, 13th. January 1902. He wrote:

"May all your efforts in behalf of Reform in your country be also abundantly blessed".

28th January, 1902. Dr Sun Yat-sen arrives in Hongkong by the s.s. "Yawata Maru," and stays at No. 24, Stanley Street.

3rd February, 1902. Dr Sun Yat-sen leaves Hongkong.

1st April, 1902. I receive a letter from Dr G. E. Morrison, dated Peking 17th March, 1902, sending me his address and enquiring for "news" of the movement.

16th April, 1902. My letter "Manchu Rule" appears in the *Hongkong Telegraph*.

As we depended upon the anti-Manchu secret societies to furnish the fighting material for the Revolution, I frequently contributed articles and letters to the foreign newspapers in their support.

16th May, 1902. Dr Yung Wing leaves for the United States by the s.s. "Gaelic".

23rd May, 1902. I receive a letter from D. Warres Smith, dated *Hongkong Daily Press* office, London, 25th April, 1902, assuring me of his support.

6th June, 1902. I advocate popular representation for Chinese in Hongkong. See *Hongkong Daily Press* of 6th June, 1902.

9th June, 1902. Alfred Cunningham, Editor of the *Hongkong Daily Press*, helps me to draft our Proclamation and Appeal to the Foreign Powers.

The rottenest government in existence

4th July, 1902. I receive a letter from Dr G. E. Morrison, dated Peking, 25th June, 1902, asking for "news". He writes:

> The Government of this country is the rottenest in existence with the possible exceptions of Persia and Turkey.

11th August, 1902. I receive a letter from D. Warres Smith of the *Hongkong Daily Press*, dated London, 7th July, 1902, assuring me of his support. He writes:

> But of course a reformation, and that a very complete one in the system of Government is absolutely necessary. That may be brought about by a big revolution, but I question it much; I fancy it will be a thing of slow growth. Anyhow; a beginning must be made some day and the sooner the better.

13th August, 1902. I write to Dr Yung Wing, LL D., instructing him to organize a junta in the United States, and work for the cooperation and support of American friends and sympathisers.

9th October, 1902. I write to Dr G. E. Morrison warning him to be in readiness for the coming Revolution. I also write to D. Warres Smith in London.

16th October, 1902. I discuss with my father the progress of Hung Chuen-fook's organization work.

19th October, 1902. I warn Thos. H. Reid, Editor of the *China Mail*, to be prepared for the coming Revolution, and also Alfred Cunningham, Editor of the *Hongkong Daily Press*.

2nd November, 1902. I advocate the suppression of slavery in China. See English and Chinese newspapers.

6th November, 1902. I receive a letter from Dr Yung Wing LL.D, dated No.12, Myrtle Street Hartford, Conn., 21st September 1902. He writes:

> I hold myself ready, at this end, to do all I can to meet your wants at the other end. Send on the cipher or secret code as soon as possible. It is an indispensable adjunct to our correspondence.

13th December, 1902. Dr Sun Yat-sen arrives in Hongkong by the s.s. "Indus" and proceeds to Saigon.

24th December, 1902. Alfred Cunningham, Editor of the *Hongkong Daily Press*, secretly prints our Proclamation of Independence, and in order to preserve secrecy, it is written and lithographed on stone!

25th December, 1902. My brother Tse Tsi-shau (Tse Tsan-ip) (子修 謝纘葉) arrives from Singapore by the s.s. "Korea", and I appoint him my Deputy.

Meetings with Dr. G. E. Morrison

26th December, 1902. Dr G. E. Morrison arrives in Hongkong from Haiphong by s.s. "Hoihao". We hold a secret consultation at the

Hongkong Hotel, and meet again on the 28th, two days later. I hand him copies of our Proclamation of Independence.

27th December, 1902. Hung Chuen-fook and my brother Tse Tsi-shau leave for Canton on a special mission.

29th December, 1902. Dr G. E. Morrison leaves for Australia by s.s. "Chingtu". Before parting he assured me of his staunch support, and promised to return to China immediately on receipt of my telegram.

30th December, 1902. I receive a letter from my brother Tse Tsi-shau dated Canton, 29th December 1902, reporting the results of a secret conference of eight of the important leaders of the movement at Fong Chuen.

1st January, 1903. Hung Chuen-fook and my brother Tse Tsi-shau return from their mission to Canton.

9th January, 1903. Alfred Cunningham calls to see me and reports that General Gascoigne and the Commodore are in favor of supporting our movement for Independence.

13th January, 1903. Hung Chuen-fook calls to see me, and reports that he will make the attempt to capture Canton City on the night of the 28th January, 1903 (Chinese New Year's Eve).

20th January, 1903. I discuss the situation with my father and brother Tse Tsi-shau.

The betrayal

25th January, 1903. Hung Chuen-fook and my brother Tse Tsi-shau leave for Canton via Macao to direct the operations for the capture of Canton. Not long after their departure, the

Headquarters of Hung Chuen-fook at No. 20, D'Aguilar Street, were raided by the Hongkong Police, and a number of arrests made.

26th January, 1903. I dispatch a message to Rev. A. Kollecker of the Berlin Mission at Fong Chuen requesting him to warn all friends and sympathisers in Canton and Fong Chuen. I discuss the situation with Alfred Cunningham and Thomas H. Reid, and we watch developments. I send a special messenger to Macao to search for and warn Hung Chuen-fook and my brother Tse Tsi-shau of the betrayal of our movement.

27th January, 1903. My father falls ill through anxiety and worry due to the betrayal and the failure of the attempt to capture Canton City. Perhaps it is well that the attempt failed, and God, in Whom I have always trusted, knows best.

27th January, 1903. My brother Tse Tsi-shau returns from Macao. Arms, uniforms, etc., at Canton and Fong Chuen seized by the Canton authorities and numerous arrests made. Hung Chuen-fook shaves off his beard and escapes in disguise. J. Scott Harston of Messrs. Ewens and Harston (Solicitors) is retained to watch the case of the arrested and imprisoned reformers.

31st January, 1903. The *Hongkong Daily Press*, publishes a leading article counselling protection for all reformers and their sympathisers. Alfred Cunningham and J. Scott Harston working in their behalf, all the prisoners are liberated, which causes a great sensation.

The S.C.M. Post, Ltd.

6th February, 1903. I discuss with Alfred Cunningham the promotion of *The South China Morning Post*, Limited, for the furtherance of the cause of Reform and Independence.

7th February, 1903. The *China Mail* publishes a lengthy leader in support of the "Reform" movement.

14th February, 1903. I discuss the situation with my father, and in order to prevent useless blood-shed, we decide to disband the different forces in the interior.

17th February, 1903. My father expresses fears that he will not have long to live and blames Hung Chuen-fook for not listening to his advice. Hung Chuen-fook was lacking in discretion, and my father suspected him of selfish designs.

Death of Tse Yet-chong

11th March, 1903. Death of my father Tse Yet-chong in Hongkong at the age of 72.

16th March, 1903. I meet Dr G. E. Morrison at the Hongkong Hotel, and we discuss the political situation in China. He assured me of his unswerving support.

1st April, 1903. The *South China Morning Post*, Limited, is successfully promoted and I am appointed to be Compradore of the Company.

Owing to the failure of the attempt to capture Canton City and the death of my father, I decide to allow Dr Sun Yat-sen and his followers a free hand, and to devote my time to the furtherance of the cause of Reform and Independence through the columns of the *South China Morning Post*, and other newspapers.

The *South China Morning Post* is now recognized to be the leading newspaper of South China.

28th April, 1903. My letter "Russia and Manchuria" signed "Indignation" is published by the *Hongkong Daily Press*.

7th August, 1903. The *China Mail* and *Hongkong Daily Press* publish at my request strong leading articles in support of the "Supao" prisoners, who were arrested in Shanghai.

22nd July, 1904. I published the first Chinese Diary of the Russo-Japanese War, and received appreciations from high Japanese officials.

22nd August, 1904. I advocated the formation of an International Society for the protection of Ancient Historical Relics, and the universal suppression of vandalism. See world's newspapers and Hongkong newspapers of 22nd August, 1904.

The World's Chinese Students' Federation

1st October, 1904. I advocated the formation of the World's Chinese Students' Federation. See letters to my old friend Dr Wu Lien-teh, M.A., M.D., LL.D. (伍連德博士). Dr Wu Lien-teh is the world-famed Plague Expert of China, and the founder of the Peking Central Hospital and Medical College. He is one of the brightest gems in China's medical history.

28th December, 1905. I advocated a scheme for the termination of the United States boycott movement in China. See *South China Morning Post* of 28th December, 1905.

26th April, 1907. Dr Sun Yat-sen, Wong Hing (黃興) and others raise the flag of revolt at Wong Kong and Yam Lim in S.W. Kwangtung [Guangdong].

18th July, 1907. I receive a letter from Dr Yung Wing, dated South Windsor, Conn., 7/6/1907, assuring me of his continued staunch support.

24th September, 1907. In order to frustrate Russian designs, I urged the immediate colonization of Manchuria and the development of its mineral resources. See *Sheung Po* of 24th September, 1907.

Dr Yung Wing's scheme

22nd October, 1907. I receive a letter from Dr Yung Wing, dated 771 Asylum Avenue, Hartford, Conn., 17/9/1907, submitting his scheme for a successful revolution in China.

25th January, 1908. I meet Dr G. E. Morrison at the Hongkong Hotel, and we discuss the political situation in China. (See lengthy interview in my Diary.)

12th May, 1908. Dr Sun Yat-sen, Wong Hing, Wu Han-man (胡漢民), Wong Chin-wei (汪精衛) and others raise the flag of revolt at Ho Hau, on the borders of Yunnan province.

17th August, 1908. I receive a letter from Dr Yung Wing, dated No. 310, Sargeant Street, Hartford, Conn., 14/7/1908, advocating the union of the reform parties, and condemning Kang Yu-wei and his Po Wang Whui (Protect the Emperor Society) Party.

30th June, 1909. Claimed that the Chinese were the first to discover Northern Australia during the Ming Dynasty, and advocated an investigation by the Chinese Government. See *China Mail* of 30th June, 1909.

17th May, 1910. I receive a letter from Dr Yung Wing, dated 16, Atwood Street, Hartford, Conn., 13/4/1910, strongly denouncing Kang Yu-wei and his disciple, and informing me of his meeting with Dr Sun Yat-sen.

24th October, 1910. I advocated a closer understanding between the United States and China, and discussed the future control of the Pacific.

See *South China Morning Post* of 24th October, 1910.

22nd February, 1911. My Open Letter "Russia and China" is sent to the Governments of the Foreign Powers, the Foreign Ministers at Peking and all the Foreign newspapers, in order to pave the way for the Great Revolution in China.

8th April, 1911. Tartar General Fu Chi (孚琦) of Canton, assassinated.

27th April, 1911. Attack on Viceregal Yamen and attempted capture of Canton by Wong Hing and others. Seventy two revolutionaries lose their lives in this attack.

Sir Hiram S. Maxim

14th June, 1911. I receive a long letter from Sir Hiram S. Maxim, dated London, 13/5/1911.

He offers China a new rifle, and refers to the importance of flying machines.

He discusses flying machines vis-a-vis dirigibles.

Sir Hiram always supported the Chinese in speech and writing. He greatly sympathised with the Chinese in their struggle for Freedom and Independence, and went so far as to offer his valuable services to the Republican Government of China.

In a letter to me, dated 14th April, 1913, he wrote:

"I could do a great deal for China if the Chinese would give me the opportunity.

I am regarded as the greatest expert on fire-arms in the world.

I took the personal Grand Prix for artillery at the last Paris Exposition.

Notwithstanding that I am an old man I am still very active and able to do a lot of work.

I have long been in strong sympathy with the Chinese, and I would like to finish up my career by making myself very useful to them".

I strongly recommended Sir Hiram to President Yuan Shih-kai direct, and also through my friend Dr G. E. Morrison, but Yuan Shih-kai failed to take advantage of Sir Hiram's offer. It was to Sir Hiram that I sent my plans of a dirigible airship in 1899. The problem of aerial navigation by dirigible air-ships, propelled by motor-driven fan propellers fore, aft and deck, was solved by me in 1894. The three deck propellers embodied the gyroscopic principle of ascending and descending. Sir Hiram believed in flying machines and had no faith in dirigibles. The design of my dirigible air-ship was published in many of the world's illustrated newspapers and magazines of this period.

25th August, 1911. I expose "Lin Shao-yang", the author (European) of "A Chinese Appeal to Christendom", in the *Hongkong Daily Press*. He apologises in the columns of the *North China Daily News*.

The revolution
The Wuchang Revolt and Li Yuan-hung

10th October, 1911. The foreign drilled troops of Hupeh province mutiny, and cooperating with the revolutionaries succeed in capturing Wuchang.

Historical documents reading

The Revolution spreads quickly throughout the whole Empire, from Chihli in the north to Kwangtung in the south and from Shantung in the east to Sze-chuan in the west. So swift and overwhelming was the progress of the Revolution that consternation reigned in Peking, and in despair the Manchu Court turned to Yuan Shih-kai (袁世凱) for assistance in quelling the rising and saving the dynasty.

In fifteen days all the lower Yangtze provinces were lost to the Empire, and by mid-November fourteen provinces had declared their independence.

Li Yuan-hung (黎元洪) is elected by the Revolutionary Committee to be President of the Provisional Government at Wuchang.

25th October, 1911. Tartar General Fung Shan (鳳山) is killed by a bomb at Canton.

3rd November, 1911. I reply to Sir Hiram S. Maxim's letter of 29th September 1911, thanking him for his support and offer of a new rifle.

4th November, 1911. Shanghai captured by the revolutionaries.

9th November, 1911. Independence of Canton declared.

21st December, 1911. Dr Sun Yat-sen arrives in Hongkong by the s.s. "Devanha". We meet on board and exchange greetings.

Dr Sun Yat-sen leaves for Nanking.

Dr Sun Yat-sen elected Provisional President

29th December, 1911. Dr Sun Yat-sen is elected Provisional President of the Republic of China by the Military Assembly at Nanking.

15th January, 1912. I interview my Editor friends Thomas Petrie of the *South China Morning Post* and B. A. Hale of the *Hongkong Daily Press* and urge them to advocate the early recognition of the Republic of China by Great Britain. I also write to Dr Yung Wing LL.D., Dr G. E. Morrison, *London Times* correspondent, D. Warres Smith and Sir Hiram S. Maxim.

Dr. Yung Wing's advice

23rd January, 1912. I receive a letter from Dr Yung Wing, LL.D., dated, 284, Seargeant Street, Hartford, Conn., 22nd December, 1911. He writes as follows:

"284, Sargeant Street,

Hartford, Conn.

22nd December, 1911

My dear Tse Tsan-tai, – As you are one of the leaders of the Revolution, I have enclosed one of my type-written letters for formality's sake more than for anything else.

What I am anxious now is that the predatory Powers now in Peking, will have a preponderating influence with the Yuan Shih-kai, Tang Shao-yi crowd, that they will leave no stone unturned to influence the Convention in Shanghai to adopt a constitutional monarchy and have Yuan Shih-kai and Tang Shao-yi have the control of the new Government. This would be just as bad as to have the Manchu regime back again in power.

A new China should be in the hands of pure Chinese, and not in the hands of trimmers and traitors with European predators to intermeddle in our civil and domestic affairs; if foreigners are employed, Americans are far preferable. We can have them under contract, on the basis of retention or dismissal, as we think best. Such an important question should; be calmly discussed and firmly decided upon in National Convention, by delegates to meet in a central city.

A Provisional Government at once be organized, and established so as to start the wheels of government at work, and to restore order and peace of society in their normal condition. Let me hear from you.

Christmas greetings and happy New Year congratulations to you. – Yours faithfully,

Yung Wing (Enclosure)"

"Hartford, Connecticut,

December 19th, 1911.

Gentlemen. – You have been providently called upon to head this wonderful Revolution which, within a short time, has reduced the Manchu regime to a cringing suppliant.

On the one hand, you have in [sic] behalf of 450,000,000 of the people of China, who have suffered oppression and depression for nearly three centuries, cried for a Republic, to give them freedom and independence for relief. Now that you have got these Manchus under your heels, let no political trimmers, however able and plausible their representations may be, entice you from your original and steadfast purpose of calling for a Republic. They may tell you that constitutional monarchy is more in consonance with your national antecedence. more in harmony with your national tradition and associations; that a constitutional monarchy with a Privy Council, headed by such a man as Yuan Shih-kai as Premier, would guarantee you all the political safeguards promised.

Don't believe a word of this. Put no trust whatever in what Yuan Shih-kai may say to you through Tang Shao-yi, his mouthpiece. You may be sure they are all on the make. Who is Yuan Shih-kai? Did he not play the traitor to his master, the Emperor Kwang Hsu, in 1898? Ought a traitor to be trusted? He is the man so much admired by the foreign diplomats in Peking, who took advantage of the crumbling Manchu Dynasty exacting by all manner of ingenious feignings till he got hold of the premiership of the miserable opium sot, Prince Ching: then his lame leg all at once got well, he was able to move about trying to prop up the odious Manchu machine, to take in China once more, having him as the chauffeur, to manipulate.

Is such a man of deep designs to be trusted? He ought to be banished with the banished Manchus. His name "Yuan" ought to be expunged from the national record of family names. He ought to be branded as a traitor in history, and forever held in execration by posterity.

The people of China in the plenitude of its sovereignty have called for a Republic and you, their leaders, have seconded the call. The people's voice is the voice of God (Vox Populi, Vox Dei). Therefore follow that voice and you will be all right.

But there is yet another still, small voice, humming in my mind, which demands peremptory enunciation. It is this: After you have finished your glorious work of the disposal of the political power of the Manchus in China, it is absolutely necessary that you should cling to each other closer than brothers.

Under no circumstances and under no provocations whatever should you fall out with each other, plunge into intestine feuds and Civil War.

I need not picture to you the dire consequences of anarchy and chaos. You know what they are yourselves. An internecine war is sure to bring on foreign intervention, which means partition of this magnificent country which a wise Providence has kept in reserve for the Chinese race, to build up a model Republic.

Think of the glorious work your revolution has opened up for you and posterity.

May He who rules all things keep you in His fear and aw, and finally gather you all in the fold of Christ Who is the sum and substance of all things. – Faithfully Yours,

Yung Wing"

30th January, 1912. I telegraphed to President Sun Yat-sen to prevent the sale of ancient curios and pictures (historical treasures) of the Peking and Fengtien palaces. This was done in order to preserve China's historical treasures and prevent the Manchus from raising war-funds.

2nd February, 1912. Dr Yung Wing, LL.D., sends his congratulations to Dr Sun Yat-sen, and writes as follows:

"284, Sargeant Street,

Hartford Conn.,

29th December, 1911.

My dear Tse Tsan-tai. – Your letter of November 21st received, also the first, and perhaps the last number of the (journal), which ends, and the Dynasty will abdicate with it, as you find no more to send me. You will have to wait till the new President of the New China Republic, Mr Sun Yat-sen, is inaugurated: you can then send me a report of his inauguration and a complete list of his Cabinet. Should you see him in Nanking in the inauguration, by all means tender him my hearty congratulations.

Tell him I am improving and perhaps will make my way to China, and have a sight of the New Republic.

I hope I may be spared to live to see the day when my friend may be elected the next President, who has laboured for China and the Chinese for the space of 22 years.

I wish very much to have a personal acquaintance with all the other leaders of the Revolution before I die.

Their memories ought to be embalmed in the memory of the people.

My son Morrison and Ada have not arrived from Europe. I do not expect to see them till February. The last I heard from them was Egypt. They are having a fine time among the mummies in Upper Egypt.

By this time they must be in Rome. – Yours sincerely,

Yung Wing.

Merry Christmas and Happy New Year to you and to the Mother of Mrs Morrison and her sisters in Hongkong. Hope they are all well. – Y. W.".

Abdication of the Manchus
China becomes a republic

7th February, 1912. Abdication of the Manchu Emperor Hsuan Tung, which was hastened by the "machinations" of Yuan Shih-kai.

12th February, 1912. China becomes a Republic. End of the Manchu Dynasty.

On this day three abdication edicts were issued. The first runs in part as follows:

> To-day the people of the whole Empire have their minds bent upon a Republic, the Southern provinces having initiated the movement and the Northern generals having favoured it subsequently. The will of Providence is clear and the people's wishes are plain. How could I for the sake of the glory and honour of one family thwart the desire of teeming millions? Wherefore I (the Empress Dowager) with the Emperor decide that the form of government in China shall be a Constitutional Republic to comfort the longing of all within the Empire and to act in harmony with the ancient sages, who regarded the throne as a public heritage.

The following appeared in the *London Times*, February 16, 1912:

> The 'Son of Heaven' has abdicated, the Manchu dynasty reigns no longer, and the oldest Monarchy of the world has been formally constituted a Republic. History has witnessed few such surprising revolutions and none perhaps of equal magnitude, which has been carried out in all its stages with so little bloodshed. Whether

the last of these stages has been reached is one of the secrets of the future. Some of those who know China best cannot but doubt whether a form of government so utterly alien to Oriental conceptions and to Oriental traditions as a Republic can be suddenly substituted for a Monarchy in a nation of four hundred millions of men, whom kings with semi-divine attributes have ruled since the first dim twilights of history. China or, at all events, articulate China, has willed to have it so. She has embarked with a light heart upon this great adventure and we heartily desire that it may bring her the progressive and stable government she craves.

15th February, 1912. Dr Sun Yat-sen resigns the Presidency. The resignation of Dr Sun Yat-sen, was followed by a meeting of the National Assembly at Nanking, which elected Yuan Shih-kai to be First President of the Republic. Everything was pre-arranged! In fact, Dr Sun Yat-sen was "engineered" out of the Presidency by Yuan Shih-kai and his satellites.

D. Warres Smith's remarkable letter

15th March, 1912. I receive a remarkable letter from D. Warres Smith, dated London 23rd February, 1912, in which he deals with the political situation in China, and gives his opinion of Yuan Shih-kai and others. He writes as follows:

"Hongkong Daily Press" Office, 131, Fleet Street, London, E. C., 23rd February, 1912

Dear Mr Tse Tsan-tai. – I thank you very much for your kind letter of the 16th ult. I received it sometime since but was induced to delay an acknowledgment as every day brought us fresh telegrams and I was anxious to see how things were developing. The latest is that Dr Sun is to come as Minister to London. I am sure that the present Minister here, H. E. Lew, is heart and soul with the new Government. I have not seen him since he came back here to his present high post, as I do not seek to intrude myself into such aristocratic circles. (But you will have no aristocracy now you have a Republic!), but I saw him in 1900 just after I came home, when he was Secretary of Legation, and although I did not recognise him he did me at once, as I used to spend my summer "week-ends" in Macao, where he had and probably still has a house on the Praya Grande and where his family lived. He was very kind, and rendered me considerable help. No doubt Dr Sun would make an able and discreet Minister, but may not be of a lively enough disposition and I should think would not care much for the gaieties of London society, an almost necessary qualification. Dr Wu Ting-fang (whom by the way I knew in the very old days, when known by his Cantonese name of Ng Choy, as he was at one time lessee of the Chung Ngoi Sun Po) is more suitable in that respect, but I suppose he will be required in China as I should think Dr Sun would be also.

The former would be the more likely to ngratiate himself with the people of the North, as he has been so much in Peking, and they, judging from what I saw and heard of Tientsin men during my ten years in Shanghai, are an independent and self-assertive people.

I presume you will to a considerable extent follow the old policy of having the head officials men belonging to other provinces than those in which they hold office, yet on the other hand avoid the danger of a disproportionate number of Kwangtung men. A great trouble will be, as in other countries, monarchical as well as republican, the hordes of office seekers.

What has become of Kang Yu wei? I suppose you Southerners do not like him, or rather his policy, much, but better have him as a friend than as an enemy.

It is difficult for Chinese and impossible for foreigners to know the real merits of the different men and how they are likely to behave under entirely new conditions, but I should have more faith in Kang than in Yuan, as I do not forget that it was the latter who betrayed Kang's party to the old Empress; and although his purpose is no doubt good he seems to us, who can get only very imperfect and colored information, somewhat of a shuffler and time server. But I must not speak disrespectfully of the President of the greatest Republic in the World. Personally, while I rejoice that the Manchu usurpers are done with for ever, I think it would better have ensured stability had a strong man been found as a Constitutional Monarch. But you do not want to be bothered with any opinions. I only express them because they are those generally held by "old China hands" here. I fully believe that what all of you desired was not so much a Republic as relief from the Manchu corruption.

A statement came from Berlin yesterday that the German Government will recognise the Republic as soon as the National Assembly has confirmed the Constitution and definitely elected a President; but I do not think it is likely until all the chief Powers have agreed, and I think haste is to be deprecated. It would make no practical difference. At the same time I should like Great Britain to be the first, as she was in the case of Japan.

I do not write for the papers here and have no influence of any kind, nor if I had would it be of any use.

An effort is no doubt being made to keep Peking as the Capital, but I hope it will not succeed, as both historically and geographically Nanking is much more suitable. But I fear there will be trouble in the North, if not elsewhere, for years to come. Consolidate but do not rush things, let *festina lente* be your motto.

Wishing the cause and you personally every success. – I am, yours sincerely,

D. Warres Smith"

Death of Dr Yung Wing, LL.D.

20th April, 1912. Death of Dr Yung Wing, LL.D., at his home in Cambridge, Massachusetts, United States of America. Dr Yung Wing was a true patriot and dearly loved his fatherland, and he longed to come back and serve China in his old age. It may be said of Dr Yung Wing that he was born too soon and before his time.

24th April, 1912. Dr Sun Yat-sen arrives in Hongkong from Nanking and is welcomed by the representatives of about sixty public Societies and Associations. I am elected spokesman, and introduce the Committee of Representatives to Dr Sun Yat-sen.

18th June, 1912. I send a letter to Dr G. E. Morrison urging the early recognition of the Republic.

Dr Timothy Richard on China

18th June, 1912. – I received a letter from Dr Timothy Richard, dated Shanghai, 13th June, 1912, dealing with the political situation in China. He writes as follows:

"Christian Literature Society for China,

143, North Szechuan Road. Shanghai,

June 13th, 1912

To Tse Tsan-tai, Esq., Hongkong.

My dear friend, – Yours of the 24th came duly to hand, for which I thank you. I rejoice with you in the removal from power of those who have obstructed the progress of China for the last hundred years. But as I conceive it, the destructive is only half the work. By far the most difficult task is the constructive, on lines that are in harmony with the will of God and the best thought of the leading men of the world.

Instead of joyful cooperation on the part of Young China on these lines, I am greatly distressed to find so many ill-informed thrusting themselves forward, while incompetent to lead or to win the confidence of their fellow countrymen by noble examples of highest service. Still we must not be discouraged, for in the long run God will be sure to make right overcome might.

I am sorry that your health is not good, otherwise a man like you would be of incalculable service at the present time.

In view of the new conditions in China at present I have thought that a service of biographies of the most eminent Christian statesmen might be of service to the open minds among China's leaders, and the series is passing through the press at present.

Herewith I take the liberty of sending you a brief outline of what I have endeavoured to do in order to place China abreast of any nation on the face of the Earth.

Trusting your health will soon be restored again and that you will be able to put your shoulder to the wheel once more, till China is in a fair way of being second to none in any department of life. Then we may soon expect to see the Kingdom of God being established on all the Earth, and instead of the present unrest all the world over we should have peace and prosperity from the rising to. the setting sun. – Ever with kindest regards, I remain, Yours most sincerely,

Timothy Richard"

Rev. Dr Timothy Richard has done much good work for China and the Chinese. The present generation cannot realize the true value of his work, but future generations will know how to appreciate his noble and unselfish Christian services.

A Chinese national anthem

2nd July, 1912. I suggest to Padre Jacob Lao (劉雅覺) of St. Joseph's Seminary, Macao the composition of a Chinese National Anthem, which was played on a piano and by a band at Mr Francisco Tse Yet's (謝詩屏) house on the 17th September, 1912. I sent the wording and music of this National Anthem to President Yuan Shih-kai for consideration and approval on the 19th September, 1912.

The national flag of the republic

15th July, 1912. In order to preserve and perpetuate the original flag of the Revolution (a white sun on a blue ground), I send my design of the national Republican flag to President Yuan Shih-kai for consideration and approval. My design consists of a twelve-rayed or rayless white sun on a blue ground superimposed upon the five-barred flag and occupying the top corner near the bar. The flag of the Army consists of a twelve-rayed or rayless white sun on a blue ground, superimposed upon a red field and occupying the top corner near the bar. The flag of the Navy consists of a twelve-rayed or rayless white sun on a blue ground, superimposed upon a white field, and occupying the top corner near the bar.

25th July, 1912. Dr G. E. Morrison is appointed political adviser to President Yuan Shih-kai.

3rd October, 1912. I received a long letter from Mrs Archibald Little, dated 69, Grosvenor Street West, London, September 8th, 1912.

The following is an extract. – "I must not tire you with a long letter as I hope to see you before very long. Whenever I get opportunity I write and speak for China's real good. I have spoken at many meetings in the last few years".

Thos. H. Reid on the political situation

29th October, 1912. I received the following letter from my old friend and colleague Thomas H. Reid:

"88, Cannon Street, London, E.C.,

October 9th., 1912

My Dear Tse Tsan-tai. – I was delighted to hear from you again. After such a long interval since we met, it is indeed gratifying to find that one is not forgotten by old friends. I trust you are well and that the world is using you well.

It is interesting to read the printed record (Biography by Chesney Duncan) you sent me. It recalls our mutual early struggles to bring about reform in China, and I personally am proud to think that I was the first to support the movement publicly in the *China Mail* when other English newspapers in China and the Far East scoffed at the movement and the men who have been instrumental in bringing it to a successful issue. I use the word 'successful' because, though there is yet much to be done before China can be said to be on the highroad to complete reform, the first great step forward has been taken in the unseating of the Manchus.

Since I left Hongkong in 1904, I have had opportunities of preaching the cause of reform and of China. In 1905 I had an article in the *Contemporary Review* showing that Germany was a greater danger to the peace of the Far East than China or Japan. During my editorship of the *Straits Times* (1906–8) – when I had the pleasure of renewing association with Sun Yat-sen – again took up the gospel of the reform of China, and when the revolution occurred in the end of last year, I wrote several articles for the *Daily Chronicle* (London) and elsewhere supporting the Reform Party.

I still have faith in the future of China so long as the motive force behind the reform movement is Sun Yat-sen and men like yourself; and I hope to see you take a more active share in public work there within the next few years.

It is a good thing to see the party in power introducing foreign advisers to aid in the initial work. Dr Morrison, my old friend, should be of infinite help to China at the present time.

The Chinese are a very capable people. They were always better than their rulers; and I do not despair – as some do – of China's ultimate success as a Republic. But as the people under the old regime never had a chance of learning the rudiments of self-government, it is only natural that they have a lot to learn.

During their tutelage under foreign advisers they will learn quickly, and some of us may live to see the day when the Chinese will have earned the respect of the whole civilized world as a capable self-governing people, possessed of all the qualities which make for individual prosperity and national greatness.

One of the Malacca canes you gave me when I left Hongkong is my constant companion and is lying beside me in my office here. It constantly reminds me of my old friend in Hongkong to whom I send my kindest greetings and best wishes. – Yours very sincerely,

Thos. H. Reid"

Yuan Shih-kai elected president

6th October, 1913. A Provisional Constitution is adopted, and Yuan Shih-kai (袁世凱) is elected President of the Republic.

After Yuan Shih-kai's election, his first move was to order the expulsion from Parliament of all the members who had been identified, directly or indirectly, with the Revolution, and this resulted in the suspension of Parliament.

Matters remained in this condition throughout 1914, Yuan Shih-kai playing the part of a dictator.

In obedience to the "secret" wishes of Yuan Shih-kai, a movement (Chou An Hui) was started in 1915 to make him Emperor. However, Yuan Shih-kai miscalculated his strength, and when he announced his intention of becoming Emperor, his most intimate colleagues opposed his project and the Ministers of the foreign Powers unanimously counselled him to abandon it.

But Yuan Shih-kai seemed unable to understand the magnitude of the hostility he had aroused, and continued to make lavish preparations for his enthronement.

Opposition was strongest in Yunnan, which declared its independence under General Tsai Ao (蔡鍔) [Yuan's secretary in 1912].

In a mandate issued on March 21st, 1916, Yuan Shih-kai announced that the Republican form of government would be maintained, and that *"the official acceptance of the throne is hereby cancelled"*. But the mischief had already been done, and it was too late!

Death of Yuan Shih-kai

Yuan Shih-kai never recovered his lost prestige, and his death on 6th June, 1916, shortly followed from chagrin and disappointment. The Chinese consider Yuan Shih-kai to be a traitor and the man chiefly responsible for the civil war in China.

On the 29th September, 1915, I received the following letter from Dr G. E. Morrison, Political Adviser of President Yuan Shih-kai:

"Peking, China,

20th. September, 1915

Dear Mr Tse, – I was much interested to receive your letter of the 24th August and to learn that you had written a new work on the 'Creation and the Deluge', and that you are going to publish it after this terrible war (European War) is ended. But why wait till then? A book of such absorbing interest ought to be published without any delay. In fact, on receiving your letter, I thought at once of telegraphing to you and asking you to delay no further: every hour is of importance.

I would suggest with regard to the title that you ought to lay emphasis on the fact that the work is by a Chinese philosopher. This, I think, is most important, and I would suggest that it would be a friendly act if you were to dedicate your book to the Allied Rulers, sending each one of them a copy. Their acknowledgments would give material assistance in making the book more widely known.

I have been waiting, with much expectation, for your pronouncement upon the activities of the Chou An Huei, who, I understand, are putting forward three proposals:

1. That the President shall become Emperor.
2. That the President shall become Hereditary President.
3. That the President shall be Hereditary President vis-à-vis foreign countries and Monarch in the eyes of his people.

Believe me,

Very sincerely yours,

G. E. Morrison"

Regarding the activities of the "Chou An Huei", I replied to Dr Morrison's letter on the 11th October 1915, as follows:

"I have nothing to say regarding the situation in China, and as I have told you already, I have washed my hands of politics. What I dread is a Civil War in China. The Civil War is coming, and you know who is responsible for it.

The blood of the people will be on this man's (Yuan Shih-kai) head.

My dear friend, I have already warned you of what is coming, and I should not like to see such words as 'the rat and the sinking ship' applied to you – my wise and learned friend!"

The following telegram appeared in the *Tsun Wan Yat Po* (Chinese Circulating Herald) of Hongkong on 18th February 1916:

"Dr Morrison, after investigating the conditions in the provinces, suggests a postponement of the ascending of the Throne".

Death of Dr G. E. Morrison

Dr G. E. Morrison resigned his appointment as Political Adviser in the Spring of 1918, and left Peking for England in order to undergo an operation. He was operated upon in June 1919, and again in January 1920. He did not recover and died at Sidmuth [sic. Sidmouth] on 31st May, 1920.

The *Times*, in paying a tribute to him said:

> "Even his last months were devoted to working the best he could from the sick-room in the interests of China".

I am proud of the late Dr G. E. Morrison's sincere friendship, and know that he was a true friend of China and the Chinese. He was acknowledged and recognised to be the greatest living authority on China, and in his sad and untimely death, China has lost one of her greatest and best of friends .... .[65]

***

II. The Creation. The Real Situation of Eden and The Origin of the Chinese. Hong Kong: Kelly & Walsh, 1914.[66]

Introduction

For many years, ever since the day I could read and understand the Bible, the question of the Cradle of the Human Race and the Origin of the Chinese has been receiving my fervent and serious attention. Although I have read much ancient history, and carefully considered and weighed the theories of different writers, and studied the results of the archaeological and geographical investigations and excavations which have been made in all parts of the world, they have not been able to convince me that the Cradle of the Human Race is in either of the two spots, in (1) Armenia and (2) the Euphrates Valley, as stated in the Bible translation of Genesis and fixed by past authorities, and as is generally taught and believed by mankind throughout the world.

This has always caused me much worry of mind and anxiety of heart.

And, during my study of the Bible and Ancient Chinese History, on Sunday the 25th October, 1914, I discovered a clue to the unravelling of the mystery, and it suddenly dawned upon me, like a flash of light, that the Cradle of the Human Race was not where it is now reputed and believed to be, but, in Chinese Turkestan (新疆) [Xinjiang] in the plateau of Central[67] Asia and also that the Chinese race originated there.

I felt so happy and delighted with my discovery, that I immediately followed up the clue, and commenced writing this, my book, and forgetting food and sleep, finished the draft at 8 a.m., on Wednesday, the 28th October, 1914, when the thunder pealed and the Lightning flashed. The revision and re-writing of my book was completed after seven days and seven nights ceaseless labour, on the 1st November, 1914, after which, I rested for three days. I know that without God's inspiration and help it would have been impossible for me to write this book as I have done.

It is now my earnest hope and prayer that archaeological and bibliographical investigations will be carried on in this part of the world, and that the result will be, as I have said.

And, further, I fervently beseech all those, who think with me, to spread the good tidings contained in this, my book, so that, henceforth, all men will believe in God and the Bible and love each other as brothers; and peace and happiness shall reign for ever on Earth.

Tse Tsan Tai, 1st November, 1914

The Garden of Eden and the Cradle of the Human Race

… That the Cradle of the Human Race is in Asia is beyond doubt, but, the question is – Where is this Cradle?

The Bible *translation* of Genesis says that the parent stock of the human race saw the light in the "Garden of Eden" in the Euphrates Valley. Archeologists and bibliographers have also located the Garden of Eden in (1) Armenia, and in (2) the valley of the Tigris and Euphrates, comprising that portion of the Mesopotamian Plain at the head of the Persian Gulf.

Is it likely that Almighty God would create man and place him in such a corner of the World?

I say the Cradle of the Human Race – "The Garden of Eden" – is in Chinese Turkestan (新疆) in the plateau of Central Asia and I will now state my reasons.

The Garden of Eden

When the north of the Asiatic Continent was not so cold and frozen as it is at the present day, and when gigantic beasts, reptiles, and strange birds roamed its vast plains and inhabited its dense forests, the primitive ancestors of the human race were created and first saw the light in that crescent-shaped oasis of the plateau of Central Asia by the Tributaries of the Tarim River, bounded on the north by the Tien-shan Mountains (天山) [Tianshan], on the west by the Pamir Tableland, on the south by the Kuen Lun Mountains (昆侖山) and the highlands of Tibet, and on the East by the Gobi desert, and now called Chinese Turkestan (新疆).

No doubt, the close proximity of Tibet to the "Garden of Eden," accounts for the similarity of the religious "ceremonies" of the Tibetan Buddhistic "Church" to those of the Roman Catholic Church, which must have sprung from the same source.[68]

The following Bible proofs support my discovery:

Genesis 11.8. "God planted a garden eastward in Eden; and there He put the man whom He had formed".

And, further –

Genesis 11.10. "And a river went out of Eden to water the garden; and from thence it was parted, and became into four heads".

Gold and precious stones are also mentioned in Genesis II. 11–12. This spot, "eastward in Eden", must, therefore, be in Central Asia and not in Asia Minor, and this is one of my principal reasons for locating the "Garden of Eden" in Chinese Turkestan.

The Cradle of the Human Race

And, what is more convincing proof: the river Tarim, with its four tributaries or "heads",[69] flows eastward through the crescent-shaped oasis of Chinese Turkestan, and empties itself into the Lob-nor (lake); and the country traversed by the river and its four tributaries is well known to be full of gold and precious stones. The bed of the Yarkand River is covered with precious jade pebbles of different colors, and some of the mountain sides also contain jade of various colors, which have been quarried in ancient times. According to the Ancient Chinese Record of the Deluge, the stones quarried by (女娲氏) Noah, after the Deluge, were of five different colors from the Tienshan Mountains (天山).

It is noteworthy that Chaldea and Mesopotamia produced no precious Stones or minerals of any kind. But, the country yielded an abundant supply of clay and bitumen!

Again, the following proves beyond doubt, that the "Garden of Eden" – the Cradle of the Human Race – was not in Western Asia (Asia Minor):

Genesis XI. 1–2. "And the whole earth was of one language, and of one speech. And it came to pass, as they *journeyed from the East*, that they found a plain in the land of Shinar, and they dwelt there".

It would be interesting to know whether this land of Shinar (China) was in the Mongolian plain north of the Hwang Ho (Yellow River) bend, or refers to the lowlands of Shensi (陝西) [Shaanxi] province in China, where the ancestors of the Chinese race first settled down and made their home.

After the Flood, the sons of Noah must have journeyed further East **along the shores of the upheaved inland sea** in the direction of **the Great Khingan Mountains of** the Mongolian Plateau, and "journeying from the East" finally settled in the **plain of Shinar (China)**,[70] where they started making bricks for the building of the "Tower of Babel". They probably traversed the same stretch of territory as the Chinese of the Han (漢) dynasty – who conquered Turkestan in 76 B. C. – with the exception of what is now known as China proper.

Genesis XI. 3.4. "And they said one to another, go to, let us make brick, and burn them thoroughly. And they had brick for stone, and slime had they for mortar.

And they said, go to, let us build us a city and a tower, whose top may reach unto heaven; and let us make us a name, lest we be scattered abroad upon the face of the whole earth".

Ancient ruins exist in the province of Shensi (陝西); and, strange to say, China is the land of bricks, high towers (pagodas), and strange dialects.

The Tower of Babel was built by Nemrod, the son of Chus, a nephew to Shem, about three score years after the Flood.

He began a new sect of infidels, but the godly men refused to join these infidels.

God confounded them, and they were separated into many nations, about 140 years after the Flood (Genesis XI. 8.9).

After Nemrod, his son Belus reigned in Babylon about B.C. 1871, 215 years after the Flood.

Therefore, I say, again, the "Garden of Eden" – the Cradle of the Human Race – is in Chinese Turkestan.

And, consequently, it will now be necessary to revise the *translation* of the Hebrew Text of the Bible, and certain "add tions" (translator's) wi have to be expurgated. And, also, it will be necessary to revise Ancient History, and particularly China's Ancient History, as names and dates are so confused.

Noah must have lived near "Eden" at the time of the Deluge, and this I will prove by the Ancient Chinese Record of the Deluge, and by subsequent geological, archaeological, geographical, and zoological discoveries.

In order to prove that the Chinese are the descendants of Adam and Noah, I will now give a brief history of the Ancient Chinese Record of the Creation and the Deluge.

The Creation

According to ancient Chinese tradition and the written records of the Creation and the Deluge, which have been handed down from time immemorial, the story is as follows:

天地初開張
In the beginning, when Heaven and Earth were created (by God)
盤古辨陰陽
Panku (Adam) was changed into a male (陽) and a female (陰).

According to Genesis II. 21–22, the first woman was made from one of the ribs of Adam.

天形如卵白
The Firmament (Heaven) assumed the position of that of the white of an egg.
地形如卵黃
The Earth assumed the position of that of the yolk of an egg (Genesis I. 1–10).
五行生萬物

The Five Elements (土火水木金), i.e. the Earth, brought forth all living things, i.e. all living things were created by God.

In the beginning God created Heaven and Earth, and all living things therein, in six days, man being created in the sixth and last day (Genesis I).

The six "days" of the creation must have been six "periods," meaning, perhaps, millions of years.

六合運三光

The Three Lights (Sun 日, Moon 月, and Stars 星) revolved in space (六合) – the limitless space contained in the (六合) six points, viz., North, South, East, West, Zenith and Nadir – i.e. God created the Sun, Moon and Stars, and set them in the firmament of the heaven to give light upon the earth (Genesis I. 16–17).

The peopling of the world

三皇紀

The Record of the Three Patriarchs of China

1. Adam (天皇)
2. Cain (地皇)
3. Seth (人皇)

   天皇十二子

1. Adam (天皇) had twelve "successors" (子).

   The generations from Adam to Noah are: – Seth, Enos, Cainan, Malaleel, Jared, Henoch, Mathusala, Lamech, Noah, Shem, Ham and Japhet – twelve in all.

   Adam was created by God, and this is why the Chinese called him 'Tien Hwang' (天皇).

   地皇十一郎無為而自化歲起攝提綱

2. Including himself, Cain (地皇) had eleven "brethren" (郎).

   His generations are those without notice of the time when they were born or died.

   Cain was a husbandman (Genesis IV. 2.). This is why the Chinese called him "Ti Hwang" (地皇).

   Being a murderer, his generations are unnoticed and forgotten.

   人皇九兄弟

3. Seth (人皇) and his eight "successors" (Enos, Cainan Malaleel, Jared, Henoch, Mathusala, Lamech, Noah.) Nine in all.

Seth peopled the Earth, and this is why the Chinese called him "Jen Hwang" (人皇).

受命最延長

Were most long-lived.

All were nearly one thousand years old, when they died. See Genesis V.

各萬八千歲

Each lived to eighteen thousand "years," (歲) ("full" moons, i.e. months).

It is not known how many days or months constituted one of these "years" (歲), there was no calendar in existence then.

一人興一邦

Each established a tribe or nation.

Cain and Seth's descendants must have inhabited the whole district, now known as the Gobi Desert and Mongolian plateau to the east of the Tarim River district ("Garden of Eden") of Chinese Turkestan, and north of the Hwang Ho [Yellow] River.

See Genesis III. 24. "So He drove out the man; and He placed at the east of the Garden of Eden Cherubims, and a flaming sword which turned every way, to keep the way of the tree of life".

分掌九州地發育無邊疆

They separated and occupied nine continents, and flourished and spread throughout the World.

At the time of the Creation there were certainly nine continents in existence, viz.,

1. Europe – Inhabited by primitive man before the Deluge.
2. Asia – Inhabited by primitive man before the Deluge.
3. Africa – Inhabited by primitive man before the Deluge.
4. N. and S. America (2 Continents) – Inhabited by primitive man before the Deluge.
5. Australia – Inhabited by primitive man before the Deluge.
6. N. Polar Continent – Inhabited by primitive man before the Deluge.
7. S. Polar Continent – Uninhabited from the time of the Creation.
8. Malaysian Continent – Inhabited by primitive man before the Deluge.
9. Polynesian ("Pacific") Continent – Inhabited by primitive man before the Deluge (Cretan Archipelago).

The Nine continents were originally connected with each other, and, therefore, became inhabited by primitive man.

The South Polar Continent being an island and separated by a wide expanse of ocean, primitive man had no means of reaching it, and, therefore, it has remained uninhabited up to the present day.

Some of these continents must have become submerged at the time of the Deluge,[71] and this accounts for the bones of extinct animals, and primitive man being found in the geological deposits (loess) of the different continents of the World. And, it is possible that there were further seismic disturbances and subsidences after the Deluge. Easter Island with its rude stone statues, and stone houses with interiors bearing paintings of birds, animals, etc., are the remains of one of these submerged continents.

The beginning of civilization

有巢氏以出
At the time of Yu Chao (Shi).
食木始為糧
Men ate fruits and plants as food.
構木為巢室
Wood was used for making huts.
襲葉為衣裳
Leaves of trees were patched together and used for clothing.
燧人氏一出烹飪得其方
Sui Jen (Shi) invented the process of cooking.
鑽木取改火
He obtained fire by friction from the drilling or rubbing of wood.
飲食無所妨
Drinking and eating was now a convenient matter.
結繩記其事
He invented knotted cord-symbols for recording events.
年代難考詳
It is difficult to fix the date of these inventions.

五帝紀 The Record of the Five Patriarchs of China

1. Fuhi-(Henoch) – (伏羲太昊) Born B.C. 3382, "Died" B.C. 3017. (Translated to Heaven.)
2. Nü Wa-(Noah) – (女媧氏) Born B.C. 2948, Died B.C. 1998.
3. Shen Nung-(Shem) – (神農炎帝) Born B.C. 2448, Died B.C. 1848.
4. Hwang Ti-(Arphaxad) – (皇帝軒轅氏) Born B.C. 2346, Died B.C. 1908.
5. Yao-(Reu) – (帝堯陶唐氏) Born B.C. 2217, Died B.C. 1978.

Note. – In Ancient Chinese History, full notice was only taken of godly men.

I.–Fuhi (Henoch)

伏羲太昊立聖憲播宣揚

Fuhi, i.e. Henoch, "ruled". His godliness was "overflowing".

蛇身如牛首

His body was scaly like a snake, and his head was like that of an ox, i.e. his eyes were large and his forehead and facial bones prominent.

形容子異章

His mien was extraordinary in appearance.

命倉頡制字後代習成章

He ordered Tsong Chi (倉頡) to design a script. The generations which followed derived their Alphabets and Literature from this (hieroglyphic) script.

He was guided in his task by the imprints of the feet of animals and birds. (See Commentary). The Assyrian Cuneiform Script was doubtless based upon these ancient hieroglyphics.

河圖龍馬獻

A drawing of the river (Hwang Ho) [Yellow River] revealed the form of the dragon and the horse to him.

This is how Chinese Art originated. The dragon must have been one of those gigantic, extinct, four-footed, antediluvian reptiles of Northern Asia and America.

畫卦明陰陽

He designed the "Eight Trigrams" (八卦) and knew life, i.e. he was able to divine.

Genesis V. 24. And Henoch walked with God: and he was not; for God took him.

男女教嫁娶儷皮為禮將

He legalized marriage, the skins of wild animals being used for betrothal purposes.

養牲供庖食畜馬牛豬羊

He taught the people how to rear horses, oxen, pigs, and sheep for purposes of trade and for food.

It is a noteworthy fact that these animals are frequently mentioned in the Bible, and, besides, the Central Asian plateau is known to be the home of the wild ancestors of several of our domestic animals, viz., the wild horse, ox, camel, donkey, goat, sheep, pig, etc.

The Deluge

Tubal-cain

祝融共工氏交兵相戰爭

During the time of Chu Yung Kung Kung (Shi), i.e. (Tubal-cain), the land was disturbed by violence and internecine strife.

Tubal-cain was an instructor of every artificer in brass and iron. The characters (共工) mean artificers in all trades. (See Genesis IV. 22.)

共工不勝怒頭觸周山崩

Men became exceedingly incensed with each other. And, there was *great wickedness* (in the World).

上(帝)驚

God became alarmed, and angry (with the World).

天(山)柱折下震地維穿

He visited his wrath upon the Earth by a great universal and terrestrial upheaval. The pillars[72] of Tienshan (天山) collapsed and fell, and great chasms formed in the earth. (This resulted in the Deluge. Genesis VI. 1–8.)

II.–Nü Wa (Noah)

女媧氏以立鏈石以補天(山)

Nü Wa (Shi), i.e. Noah "ruled". He (after the subsidence of the waters, which had deluged the land), quarried stones for the repair of Tienshan (天山), i.e. the repairing or damming up of the mouth of Gaib gorge.

斷鼇足立極地勢得其堅

Having cut the foot of the gorge and strengthened the foundations, the safety of the land was secured.

聚灰止淹水天(山)地得依然

Having dammed and trained the waters of the channels, the locality of Tienshan resumed its former state.

傳位十五氏不可考根源

He had fifteen successors, but it is difficult to trace their history (Genesis IX).

The generations of Noah, and his three sons Shem, Ham and Japhet, are as follows: …

The fifteen generations of Noah and Shem in the direct line, are as follows: – i.e. Shem, Elam, Asshur, Arphaxad, Lud, Aram, Hus, Hul, Gether, Mosoch, Sale, Heber, Phaleg, Jectan, and Reu – fifteen in all.

The Continent of Asia was named after Asshur.

The Chinese Record of Ta Yu (大禹) [Da Yu] and the "Flood" is, now, quite clear. He merely drained that portion of the basin of the Hwang Ho, which had been devastated by one of those terrible floods for which this river is famous. It is noteworthy that the portion of this river in Shensi (陝西) and Shansi (山西) has *nine* tributaries, which are referred to in Chinese History.

At the time of the Deluge, Noah was 600 years old, and Shem 100 years.

The Chinese Record of the Creation and the Deluge from Adam to Noah ends here.

It appears that all the Chinese commentators have failed to decipher the true meaning of much of this Ancient Chinese Record of the Creation and the Flood. And, not being able to understand, they allowed their imagination to run riot. The Chinese commentators made a great mistake in believing that Nü Wa (Shi) (女媧氏) was a woman and the consort or sister of Fuhi, and an imaginary female deity! This is why this particular portion of China's ancient history is so confused and vague, and why dates are in disagreement with those of the Bible.

Disregarding all the mythical and fictitious portions of these ancient commentaries of the Creation and the Flood, it is noteworthy that the main chronological facts agree with the more important events of the Creation and the Flood as recorded in the Bible.

Now, this terrestrial and universal upheaval, which is mentioned in the Chinese Record of the Creation, and the Deluge, must have altered the beds of seas and rivers, and caused continents to rise and fall, resulting in a Deluge (tidal wave), which flooded the whole world, and turned that portion of the Asian **(Continental)** plateau, now known as the Gobi Desert, and Chinese Turkestan, into a vast Inland Sea. It is impossible for rain itself to submerge the whole earth, because only a percentage of the water that is evaporated by the sun returns to the earth again as rain. This is one of the reasons why scientists and geologists doubt the truth of the Bible story of the Creation and the Deluge.

This mighty **cataclysmic** upheaval **must** have been due to some seismic disturbance, **leading** to the changing of the slope[73] of the Earth's axis, due to upheavals or subsidences of **land, resulting** in a Tidal Wave and the sudden freezing of the northern parts of the continents of Asia and America (N.W.), and the sudden death by freezing or drowning of all those gigantic mammals, saurians, etc., of the antediluvian age. This accounts for mammoths and other extinct animals being found in Siberia under the ice and snow, and quite near the surface of the ground, and for the strong glacial indications, and deposits found in certain parts of the world – the *North Polar regions of The Creation*.

I firmly believe that at the time of the Creation, and before the Deluge, the North Pole[74] was in the **region of** North **Central** Greenland, and this accounts for the Polar glacial indications found in the N.E. portion of North America, Scotland, Ireland, Norway, and Northern Europe.

According to geologists, in no part of the World are evidences of glacial action more extensive or more interesting than in the northern two-thirds of North America. The Labrador peninsula is in the main, a most forbidding and desolate expanse, covered with rocks and precipices, and having a winter far more rigorous and inhospitable than that of Lapland or even Siberia.

The northern parts of Siberia show no evidences of Polar glacial action. The whole of West Siberia, between the Alpine belt and the shores of the Arctic Ocean, is an immense lowland. The southern part of these lowlands – the prairies of Ishim, Upper Tobol, and Barata – is extremely fertile. The soil is a *thick layer of black earth*, which also penetrates into the lower valleys of the Altai, and the traveler finds there (within 16 degrees of the Arctic Circle), to his astonishment, a territory, nearly as large as Great Britain, entirely covered with a luxurious grass vegetation, with masses of *deciduous forest*, which is even now the granary of Siberia. Labrador is similarly situated in latitude, but, note the *great difference* in geological and climatic conditions. Farther north still begin the *tunaras*, which extend along the Arctic seaboard as far as Kamchatka, and cover an aggregate area of some 450,000 square miles. The soil is *alluvial and agricultural*, but, owing to the terrible cold of December and January – 15 to 35 degrees below zero – trees and vegetation are, now, scarce.

These are all indisputable proofs that the freezing of Northern Asia has been due to a change in the inclination of the Earth's axis, and the shifting of the position of the North Pole from the north of Greenland to its present position.

As the result of the numerous explorations and archaeological excavations which have been made in Chinese Turkestan, it has been found that the Takla Makan Desert was once an immense lake. Fossils, gravel, sand, chalk grypœa, carboniferous deposits, and "mesozoic and tertiary transgressions" have been found, all indicating that the land was once convulsed by some seismic disturbance, and finally submerged.

Ruins of ancient cities abound in the Turfan Oasis, and in the Oases along the Tibet border, and interesting manuscripts have been found written in alphabets unknown to linguists.

What if they are the hieroglyphic script of Tsong Chi (倉頡)? Perhaps some of the ancient ruins in the Mongolian Plateau **or the submerged Continent of Polynesia** may yet prove to be those of the City of Enoch built by Cain.

Genesis IV. 16–17. "And Cain went out from the presence of the Lord, and dwelt in the land of Nod, on the *East of Eden*.

And Cain knew his wife; and she conceived, and bore Enoch: and he built a city, and called the name of the city, after the name of his son, Enoch".

Lake Bojante-kul, south west of Lukchun, at the foot of Eastern (天山), is 56 feet below sea level, and must be one of those subsidences or depressions recorded in the Chinese Record of the Deluge (天(山)柱折下震維穿). There are other large depressions at the foot of the Tienshan Mountains. Obrucheff has shown that a local subsidence of the rocks took place at Lukchun, along a narrow strip parallel to the Tienshan Mountains. It is noteworthy that earthquakes desolate Central Asia with ever-increasing frequency. The Russian explorer, G. Grum-Grzimailo has also described immense boulders of a fine-grained grey granite, 14 to 17 feet high and 100 feet in circumference, which he found lying at an altitude of 3,200 feet about the mouth of the Gaib gorge, which descends from the Karlyktagh Mountains (12,000 feet) of eastern Tienshan in the N. E. of Hami. The rocks of this gorge consisted, both at this spot and higher up, of quite a different sort of granite and crystalline slates.

No doubt, these immense cylindrical boulders of a fine-grained grey granite were the stones quarried by Nü Wa (Shi) (Noah) (女媧氏) for repairing or damming up the Gaib gorge of Tienshan (煉石以補天(山)) so as to prevent the flooding of the plateau. Again, it is mentioned that it has on its north-western borders several broad trenches which are cut in its mass, like gigantic railway trenches leading with an imperceptible gradient from the lowlands to the heights of the plateau, and supposed to be channels for the drainage of the waters discharged by the plateau.

And, doubtless, these were also the channels which Nü Wa (Noah) trained and utilized for draining off the waters from the Gaib gorge, and the plateau (聚灰止淹水天(山)地得依然).

Thus is the authenticity of the Ancient Chinese Record of the Deluge substantiated, and the incidents proved, for all time.

The real Mount Ararat

And, again, there are the Sarikol Mountains containing Mustaghata Peak (25,000 feet), which joins the Ulug-art (Ararat?) range of the Tienshan mountains. Close by there is also a range called the Narat Mountains. Mustaghata Peak must, therefore, be the Mount Ararat of the Bible, because it is the highest peak of these mountain ranges.

If the Bible story of the Flood is to be believed, how was it possible for Noah in his Ark to survey the submerged Earth from the top of Mount Ararat of Asia Minor?

It is now clear that the Deluge was *a real fact*.

The re-peopling of the world

After the waters of the Flood had subsided, the descendants of Noah and his three sons Shem, Ham, and Japhet, migrated eastward, in the direction of the Mongolian Plateau and must have multiplied, and spread in all directions, journeying North, South, East, and West, along routes which offered the least resistance, gravitating to warmer climes, and establishing nations and civilizations distinct from each other, and undergoing changes in color and features brought about by the temperature and the climatic conditions of their natural surroundings. This, no doubt, is accountable for the universal story of the Deluge, which appears to be the common property of all the races – savage and civilized – of the World.

Naturally, the migratory tendency of these tribes was to flee from the cold and arid regions of the North, and to go toward the East, West, and South. The descendants of Shem (神農炎帝) established the Chinese, Chaldean, Assyrian, Median, Persian, Babylonian, Hebrew, Lydian, Mongolian, Manchurian (Tunguse), Japanese, Corean, and North and South American Indian nations; and the Yakuts, Voguls, Ostiaks, Samoyeds, and Esquimaux of the North Polar regions, and the Tibetans, Nepaulese, Indian **races** of Northern India, Burmese, Siamese, Annamites, Malays, etc., are, likewise, descended from them, as also the natives of Australasia and Polynesia. And it is a remarkable fact that images resembling Chinese idols have been found in Arkansas (U.S.A.) **and Mexico**.

The descendants of Ham established the Egyptian, Ethiopian, Hindoo (Dravidian), Arabian, and other kindred nations.

The descendants of Japhet established the Modern European nations, whose ancestors did not become thoroughly civilized, until the advent of Jesus Christ.

The great antiquity of the Chinese

Proof of the great antiquity of the Chinese people is the fact that porcelain vessels, having Chinese mottos upon them, have been discovered in the ancient Egyptian tombs, in shape, material, and appearance, exactly resembling those made in China. Rosellini, the great Italian antiquary, believed them to have been imported into Egypt from China by kings who reigned in Egypt about the time of Moses or before.

It appears that at the time of the Deluge the human race was only able to record events by knotted cords and the hieroglyphic script of Fuki (Henoch) and Tsong Chi. After the Deluge, the Chinese, owing to their isolation and continuous civilization, succeeded in evolving from the knotted cord-signs and hieroglyphics their present modern script.

The ancient Egyptians did not get much beyond their hieroglyphics, and all the other dead nations, and the Mongolians, Manchurians, Hindoos, Turks, Persians, Arabians, Malays, etc., evolved and adopted scripts based upon the ancient hieroglyphics or knotted cord-signs and symbols.

While great empires have successively risen and fallen in other parts of the world, China has remained the same for at least five thousand years, surviving all the great nations of Western Asia, Northern Africa, and Europe.

China is the only ancient empire which has continued to the present time.

Being surrounded by high and massive mountain chains, and extensive deserts, and a wide expanse of ocean, it is no wonder that its existence and civilization remained a mystery to the surrounding nations for so many centuries.

China's civilization[75] has existed without change from time immemorial, and before that of the Nile Valley; and, at the time when the Egyptian kings were building their pyramids, China had a settled Government, and was enjoying a high state of civilization.

The origin of the Chinese and the religion of the Chinese

The Chinese are the descendants of Shem. Shem (Shen Nung) (神農炎帝) and his descendants established themselves in the Hwang Ho (Yellow River) basin, where the provinces of Shensi (陝西), Shansi (山西), and Honan (河南) now stand, thus founding the Chinese nation, and being God's chosen people. He led them into this "Land of Milk and Honey" to thrive and flourish, and to civilize the surrounding barbarous nations.

Genesis IX. 26. And he (Noah, i.e. Nü Wa) said Blessed be the Lord God of Shem; and Canaan shall be his servant.

This accounts for the ancient Chinese reverence and respect for Almighty God – the Supreme Ruler (上帝) – embodied in the word "Tien" (天), i.e. Heaven.

This great reverence for Heaven, i.e. God, dates from time immemorial, and can be traced to the earliest records of Chinese History.

Confucius, the Heaven-sent Sage and Teacher of China, had always the greatest reverence and respect for Heaven (天), i.e. God, and it has been the same with all the sages and wise men of China, who went before, and who came after him. And, this is why God has protected and preserved the Chinese nation for so many thousands of years.

The religion of the ancient Chinese was a pure and unadulterated Theism, similar in every respect to that of the Jews, whose ancestors migrated into Chaldea from China, about B.C. 2000.

The religion of the Chinese

Owing to the favorable position of this chosen land, and the formidability of its natural surroundings, the Chinese race began to develop and flourish in peace, under the wise and beneficent rule of the Five Patriarchs, and the Emperors of succeeding dynasties, and to evolve a civilization and ethical culture distinctly its own.

III.– Shen Nung (Shem)

神農炎帝立

Shen Nung (Shem) ruled.

其始教民耕

He was the first to teach farming to the people.

斲木為耒耜

He was the first to invent farming implements.

衣食在桑田

Clothing and food were obtained from the mulberry and the fields.

From this we gather that the Chinese were already wearing silk, as deducted from the words "clothing" and "mulberry".

Cream colored silk of the 1st Century A.D., from Yen Cheng, Shantung, was found by Sir Aurel Stein in the ruins of Lop Nor – 1 foot 10 inches wide – of remarkable degree of finish, and proof of the high state of culture and standard of living which existed there at that period. And, further, a specimen discovered near Tun Huang bore a date contemporary with B.C. 94.

親口嘗草木醫藥得相傳

He personally tasted herbs and plants, and this resulted in a knowledge of medicine, and the cure of sickness.

教人為貿易貨物並橫權

He taught the people how to do business, and introduced weights and measures for the weighing and selling of commercial products.

傳代凡八世五百廿五年

His descendants consisted of eight generations – 525 "years".

(i.e. Arphaxad, Sale, Heber, Phaleg, Reu, Sarug, Nachor, Thare.) (See Genesis.)

It is not known how many days or months constituted one of these "years".

VI.–Hwang Ti (Arphaxad)

皇帝軒轅氏人事漸完備

When Hwang Ti (Arphaxad) ruled, all things required for the use of man were practically complete and in existence.

諸侯始爭雄適習干戈起

It was then that the feudal lords began to become ambitious for power, and this resulted in war.

蚩尤嘗作亂作霧迷軍旅

Chi Yu attempted to rebel, and took advantage of a fog to screen the movements of his army.

帝造指南車起兵相戰敵

Hwang Ti invented a Compass-chariot, and assembling his forces, he advanced south and attacked Chi Yu.

蚩尤被帝擒殺於涿鹿裡

Chi Yu was defeated and captured by Hwang Ti and executed at a place called (涿鹿裡).

軒轅作內經素問靈樞出岐伯徹精微，發明醫道理後人始得傳疾病沉屙起

Hwang Ti Composed a Treatise on Medicine and the Art of Healing, and ever afterwards people were able to diagnose and cure diseases.

伐木作船車水埕皆通濟

He used wood for making boats and chariots, thereby enabling the people to travel on water and on land.

隸首作算數九章演算法起

Ti (隸) was the first to invent the abacus and methods of reckoning (Mathematics).

帝遊河洛間魚負天文志

When Hwang Ti was journeying along the Hwang Ho, in the neighbourhood of Loh (洛間) Yu (魚) presented him with a Chart of the stars and a Treatise on Astronomy.

即命師大撓造成花甲子

He immediately ordered Su Ta Lao (師大撓) to compute a "Cycle of Time" (花甲子).

伶倫制竹筒陰陽調律呂，遂有管弦聲音樂從此始

Leng Lin (伶倫) invented bamboo instruments for the production of the tones (twelve), and music originated therefrom.

采銅鑄鼎成

Hwang Ti mined for copper for the casting and making of tripods.

騎龍朝天帝在位一百年壽元百十一

He rode upon a dragon and ascended into the presence of God, i.e. he died at the age of 111 years. He ruled for 100 years.

V.– Yao (Reu)

帝堯陶唐氏仁德宏天地，茅茨不剪伐土階為三級

Yao (Reu) was renowned for his benevolence and virtue. He lived in a plain thatched palace with three flights of apartments.

蓂荚生於庭觀驗旬朔日

The Ming Keh (蓂荚) plant grew near this palace, and on examining it, Yao was able to know the days of the month **(i.e. the Four Seasons)**.

洪水泛九年使禹而疏治

A great flood desolated the land for nine years, and Yao ordered Yu to drain of the waters.

居外十三春未入家門視

Yu remained abroad for thirteen years, and all this time he never visited his home.

通澤疏九河引水從東逝

He drained morasses and swamps, dredged and conserved the nine tributaries of the Hwang Ho, and caused the waters to flow eastwards.

舉益治山澤猛獸皆逃避

He appointed Y (益) to deal with the forests and jungles, and the wild beasts fled and hid themselves.

百姓樂雍熙擊壤而歌戲

And, henceforth, the people lived in peace and happiness; and they sang, and enjoyed life.

大舜耕曆山堯聞知聰敏二女嫁為妻

Ta Shun (大舜) was a farmer of Li Shan (曆山). Yao learnt of his great ability and learning, and gave him his two daughters in marriage.

九男遣奉侍器械並百官, 牛羊倉廩備事舜畎畝中

He also ordered his nine sons to serve Shun, and furnished him with all necessary farming implements and one hundred servants, together with cattle, sheep, and granaries.

取舜歸帝裡

Yao subsequently invited Shun to the palace, with the object of appointing him to administer the affairs of the country.

堯老倦於盡四嶽舉舜理, 堯立百二年一百十七歲

Yao, becoming old, was unable to carry on the administration of the country, so he abdicated in favor of Shun. Yao ruled for 102 years, and lived to 117 years.

舜見堯升遐避位南河地

But, when Yao died, Shun fled from the locality south of the Hwang Ho (so as not to be in the way of Yao's sons.)

百姓感舜恩從者入歸市,天與人歸之回宮節帝位

However, the people, being deeply grateful to Shun for his beneficent rule, were anxious to become his faithful and loyal subjects.

Heaven and the people favored Shun, and so he became Emperor.

The origin of the Jews

Yao (堯) (i.e. Reu) abdicated in favor of Shun (舜), who in turn, abdicated in favor of Yu (禹). Yao's grandfather, Chwan Hu Kao Yang (Heber) (顓頊高陽氏) invented a Calend[e]ar, and fixed the year and the Four Seasons, but, history records very little about his father Ti Kuh Kao Sin (Phaleg) (帝佶高辛氏), as the country was then in the enjoyment of peace. This accounts for the Hebrew Record of the Creation and the Deluge being more detailed and accurate than the ancient Chinese Record.

It was after Yao's abdication, and about the year B.C. 2,000, that his great grandson Thare and his family (a small band of nomads) migrated westwards to Chaldea and established the Hebrew nation; and no doubt they were forced to leave China owing to the terribly devastated condition of the Country. Even at the present day there is a Colony of Chinese Jews in Honan (河南) [Henan].

Yu (禹) journeyed further east to Honan (河南) and Shantung (山東), and founded the Empire of the Hsia (夏) Dynasty (B.C. **2205** to B.C. 1797).

I have abstained from making long and detailed references to the later rulers and events in Chinese History, as I wish to make my message as brief and as clear as possible.

The high morality of China's sages and historians is noteworthy, and is proved by the complete absence of profane and obscene records or references; and Chinese History may be read by children, and the most fastidious persons, without, in any way, hurting their feelings of propriety.

China's indigenous civilization

Having established beyond doubt the real situation of The "Garden of Eden",[76] and the origin of the Chinese, I will now prove that the civilization of China is indigenous, and distinctly different from all other civilizations, ancient and modern.

China (ancient) has influenced other civilizations, but has never been influenced by others. In fact, China and its institutions have outlived everything else in the World.

Writers have, in the past, assumed that the Chinese came originally from the West, probably from the Sumerians of Babylon, believing that the similarity between some of the Sumerian and Chinese roots and hieroglyphics was sufficient proof! This theory is contrary to all the known facts, and as I have already stated and proved, the origin of the Chinese is indigenous to the land now occupied by them.

The ancient Chinese hieroglyphics are distinctly Chinese, and the evolution from the hieroglyphic stage to the modern script has been continuous. No other dead nation has possessed a similar script. This is proof that the Chinese script is indigenous and not Sumerian.

The Han (漢) Dynasty (B.C. 206) Historical Bas Reliefs of Fuhi, Shen Nung, Hwang Ti, Yao, and Shun illustrate the costumes, head-dress, and foot-wear, etc., of the ancient Chinese, and show that they are purely Chinese, and more refined than the costumes of the Egyptians, Assyrians, and Babylonians.

Again, a careful study of the horses, carriages, chariots, etc., is sufficient proof of the high state of China's indigenous civilization at this epoch of her existence as a nation and an Empire.

The "Dragon" and the "Phoenix" are also purely Chinese, and no other ancient nation has similar emblematic representations, unless it has been influenced by Chinese civilization.

Regarding architecture, China, possesses a style distinctly her own. No other ancient nation possessed architecture anything like that of the Chinese. The pointed and tapering roofs and upturned eaves, were no doubt copied from the designs of the tents of their nomadic ancestors, and have been tenaciously adhered to throughout the thousands of years of her existence.

The artistic and beautiful bronze and iron temples and pavilions (at least, B.C. 100) on the top of the sacred Taishan (泰山) mountain of Shantung (山東) province are world-famous, and the wonder and admiration of all visitors.

China's Art is also indigenous, and distinctly different in conception, style, and execution, from that of the West, and paintings on silk, representing the civilization, architecture, and historical events of two thousand years of her national life, are still in existence.

I hope I have, now, also, satisfactorily proved the antiquity of China's indigenous civilization.

Universal peace and the brotherhood of man

The Creation and the Deluge are, now, as clear as day, and, in spite of scientists and geologists trying to prove the contrary, and the support which the Darwinian theory of "The Origin of Species" and "The Descent of Man" has been accorded, the truth of the Creation and the Deluge has been proved beyond doubt.

And, now, that the Ancient Chinese Record of the Creation and the Deluge is found to be the same as Genesis, I fervently hope and pray that, the whole human race will soon learn to believe in God and the Bible, and that, henceforth, men will love and treat each other as brothers.

In conclusion, I fervently beseech all those, who think with me, to work for the following:

1. Universal Disarmament.
2. Universal Peace.
3. The protection and civilization of all the weak and savage races of the World.
4. The Brotherhood of Man.

And, when the nations and governments of the World have reached a state fit to be Federated, I hope and pray that China will take the lead in turning the "Garden of Eden", i.e. "Chinese Turkestan, into an "International State," and that the Parliament of Nations will be established there (in China).

Then will there be Peace on Earth.

The End

Appendix: Why God has punished Europe

This[77] terrible fratricidal war, which is convulsing and devastating Europe, is not due to trade rivalry, mutual fear of aggression, or the ambition of Kings and Emperors to become supreme in this world.

It is the punishment of God for the crimes of Europe.

There must be many ungodly men, to-day, who are blaspheming God, and crying out with uplifted hands – "There is no God. If God exists, why should He make the innocent suffer with the guilty, and, why should Europe be made to suffer so much misery?"

God is a just God, and He rewards the good, and punishes the wicked. If the punishment does not come to-day, it will come to-morrow. But, sooner or later, it is bound to come.

We should always remember that the crimes of the father are visited upon his children, and this applies to nations as well as individuals.

See Exodus XX. 5–6. "God visits the iniquity of the fathers upon the children unto the third and fourth generation of them that hate Him.

And shows mercy unto those that love Him and keep His Commandments".

The nations of Europe have sinned against God, and broken His Commandments:

1. *Thou shalt not kill*
2. *Thou shalt not steal*

3. *Thou shalt not covet thy neighbour's house or anything that is thy neighbour's*

If the Christian nations of Europe believe in the Bible, they must acknowledge that Militarism is a crime against God, and that the savages of the World are their brothers. ...

Therefore, the crimes of Kings, governments, and the leaders of men have been visited upon the people, and this is the reason for the punishment which Almighty God has inflicted upon the nations of Europe.

It is a terrible warning for the future.

***

III Ancient Chinese Art. A Treatise on Chinese Painting. Hong Kong: South China Morning Post, pp. 18, 1928.

Introduction

Owing to the wonders of Wireless Telegraphy, Telephony, Television, and Telephotography, and the great strides which are being made in Aviation, and consequent on the exploding of Sir Rudyard Kipling's false and misleading dictum *"For East is East and West is West and ne'er the twain shall meet"*, which has resulted in so much ill-feeling and misunderstanding in the past, the peoples of the different countries of the World are being brought into closer contact with each other, necessitating the fostering of good-will and friendship and the acquiring of a better knowledge and understanding of each other.

Not only should nations have a friendly understanding of each other as individuals, but it is important and necessary that they should get thoroughly acquainted with each other's civilization, In order to hasten the realization of universal peace and brotherhood, which is the World's desire, and the goal of all pacifists and the representatives of the Hague Peace Tribunal.

It is purely with this object in view, that I have made the attempt to place before the Western world a brief outline of the history of the Art of Ancient China, because Art is Civilization and Civilization is Art.

And, my best thanks and acknowledgments are due to the well known art critics from Whose writings I have made extracts and quotations. …

Chapter 1: Origin

Art is Civilization and Civilization is Art.

The standard and greatness of a Country's Civilization is measured by its Art, which unerringly unfolds to the World the thought and life of its people, its religious inclinations, and the stages of its material progress and advancement.

It is only savages and the barbarous races of the World, who have no knowledge of Art, and are ignorant of its importance and civilizing influences.

China's Art is indigenous.

China has had her designers and artists from time immemorial.

We read in the earliest records of China's history (史記) that Fu Hi (伏羲 – about B.C. 3300) designed and drew the Eight Trigrams (八卦) and a map of the Whang Ho River (河圖) [Yellow River], and that he also ordered Tsang Chieh (倉頡) to design a pictographic script. Therefore, it is evident that simple line-drawing originated and came into existence at the same time.

The earliest mention of Color dates from the Emperor Shun (舜 B.C. 2000). It is recorded in the Shu King (書經) or Book of History that His Majesty ordered the twelve symbols of power to be embroidered in the five colors on his sacrificial robes, and painting is also mentioned.

Chapter 2: Development

The early painters were more draughtsmen [sic] and designers than artists in the modern sense. Their craft was the designing and drawing of palaces and buildings and frescos for the decoration of the walls. It was all line work, and colors (natural mineral oxides) were added to make the human figures, &c. more realistic and conspicuous.

We have examples of this line-drawing in the sculptured walls of the Lung Men [Longmen in Luoyang] Caves, the sculptured Han (漢) bas-reliefs (B.C. 100), and the magnificent fresco paintings which adorn the walls of the Tai Temple (岱廟) of the sacred Tai Shan (泰山) mountain in Shantung province, and which have not been retouched for over one thousand years. We have also the fresco paintings which have been discovered by Sir Aurel Stein, Dr Sven Hedin and other modern explorers in the sand and *Loess* buried cities of the deserts of Chinese Turkestan and Mongolia, which I have proved in my books (1914) and pamphlets

(Published by Messrs. Kelly and Walsh, Ltd.) to be the "Garden of Eden" and the Cradle of the Human Race. (See pamphlets proving the Upheaval of Central Asia and subsidence of the Pacific continent, the flooding of the World by a devastating Tidal Wave, and a change of 15° in the Antediluvian North Polar regions, resulting in the retreat of the Frigid cold from North Europe, and the sudden freezing of Alaska and Northern Asia.)

The next Evolutionary Stage in Chinese Art was the transfer of these designs and drawings to cloth and silk, when it was possible to manipulate the brush and play with the colors with greater freedom.

It was then that the true artist began to delight his Imperial master the Emperor and the people with proofs of his genius, and to permanently record the customs and the civilization of his times.

It is during the Han (漢) dynasty (B.C. 200 to A.D. 200) that we read of artists who painted portraits, dragons, birds, beasts, horses, and pavilions, &c.

In B.C. 51 it is recorded that the Emperor Yuan Ti (元帝) ordered the portraits of eleven of his most eminent warriors and statesmen to be hung in the Unicorn Pavilion of the Palace.

Portraits and paintings by Lieh I (烈裔) (B.C. 220) and others of earlier dates are also mentioned.

According to these records, the art of painting in China had its origin early in the Classical Period, which opened five centuries before the birth of Jesus Christ.

The Golden Age of Chinese Pictorial Art dates from the 4th Century, and reached its zenith during the Sung (宋) dynasty (969–1279 A.D.).

One of the earliest Chinese paintings known to the European Art World is the silk scroll painting "The admonition of the female historian" by Ku Kai Chih (顧愷之) (A.D. 400) in the British Museum. Regarding this artist's work Mr Laurence Binyon of the British Museum one of the greatest of living Chinese Art critics, ably and truthfully writes:

> Though of so early a period, there is nothing primitive about the workmanship; on the contrary, the painter has perfect mastery over his materials, and his delight in it overflows in the exquisite modulations of the brush with which the draperies are expressed.
>
> For beauty of sweeping and yet sensitive line, few paintings in the World approach this. Yet charming touches of actual life prevent the art from being over-calligraphic. Note the sense of dignity, of refinement – still more apparent in other scenes of the roll – pointing to an age of culture. Chinese art must have been flourishing for many centuries before work so mature could be produced.
>
> As writers on the subject have assumed that no work of this period remains, and have conjectured that only rude beginnings existed before the introduction of Buddhism and Indian art, this painting of Ku Kai Chih is of extreme importance to students as well as of high aesthetic value.

I would use the same language in describing the works of Chan Tzu Chien (展子虔) of the Sui (隋) dynasty (A.D. 581–617), of which I have four in my Collection. They are a set of four large allegorical paintings in monochrome (Ink) entitled and representing *Fishing* (漁), *Afforestation* (樵), *Agriculture* (耕), *Education* (讀), painted on silk, which, fortunately, are well preserved for their great age (nearly 1,500 years). They are from the Imperial "Sung" collection, and are of the greatest artistic and historical value and importance. Chan Tzu Chien's figures are full of life and vigor, and possess a subtle charm beyond that which mere technique can give. He is considered to be one of the progenitors of Tang (唐) painting, when not the actual founder; and undoubtedly the great Wu Tao Tzu (吳道子) was guided by his historical example, as I find that there is much similarity between the brush work of the two artists.

Chapter 3: Technique

Chinese Art, and particularly Ancient Chinese Art, is not yet properly understood and appreciated by European Art-lovers. Chinese Art is "calligraphic," and the coloring is harmonious, and finished in delicate and soft gradations of color. There is also a rhythmic unity and harmonious arrangement of details, which is instinctive.

An ancient masterpiece, and particularly a landscape painting, is a wonderful composition of vigorous and sinuous strokes and lines, and systematic groups of dots, representing bushes and clumps of shrubbery, or patches of moss and lichen, when applied to rocks and stones.

A real masterpiece contains nothing superfluous, not even a line, stroke, or dot. All should have their fixed and proper positions in the composition of the landscape.

All the landscape masterpieces are soft and subdued, and free from anything coarse and "fiery" (火) or distracting to the eyes of the critical observer.

Lines may be thick or wiry, and dots big or small and of various recognized shapes, but all have their designated positions in the picture, and are executed with the utmost care and precision.

Event dots must have form and life!

No line, stroke or dot is executed haphazardly by the Master.

Dots may be compared to the gems in a piece of embroidered tapestry. They help intensify lights and shades, and to regulate distances in the landscape, and only the Master knows how and where to place them.

So careful and precise is the master in the placing and execution of his lines and dots, that he does not want to give posterity the chance to detect flaws, in the shape of *weak lines* or *superfluous dots*, in his picture. Therefore, the expert eye can easily detect a genuine masterpiece at a glance. But in order to be able to properly judge and appreciate the brush work of a landscape masterpiece, it is necessary to possess a practical knowledge of Chinese painting and technique.

The ancient masters excelled in the life and vigor of their lines and dots.

They first composed their picture, and with the composition in their minds' eye, they started rapidly but cautiously to transfer the scene to silk or paper.

In the execution of all the prominent lines and strokes of human figures, and the mountains, rocks and trees, &c. of a landscape, the brush was generally held perpendicularly and firmly between the thumb and the first, second, and third fingers of the right hand, with the arm extended for freedom and rapidity of movement, and, then, then, after taking in a deep breath and concentrating the whole "mind's force" (spiritual impulse) and sending it through the rigid arm to the very point of the tightly held brush so to speak, the stroke would be begun, and the breath would not be released, until the complete stroke, whether perpendicular, curved, or modulated, had been finished! Concentration was only relaxed, when the Master occupied himself in the casual and easy task of shading and coloring his picture.

It is only by holding the brush in this way that it is possible to concentrate and sustain the strength and "force" necessary for executing the long sinuous and virile lines of a masterpiece, and it is the ability to execute such graceful sweeping lines with perfection that calls forth the admiration and delight of the Chinese calligraphist and Art connoisseur.

This "force" is a hidden concentrated movement guided by will power, solely Chinese in inception, and quite unfamiliar to foreign artists and art critics.

Such skill with the brush can only be attained by years of constant study and practice, and depends upon the genius and intelligence of the student.

It is this skill with the brush that is responsible for the impression that Chinese Art is *calligraphic*, but it should be remembered that it is applicable mainly to the free-hand calligraphic brush work of the Black and White landscape paintings and figure sketches of the Idealistic Sung Period (A.D. 960–1279).

The Tang (A.D. 618–906) painters were more practical and realistic in their marvelous compositions, and devoted most of their time and attention to coloring and details, as exemplified by their magnificent paintings of Religious and Historical subjects, Human figures, and Architectural views and landscapes.

Painters are born not made, and without inspiration and imagination one cannot expect to become a great Chinese painter; and besides it is necessary to possess the power of modulating the lines and strokes of the brush in order to give them "life" and make them express the nature, and the intensity and force of the "spirit".

Chinese painting is based on memory and founded on the great examples of the past.

Chinese painters never copy or imitate a model in the Western sense, but their art is based on reproduction and imaginative reconstruction, and perfection consists of rhythmic conception and a thorough mastery of brush strokes and dots.

Chinese Art has never been influenced by the mathematical perspective and scientific laws of European painting.

It has its own perspective, which is *isometric*, and which Chinese artists consider best suited to bring out the essential and permanent points in a painting.

Symmetry and harmony in design and composition was of great importance, and the design, the drawing, and the coloring of a painting must be in perfect unison.

To appreciate Chinese painting properly and at its true worth, the westerner must forget his own mental preconceptions of Art, and adopt a point of view totally differing from that in which he has been educated.

In order to understand and appreciate the artistic and scenic beauties of a Chinese landscape painting, the spectator must imagine himself as viewing the scene from an eminence or flying over the landscape in an aero plane.

It is only by this ingenious and clever method of perspective (Isometric) that the Chinese painter has been able to include hundreds of miles of scenery within the limited space of a few square feet of silk or paper.

Chinese methods of landscape painting are quite unique, and the art of landscape painting in all its phases, remains unsurpassed in its richness of poetic depth and feeling.

Chinese Art is governed by the following Six Canons of Hsieh Ho (謝赫), the famous painter and art critic of the Southern Chi (南齊) (A.D. 479–501), who is regarded as the first systematic writer on Art.

1. 氣運生動 Rhythmic conception and vitality of execution.
2. 骨法用筆 Structural strength and virility of brush work.
3. 應物寫形 Conformity of outline with shape of object.
4. 隨類傳彩 Harmonious coloring suited to various forms.
5. 經營位置 Perspective to be correctly perceived.
6. 傳模移寫 Representation to conform with style.

Such are the essential laws of Chinese pictorial art, which no other age or nation has ever possessed.

These six canons of the fifth century only crystallized ideals, which inspired previous artists; and their universal acceptance proves them to have been racial and native to the Chinese mind.

The theory advanced by certain Foreign art critics that Chinese painting owed its virtual existence to the inspiration of Buddhist images and pictures imported from India is entirely untenable.

Such a theory is absurd and needs rectifying.

Modern Chinese artists have lamentably failed to follow in the footsteps of the ancient masters, and this is why the lines and brush work of their pictures are so weak, and wanting in life and vigor. Indeed, the life and vigor of the marvelous brush work of the masterpieces of the Old Masters is now a lost art.

Chapter 4: Schools

The ancients were great lovers of Nature, and the mountains, the waterfalls and the streams; and they obtained their inspiration from the mountains, where they sat and drank in the scenes and natural wonders, which lay spread out before them.

They were great thinkers and scholars, and they communed with God in the solitude of the majestic grandeur of their mountains and crags, and this is why the great and incomparable Sung (宋) Landscape masterpieces so faithfully represented the towering peaks and precious crags of the Yang-tze Valley provinces.

During the Tang (唐) dynasty (A.D. 618–960) there developed two great schools of Landscape painting, the Northern School being represented by Li Ssu Hsün (李思訓) and his son Li Chao Tao (李昭道), and the Southern School by Wang Wei (王維), the aesthetic poet and painter, and the originator of the chaste and idealistic in Black and White landscape painting.

The chief characteristic of the Northern School was gorgeous and brilliant coloring and a certain virile sternness, and that of the Southern School, idealistic refinement and a total absence of vivid colors.

At this period, and previous to the introduction of Buddhism into China there existed two main currents of thought, viz. Confucian and Taoist.

The former was exemplified in the Art of the bronze ceremonial vessels, the jade symbols of rank, &c., the frescos and paintings produced in early times (Chow (周) and Han (漢) dynasties), and in the sculptured stone slabs made during the period from B.C. 200 to A.D. 200. These works of art all bore witness to the Chinese love of the Confucian virtues of social harmony, piety, and loyalty. But, we have still to unearth and bring to light the Art treasures and relics of the Antediluvian cities, which have been smothered and entombed by the 400,000 square miles of Diluvial Loess deposits of the Whang Ho River basin of North China (See my books and pamphlets).

The other current was of a different sort, and showed the idealistic and individualistic trend in the Chinese consciousness. This current flowed mainly in the South, where it flourished wild and free on the banks of the Yang-tze River, and found expression in the literary and artistic works of a group of poets and artists of the period (A.D. 618 to A.D. 1279).

About B.C. 200 rumors of Buddhism came to China over the trade route which was opened through Chinese Turkestan, but it was not until A.D. 67 that Buddhism was officially introduced into China by the Emperor Ming Ti (明帝). And this may also be considered as the period of Graeco-Bactrian influence.

With the fall of the Han dynasty, Buddhism gradually began to prosper in China. Monasteries and temples sprang up rapidly, and with them arose the need and demand for Buddhist art, which then began to influence Chinese painting.

Besides the Northern and Southern schools founded by Li Ssu Hsün and Wang Wei, other schools of Landscape painting were founded subsequently by Fan Kuan (範寬), Yen Wen Kuei (燕文貴), Mi Fei (米芾), Ma Yuan (馬遠), and Hsia Kuei (夏珪) of the Sung (宋) dynasty (A.D. 960–1279), whose art and technique will be exhaustively dealt with in a future article.

Chapter 5: Masters

For the purpose of this treatise, I am dealing principally with the Art of the Tang (唐) Dynasty (A.D. 618–906), the Golden period of Chinese Art, as exemplified by the masterpieces, which are in my collection, So far, it has been possible to see examples of the Landscape Art of the Tang (唐) and Sung (Song 宋) periods (A.D. 618–1279), but genuine Tang (唐) masterpieces are extremely rare.

Any Landscape painting ante-dating this period has not yet been found.

Tang Landscape art as represented by Li Ssu Hsün (李思訓), a grandson of the founder of the Tang Dynasty, and his son Li Chao Tao (李昭道), was grand and majestic, and bold in conception (See Frontispiece). Both father and son executed towering peaks, amidst which were located magnificent palaces and terraced pavilions, glittering in green and red and gold, from which could be observed the thundering water-falls and the meandering silvery clouds of mountains and scenery of the sublimest grandeur.

This Frontispiece Illustration is a photograph of the wonderful screen painting of Ta Tung Palace (大同殿) painted by Li Ssu Hsün for Emperor Ming Wang (明皇) in A.D. 745, now in my collection, and has been miraculously preserved. It took several months to complete, and is signed by Li Ssu Hsün. (Dimensions – Length 9 feet 9½ inches. Width 6 feet 5½ inches). It is the greatest Landscape painting in existence, and one of the priceless artistic wonders of the World.

So perfectly executed and architecturally correct is the line work and tracery of the palaces, pavilions, and bridges, and so carefully, and minutely are the leaves of the different groups of trees formed and colored, that the brush work could only be properly studied and appreciated by using a magnifying glass!

One is amazed at the stupendousness of the task, and the archaic splendor of the painting; and it is not surprising that it should have taken several months to complete.

Li Ssu Hsün's line and brush work strong and virile, but delicate and refined, when compared with the rapid, free, and vigorous brush work of the Sung (宋) masters.

Li Ssu Hsün was a Heaven-born genius, and the Master draughtsman and colorist of China: and his art fittingly represents the Ancient glory and greatness of China's civilization.

His paintings have a chrysochlorous shine about them, and when hung in the light, they give out a wonderful and mysterious green and orange (golden) glow.

This was his specialty, and was much imitated by later masters. It was on this on this account that he was looked upon as having furnished the pattern for landscape work as far as colors are concerned, and his originality in the coloring of his pictures has caused later art historians to describe him as the founder of the Northern School of Landscape Painting.

Therefore, it is not surprising that Li Ssu Hsün has been acclaimed by generations of Chinese artists to be the greatest Landscape painter of China,

In my opinion Li Ssu Hsün is the greatest Landscape painter that the World has ever known.

Li Ssu Hsün was born in the 4th year of Emperor Kai Yuan's (開元) reign (A.D. 715), and died when sixty six years of age.

He was appointed Field Marshal (大將宣), for which reason his pictures are spoken of as "Marshal Li's Landscapes" (唐大李將軍山水).

Wang Wei (王維) the famous scholar and poet of the same period, was equally famous as a calligraphist and painter, and he originated a new school of Landscape painting, which Art historians have termed the Southern School. He shunned the brilliant colors used by Li Ssu Hsün and his son, and is therefore popularly acclaimed as the originator of the Southern School of Black and White Landscape painting. Wang Wei appears to have perfected his art by direct inspiration from Nature. He generally painted his Landscape in monochrome, and excelled in snow scenes, faithfully representing clumps of snow covered trees with villages nestling amidst the snow-clad hills of the landscape, as shown by the masterpiece (From the Imperial Kuen Lung (乾隆) Collection) in my collection, bearing inscriptions by the Emperor Kuen Lung, and other famous art critics, viz., Su Shih (蘇軾) and Yen Siu (岩叟) of the Sung dynasty. (Size: Length 5 feet 6 inches. Width 2 feet 5 inches.)

His art is simple and unpretentious, and shows the carefully executed lines and brush work of the enthusiastic lover of all that is Nature. His pictures are devoid of glaring colors, and are shaded and tinted in accordance with the moods of Nature. There is nothing coarse about them, but a gentle softness pervades his peaceful and smiling Landscapes.

Wang Wei's style is distinctly different from that of Li Ssu Hsün, the magnitude, depth, and grandeur of whose compositions have never been equaled or even approached by any of the great masters of succeeding dynasties.

Li Ssu Hsün and Wang Wei are the originators of two schools of Landscape painting, but in the magnificence and majesty of design and composition, the scheme of coloring, the boldness and depth of imagination, the marvelous brush work, and the flawless execution of lines, strokes and dots, Wang Wei has never been able to approach Li Ssu Hsün.

Indeed, Li Ssu Hsün is beyond compare, and his name must live through the ages as the greatest Landscape painter of China.

Chinese Art critics and historians declare that Li Ssu Hsün's masterpieces ate protected by the Gods and Spirits of the Spirit World, for they say –

"how has it been possible for frail humanity alone to protect and preserve them from loss and destruction throughout the changing vicissitudes of so many centuries?"

Amongst painters of the human figure of the Tang dynasty Wu Tao Tzu (吳道子), whose real name is Wu Tao Yuan (吳道玄) again altered to Wu Tao Yuan (吳道元), is universally acknowledged to be the Master of Masters, ancient and modern; and he is regarded as the inspired painter of all generations, not only in China, but also in Japan, where he is known as Go-doshi. He was born toward the close of the Sixth Century at Yang-ti near Kai-feng-fu in Honan

Chinese Art historians also refer to him as the greatest painter who ever handled a brush.

Wu Tao Tzu's brush work is bold and vigorous and full of life, and he combined extreme decision with extreme quickness. He painted as he wrote, so unerringly correct was his brush work. He knew how to paint the human expression in all its moods, and he faithfully portrayed with life-like exactitude the benign features of his Gods and Goddesses, and all human forms, which originated from his brush.

Chinese artists say that it is most difficult to paint the hands and feet of the human figure, but the hands and feet of Wu Tao Tzu's figures were always perfect and matchless in form and execution. Such was the wonderful brushwork of Wu Tao Tzu, and it is no wonder that his name has been surrounded with legend, and that he should be universally acclaimed *Master of Masters*, and the greatest painter of all generations.

Wu Tao Tzu's painting of the portrait of Kuan Yin (觀世音大士像), the Goddess of Mercy, with disheveled hair and naked feet, sitting beside a flowing stream under a big clump of spreading bamboos, and with an open scroll across her lap, in my collection, is a remarkable picture, and exhibits this great Master's technique and vigorous brush work in all its phases, the brush work of the rocks and bamboos being particularly interesting and instructive.

It is painted on silk in monochrome (Ink) with the features of the Goddess slightly tinted, and is dark and scarred with age. (Size: Length 7 feet 4 inches. Width 3 feet 4½ inches.)

The knowing glance of the Goddess is wonderfully lifelike, and she appears to smile and read you through!

It is a glance that haunts and is never forgotten, like that of Leonardo Da Vinci's world-famed "Mona Lisa".

The painting bears Wu Tao Tzu's signature and Seal "Tao Yuan" (道玄), which are absent from the majority of paintings reputed to be from his brush. It is dated the 10th year of the reign of the Emperor Kai Yuan (開元), i.e. A.D. 722.

Wu Tao Tzu styles himself in this painting "Disciple of Buddha, Wu Tao Yuan" (弟子吳道玄) in the "ancient" script.

In accordance with Official etiquette, the character & in his name 玄 in his name was afterwards ordered to be changed to 元, owing to the character & in the Emperor's name 玄宗 (Yuan Tsung) being the same.

The painting all bears lengthy panegyrics by the two famous Art critics, Tseng Hsuan (曾選) and Chien Si (錢乃) of the Yuan (元) dynasty.

Chapter 6: Foreign criticism

The following are some interesting and valuable opinions of European Art critic Mr Laurence Binyon of the British Museum, one of the ablest and greatest of Chinese Art critics, writes:

"Whatever the limitations of Chinese painting, no one could deny its real qualities as pure art.

It was a world as yet not half explored, in which they continuously wondered at the freshness of the thoughts and feeling out of which it flowed, and at the suggestions and inspiration which it held for us to-day".

Mr Ralph M. Chait has given the following interesting opinion in the "*Antiquarian*":

"We look back on a period of more than 4,000 years with a feeling of wonder at the achievement of the Chinese in the arts of peace, and the light gradually dawns upon us when we begin to slowly realize the sources upon which the Chinese artist could draw. There is not in all of China a mountain, a plain, river, grove or wood that is not hallowed by some legend or poetic tale, and besides, intimately connected with the idea of immortality".

And so, in brief, the artists of China, though careless, or rather caring less for material reward, but with hearts on fire with zeal for their craft, imparted to their work a "spirituality", a certain something difficult to define.

Conclusion

In order to enable the World to properly appreciate Chinese Art, I hope it will be possible in the not far distant future to see the great paintings of Europe represented by the side of the great paintings of India, Persia, Japan, and China.

To quote Sir Charles J. Holmes, Director of the National Art Gallery:

"Only by exhibiting the great painters of the East in juxtaposition with the great painters of Europe could we properly estimate, proclaim and emphasize the place of the East in the vital artistic achievement of the World."

And, in conclusion, I also hope that I have succeeded in explaining and elucidating the intricacies of Chinese Art and technique, and that this short treatise will prove useful as a guide and companion to Western Art students and lovers of all that is beautiful and instructive in Chinese Art, and pave the way for abler works on the subject.

Notes

1. Alfred Cunningham was a special correspondent for Central News in the Sino-Japanese War of 1894–1895, founded and edited the *Review of the Far East*, was director of the *Egyptian Daily Post* in Cairo, special correspondent for the *New York Journal* with Spanish forces in the Philippines during the Spanish-American War, and in 1905 for *Daily Mail* and *New York Sun* with the Baltic Fleet during the Russo-Japanese War.

2. Data for Mitchell (1870–1947) and her lodger, Canton-born Man Cheuk (Michael) Lui (雷初覺 1899–1990), are corroborated in the *Census of England & Wales*, the *1939 Register*, and *Civil Deaths & Burials* held at *The National Archives of the UK* (TNA) (www.nationalarchives.gov.uk/), as well as in a mimeographed *Directory of Chinese Students in Britain* (1951/2) and in Clara Mitchell's name card found among the bundled papers. Lui apparently joined her during her stay in China and upon return to Leeds remained her lodger until she passed away in 1947; her will bequeathed £310 worth of "effects" to him. By then, he had become a lecturer and had, already in 1942, been married to Ethel Rowena Cawthorne (1886–1974). His extensive diary was also found alongside the papers in my possession, but still awaits detailed examination.

3. Some of Tse's works or their excepts are available online, e.g., a facsimile of *The Creation: The Real situation of Eden, and the origin of the Chinese* (1914) in the library of Harvard University. https://iiif.lib.harvard.edu/manifests/view/drs:50116629$9i (accessed on August 27, 2022).

4. Traditionally, the Han has been referred to as a coherent category of identity with over ninety percent of the populations of the People's Republic of China and Taiwan. Thomas S. Mullaney challenges such "an umbrella term that

encompasses a plurality of diverse cultures, languages, and so forth" (Mullaney, 2011).

5. In the case of Australia's federation in 1901 where Chinese immigration in the latter half of the nineteenth century was central to the evolution of Australian nationalism, historians explain: "[I]f we think of federation as the realisation of a national ideal, then the exclusion of the Chinese is very definitely part of the story. The agitation against the Chinese had given new power and cogency to the ideal of a pure, pristine, unsullied, united Australia" (Couchman, 2004, p. 19, p. 21).

6. Including English, Irish, Scottish, German, and other immigrants.

7. Sleeman was the commissioned biographer of Jack T. Lang (Labor Premier of New South Wales, 1925–1927; 1930–1932). Regarding the links between Chinese migrants in Australia, Soviet-inspired labor movements, the Communist Party of Australia, communist internationalism, and the KMT overseas branches, see Benton, 2007, ch. 7.

8. Waterhouse's story was verified by Tse Tsan Tai although the former (remembering incidents taking place nearly six decades ago) seemed to have been confused about the latter's age (who was four years old) in 1876.

9. It should be noted that until 1937, the Chinese name for *South China Morning Post* (SCMP) was a mixed use of 南清早報 and 南華早報. Hutcheon, 1983, p. 22; Tse, 1937, p. 10, 7.

10. In similar complexity, Tien-wen Kung's book, *Disporadic Cold Warriors*, reveals the making and unmaking of Chineseness, anti-Communism, Communism, and anti-anti-Communism among Philippine Chinese, many of whom hailed from Fujian in history. Kung, 2022; Yu, 1991, p. 895; Leow, 2022; Fitzgerald and Yip, 2020.

11. Tse's letter to Sir James Lockhart can be seen in Lightfoot, 2008, p. 151. See also Robert Nield, www.amazon.co.uk/dp/0773450793#customerReviews, posted on July 8, 2008

(accessed on December 18, 2022) for a critical evaluation of Lightfoot's book.

12. Dispatch from Henry A. Blake, Governor of Hong Kong (November 1898–November 1903), to Joseph Chamberlain, Secretary of State for the Colonies (June 1895–September 1903), April 30, 1903. Earlier in 1898, the British government negotiated with Qing China a 99-year lease on the New Territories (mainly a large landmass that borders China), an expansion of the Hong Kong Island and Kowloon Peninsula, territories ceded to Britain in 1842 and 1860.

13. Author unknown, "China and the Conquest of the Air." His proposal predated the first trials with comparable Zeppelins by several years.

14. See Chapter 6, Historical Documents Reading I.

15. In general, a democracy that is reasonably responsive to the wishes of the people contains at least eight institutional guarantees: freedom to form and join organizations, freedom of expression, the right to vote, eligibility for public office, the right of political leaders to compete for support and votes, alternative source of information, free and fair elections, institutions for making government policies depending on votes and other expressions of preference. Lijphart, 1984, p. 2.

16. www.marxists.org/archive/lenin/works/1914/self-det/ch09.htm (accessed on January 13, 2023).

17. Yung Wing, the first student to study in the United States on the sponsorship of the Qing government, ambassador to America, and later an anti-Qing reformer in close contact with Tse.

18. Related to George Macartney who led the British first failed mission to the Qing in the eighteenth century, Halliday Macartney was also commander of Li Hung Chang's trained military force that put down the anti-Qing Taiping Rebellion of 1851–1864, founder of the first Chinese arsenal, and for thirty years at the service of Qing China from 1877 when

the first Qing Chinese mission in Britain was established. Boulger, 1908.

19. Vol. 46, cc396–7396. TNA FO 17/1718, no. 154, handwritten draft responses by/in the name of Lord Salisbury to the questions raised in the House of Commons.

20. Britain formed military alliances with Japan (1902), France (1904), and Russia (1907) in order to contain the German menace in Europe. In a controversial rejection of this Edwardian viewpoint, historian Keith Neilson (Neilson, 1995) argues that Russia, not Germany, was the principal long-term threat to Britain's global position.

21. In the conversation with Byron Brenan (1847–1927), acting Consul General in Shanghai, Kang also stated that "The Empress Dowager has a secret compact with Russia that Russia is to Protect Manchuria and guarantee the Manchu rule of China. The talk of deposing the Emperor [Guangxü] has been going on for a year: the Empress Dowager has frequently threatened him that if he did not do what she wished she would depose him." "Memo of a conversation with Kang Yu-wei on the 25th of September 1898, on board the P&O Royal Mail Steamer 'Ballaarat' lying at Wu-sung [Wusong] below Shanghai", forwarded to the Foreign Office by the acting Consul General in Shanghai, Byron Brenan (1847–1927).

22. September 26, 1898, Shanghai, "Letter from Consul General in Shanghai, Byron Brenan to the Under Secretary of State for Foreign Affairs, Foreign Office London [Francis Leveson Bertie, 1st Viscount Bertie of Thame (1844–1919)]." Letter from R. P. Cochran, Commander & Senior Officer, Yangtse Division, to Commander-in-Chief, H. M. Ships, China, September 26, 1898.

23. December 6, 1899, letter from Lo Fêng-luh (羅豐祿) at the Chinese Legation in London to Lord Salisbury, K. G., Principal Secretary of State for Foreign Affairs.

24. Swettenham's report also contains an extract from the chief police officer in Singapore about his encounter with Kang and Yung Wing.
25. James Cantlie's and Charles Sheridan Jones's co-authored book on Sun Yat-sen published in 1912 is a hodgepodge hagiography.
26. TNA FO 17/1718, no. 354, no. 359, and no. 359A-B indicate how in August 1900 the British coordinated a tougher stance. The word "enlistment" was a code word here. What they meant was that any attempt to recruit (i.e. enlist) activists for disturbances in Canton would trigger banishment warrants with reference to the "Foreign Enlistment Act" of 1870. This followed on from Governor Blake's August 3, 1900 report (nos. 354–357) which gave a less hostile, even understanding, and more nuanced view of the situation in South China. This report and its attachments (nos. 358–359) indicate how the revolutionaries were appealing to western powers for support with reference to their shared interest in fighting the Boxers. Although the British attitude sharpened in August, they seemed to have kept open lines of communication and sought to persuade them to desist from their revolutionary designs, see TNA FO 17/1718 from October 1900 (nos. 372–374 and further).
27. Note by Francis Bertie, "Communicated by Colonial Office, 9 August 1900. Sun Yat-sen: memorandum on and report of interview with", report dated 1900-07-12 from Sir Swettenham in Singapore to Colonial Office.
28. In his interview with Sir Alexander Swettenham, W. R. Collyer, and W. E. Edgerton on July 10, 1900 in Singapore, Sun confessed he "wished to do away with the Manchus," but Kang supported the young reformed-minded Guangxü, and Sun wanted to increase his Chinese following. Sun also indicated this prize on Kang's head was three times larger than the one on Sun's head, $40,000 placed by the Qing Chinese government. TNA FO 17/1718, nos. 315–352, notes

of an interview with Sun Yat Seng [sic] at 3:30pm on July 10, 1900 in Singapore.

29. The next several paragraphs and quotations are from Wang, 2005, ch. 2, unless otherwise indicated.
30. For differences of the CCP and KMT before their open split in 1927, see Wang, 2005, ch. 2.
31. The new party charter dated September 1, 1914.
32. See Historical Documents Reading II.
33. Kelly & Walsh's advertising flyer for 1915, Dong Wang's personal collection.
34. The *Huainanzi* (The Master of Huainan), a written record in Chinese of the second century BCE, presented a cosmogonic tale of the universe where Nü Wa (Nüwa) smelted together five colored stones to patch up the azure sky and cut off the legs of the great turtle to set them up as the four pillars of heaven. In later sources from the Eastern Han (25 CE-220 CE), the legendary figure Nü Wa also created human beings by using the yellow earth (Wang, 2022b).
35. Seen from prior texts as well as later *Shiji* (The Grand Scribe's record) by Sima Qian (ca. 145 BCE), the father of Chinese historiography, many narratives of Chinese early history centered upon the three benevolent rulers/emperors/sages (Sanhuang) – Yao, Shun, and Yu the Great – and Five Sovereigns (Wudi) – Fu Xi (Ox-tamer), Nü Wa (Nüwa, mother goddess of Chinese mythology), Shen Nong (Shennong, divine farmer and creator of fire, Yandi), Huangdi (the Yellow Emperor), and Zhuan Xu, an upper echelon of different tribal leaders, all sages and ideal rulers in Chinese legends. These legends have played increasingly greater roles in the construction of Chinese nationalism and cultural identity, as shown in Tse, 1914.
36. Historical Documents Reading, III, *Ancient Chinese Art. A Treatise on Chinese Painting*.

37. In Tse's letter from Hong Kong to Lockhart of September 9, 1912, he confessed to Sir Lockhart again that he had "helped the Chinese to gain their independence", and that he had just received a letter from Lu Cheng Hsiang (Lu Zhengxiang), premier of the newly founded Republic of China "informing me that my services have been made known to President Yuan Shih Kai" (Lightfoot, 2008, pp. 151–156). Yuan Shikai was the first president of the Republic of China from 1912–1916. Although, whether at the request of Lockhart or not, Tse in the letter attached his detailed political resume and political biography, seven months after he revealed his revolutionary identity to Lockhart.

38. Correspondence between Lockhart and Tse cited in this section can be seen in Lightfoot, 2008, appendix 1.

39. Besides on Chinese paintings and other forms of art, Voretzsch also authored and coauthored several books on Indian, Ceylonese, and Japanese art, history, and culture in German. Voretzsch, 1916. Tse's collection was "critically examined and greatly admired by prince Waldemar, Prince Reuss, Dr G. A. Voretzsch, (Collector and Connoisseur) [sic], H. E. Oscar Stuebal, J. Nelson Fraser (Indian Education Service), Sir Charles Eliot (Vice Chancellor, Hongkong University), T. K. Dealy (Director of Education, Hongkong), F. Perzuski (Expert of the Berlin Museum), and others" (Duncan, 1917, p. 8).

40. Regarding prices, Lockhart clarified that "I regret to say I am not a Croesus so cannot afford much but if you hear of anything good going very cheap I shall be obliged if you will let me know." Letter 5a from Lockhart dated July 1, 1910. In the early twentieth century, ordinary workers in Hong Kong earned less than HK$15 per month.

41. Hu Han-min (1879–1936), leader of the revolutionary army in Canton and a most senior powerful KMT conservative-wing member, later in the 1920s–1930s advocated the Turkish Republic Kemalism/Altı Ok/Atatürkism, state-sponsored reforms, and modernization. Wei Yuk (韋寶珊), like Tse, also a graduate of Queen's College Hong Kong

(Central Government School), was a prominent Hong Kong businessman, comprador of Chartered Mercantile Bank of India, London, and China, and served from 1896–1917 as an unofficial Legislative Council member in Hong Kong – an extraordinary confidence and honor offered by the British government to a local Hong Konger. Lockhart was the godfather of Wei's son (Lock Wei).

42. 旗昌洋行, a leading trading firm founded in Hong Kong by Scottish Robert Gordon Shewan and American merchant Charles Alexander Tomes with branch offices and agencies in Kobe (Japan), Manila, Southeast Asia, New York, London, Shanghai, Tianjin, Hankow, etc. An important adviser and share holder of the SCMP, Shewan was also on SCMP's very small board of directors.

43. https://en.wikipedia.org/wiki/Shewan,_Tomes_%26_Co. Sometimes, Mr Tomes also received letters and parcels to Tse on Tse's behalf. (Tse, January 27, 1912, letter 41). *Chung Kwok Po* [中國日報 *China Daily*] in Chinese was founded in 1900 in Hong Kong by the radical revolutionary Chan Siu-pak (Chen Shaobai 陳少白 1869–1934), who studied at Canton Christian College and Hong Kong College of Medicine for Chinese and was an early member of the secret society the Revive China Society formed in 1895 in Hong Kong.

44. https://industrialhistoryhk.org/tse-tsan-tai-%E8%AC%9D%E7%BA%98%E6%B3%B0-founder-south-china-morning-post/ (accessed on December 13, 2021).

45. In early 2022, the century-old proposal was revived again, and the construction of the 120-kilometer-long high-speed railroad between Canton (Guangzhou), Zhuhai (part of Macau in history) and Macau is under way with the PRC state sponsorship.

46. "The Proposed Canton-Macao Railway", https://eresources.nlb.gov.sg/newspapers/Digitised/Article/straitstimes19070917-1.2.53; https://eresources.nlb.gov.sg/newspapers/Digitised/Article/straitstimes19090102-1.2.41; https://eresources.nlb.gov.sg/newspapers/Digitised/Arti

cle/straitstimes19100418-1.2.96; Typescript "Macao-Canton Railway Convention", Shanghai, William Woodville Rockhill Papers, Harvard Houghton Library, https://hollisarchives.lib.harvard.edu/repositories/24/archival_objects/458129.

47. *South China Morning Post*, "Talking about a revolution with Post co-founder." www.infoweb.newsbank.com/apps/news/documentview?p=AWNB&docref=news/149E662D82A13BA8 (accessed on May 15, 2022).

48. Offprint with Tse's handwritten dedication to Miss. Clara B. Mitchell, undated.

49. Zou, 2014, p. 158 and p. 194, but no year, month, and date were given. Chen, a leader of Hong Men (secret society, Zhigong Party), later collaborated with the CCP, remaining in mainland China, and labeled and prosecuted by the CCP as a rightist political enemy.

50. In the KMT and CCP narratives of modern China, memories of Chen have mostly been erased or morphed into a caricature of a "counter-revolutionary" warlord, due to the fact that Chen for a while ousted Sun Yat-sen from Guangdong Province in 1922 and favored Guangdong's independence rather than the unification of China.

51. "Odyssey in the South," *United China Magazine*, October 1933, pp. 434–435.

52. Probably in 1925, Tse has made corrections by hand to this original title of the 1924 first edition of his short book as *The Chinese Republic. A Short History of the Revolution. Also The Secret History of the Revolution*. In October 1933, the Shanghai-based English magazine *United China Magazine: Journal of Chinese Revolutionary Progress* (pp. 474–489) also reprinted the bulk of Tse's *The Chinese Republic* based on the 1924 published originals.

53. Pinyin and phrases in squared brackets are mine, unless otherwise indicated throughout the excerpts.

54. The Chinese characters are in the original throughout the excerpts, but they read in the left-reversed order in classical

Chinese. I also made some minor punctuation changes to adjust Tse's originals to contemporary style. These apply to all three excerpts below.

55. Tse erased the last two phrases in his hand corrections given to Ms Mitchell.
56. Located in Central, Hong Kong, the site has been now remembered as a cradle of China's 1911 Revolution since its centennial. In 2011, the place was revamped as a historic public garden memorial.
57. In handwritten corrections, Tse added the Chinese characters 盡心愛國 to the original.
58. This national flag is still in use by the Republic of China on Taiwan.
59. In King and Clarke, 1965 (p. 202), Tse's "Reform Manifesto to the Emperor Kwang Hsu" was published in Hong Kong newspapers on May 30, 1894, a year earlier.
60. This was confirmed with nearly identical lines in Duncan, 1917, p. 3.
61. Tse Tsan Tai was married in 1892 to Zeng Guihua, and they had four sons and five daughters (Tse, 1937a, p. 3). The official marriage register seems not to exist for a span of years around that time, www.grs.gov.hk/en/arrangement_and_description.html. In 2018 Andy Kwok-Cheong Tse, a grandson of Tse, gave an interview with the South Morning China Post, Dolly Li (李佩娟), www.dollyli.com/, which can be seen at www.scmp.com/video/2171150/interview-andy-tse-grandson-scmp-co-founder-tse-tsan-tai (published on November 1, accessed on September 5, 2022).
62. Alice (Archibald, Alicia) Little (1845–1926), a popular author on China and wife of a British merchant in Shanghai for twenty years since the late 1880s, wrote two letters in early 1900 to high officials in Macao and through her influence the Natural Foot Society and the Not Bind Foot Society were founded. Cameron, 1989, pp. 361–370.

63. This caused the issuance of a new banishment in 1902 after Sun made a brief visit to Hong Kong and renewed again in June 1907. Schiffrin, 1968, p. 133.
64. Li was Qing China's most powerful politician. Tse's account is corroborated in Cunningham, 1903, ch. 7.
65. To save space, the Conclusion in the original is not included here, because it is quoted in relevant places and as the front epigraph throughout this book.
66. This version of the short book is based on the copy containing Tse Tsan Tai's neat and careful handwritten revisions in red ink dated 1937 in the packet he gave to Ms Clara Mitchell that July. Tse consulted both Roman Catholic and Protestant editions of the Bible alongside *Ancient Chinese History*, *Clare's History of the World*, *Encyclopedia Britannica*, and *Chambers Encyclopedia*.
67. Tse's hand correction in place of "Eastern" in the original. Hereby Tse's insertions and corrections are in bold font.
68. [Tse's handwritten note:] Religion of God – The God of Moses and the ancient Chinese.
69. Tse's hand-added notes, the same below: The 'four heads' are as follows: 1. Yarkhand R. – Indus – (Gihon); 2. Kashgar R. – Oxus – (Hiddakel); 3. Khotan R. – Ganges – (Pison). 4. Aksu R. – Jaxartes – (Euphrates.) N. B. Before the great upheaval of Central Asia, these 4 "heads" flowed westward. (See supplementary map of China.)
70. The Great loess plain of Central China (Whang Ho River Basin) is 400,000 square miles in area.
71. Over ten groups of islands in the Pacific Ocean contain megalithic remains of an antediluvian prehistoric civilization, proving the subsidence of the "Pacific" Continent.
72. Mountain peaks.
73. List of about 15° (about 1,000 miles).
74. About Latitude 75°, Longitude 40°.

75. Great cities are buried beneath the 400,000 square miles of loess deposits of the Yellow River Valley district of China.
76. Cradle of the Human Race.
77. This text was later published as Tse, 1916.

Bibliography

Anderson, B. (1991). *Imagined Communities: Reflections on the Origin and Spread of Nationalism*. London: Verso, 1st ed. in 1983.

Anderson, B. (2016). *A Life Beyond Boundaries*. London: Verso Books.

Austin, D. A. (2004). Citizens of Heaven: Overseas Chinese Christians during Australian Federation. In: S. Couchman, J. Fitzgerald and P. Macgregor, eds.. *After Rush: Regulation, Participation, and Chinese Communities in Australia 1860–1940*. Kingsbury, Victoria: Australia Otherland Literary Journal.

Benton, G. (2007). *Chinese Migrants and Internationalism: Forgotten Histories, 1917–1945*. New York: Routledge.

Bergère, M. C. (1998) *Sun Yat-sen*. Stanford, CA: Stanford University Press.

Boulger, D. C. (1908). *The Life of Sir Halliday Macartney K.C.M.G.* London: John Lane.

Brady, A.-M. (2003). *Making the Foreign Serve China: Managing Foreigners in the People's Republic*. Lanham, MD.: Rowman & Littlefield.

Cameron, N. (1989). *Barbarians and Mandarins: Thirteen Centuries of Western Travellers in China*. New York: Oxford University Press, 1st ed. in 1970.

Cantlie, J., and Jones, C. S. (1912). *Sun Yat Sen and the Awakening of China*. New York: Fleming H. Revell Company.

Carroll, J. (2006). Colonial Hong Kong as a Cultural-Historical Place. *Modern Asia Studies*, 40, pp. 517–543.

Chueng, P. C. I. (1997). The Study of Tse Tsan Tai (1872–1938) [*sic* 謝纘泰研究]. MA thesis in Chinese, The University of Hong Kong.

Cheung, G. (2013). "Talking about a revolution with Post co-founder", *South China Morning Post* (Hong Kong), November 6. infoweb.newsbank.com/apps/news/documentview?p=AWNB&docref=news/149E662D82A13BA8 (accessed on May 15, 2022).

Couchman, S., Fitzgerald, J., and Macgregor, P., eds. (2004). *After the Rush: Regulation, Participation and Chinese Communities in Australia, 1860–1940*. Kingsbury, Victoria: Otherland Literary Journal.

Dapp, I. F. (1905). The Archaeological Congress at Athens. *Records of the Past*, IV (7), pp. 199–202.

Dietler, M. (1994). Our Ancestors the Gauls: Archaeology, Ethnic Nationalism and the Manipulation of Celtic Identity in Modern Europe. *American Anthropologist*, 96, pp. 584–605.

Duncan, C. (1917). Tse Tsan Tai. His Political & Journalistic Career. A Brief Record. *Present Day Impressions of the Far East and Prominent and Progressive Chinese at Home and Abroad*. Offprint by Kelly & Walsh in Hong Kong. London: The Global Encyclopaedia Company.

Fitzgerald, J. (1996). *Awakening China: Politics, Culture, and Class in the Nationalist Revolution*. Stanford, CA: Stanford University Press.

Fitzgerald, J. (2007). *Big White Lie: Chinese Australians in White Australia*. Sydney: UNSW Press.

Fitzgerald, J., and Yip, H.-M., eds. (2020). *Chinese Diaspora Charity and the Cantonese Pacific, 1850–1949*. Hong Kong: University of Hong Kong Press.

Goodnow, F. J. (1915). Reform in China. *American Political Science Review*, 9, pp. 209–224.

Hale, E. (2022). Taiwan Ranks Among Top 10 Democracies in Annual Index. *VOA News*. www.voanews.com/a/taiwan-ranks-among-top-10-democracies-in-annual-index-/6438806.html (accessed on November 9, 2022).

Holcombe, A. N. (1930). *The Chinese Revolution*. Cambridge, MA: Harvard University Press.

Hopkin, D. (2017). British Women Folklorists in Post-Unification Italy: Rachel Busk and Evelyn Martinengo-Cesaresco. *Folklore*, 128, pp. 189–197.

Hucker, C. O. (1975). *China's Imperial Past: An Introduction to Chinese History and Culture*. Stanford, CA: Stanford University Press.

Hutcheon, R. (1983). *SCMP: The First Eighty Years*. Hongkong: South China Morning Post.

Kang, Y. W. (康有為) (1899). Lou, Y. L. Comp. *Kang Nanhai zibian nianpu (wai erzhong)* [康南海自編年譜(外二種) The self-compiled chronicle of Kang Nanhai (plus two additions)]. Beijing: Zhonghua shuju. Reprint 2017, based on 1992 ed.

Kayloe, T. (2018). *The Unfinished Revolution: Sun Yat-Sen and the Struggle for Modern China*. Singapore: Marshall Cavendish International.

Kemenade, W. V. (1998). *China, Hong Kong, Taiwan, Inc.* New York: Vintage Books.

King, A. Y.-C. (1975). Administrative Absorption of Politics in Hong Kong: Emphasis on the Grass Roots Level. *Asian Survey*, 15 (5), pp. 422–439.

King, F. H. H., and Clarke, P., eds. (1965). *A Research Guide to China-Coast newspapers 1822–1911*. Cambridge, MA: Harvard University Press.

Knudsen, R. A. (2020). *The Fight Over Freedom in 20th- and 21st-Century International Discourse*. London: Palgrave Macmillan.

Kung, C.-W. (2022). *Diasporic Cold Warriors: Nationalist China, Anticommunism, and the Philippine Chinese, 1930s–1970s*. Ithaca, NY: Cornell University Press.

Lattimore, O. (1962). Open Door or Great Wall? In *Studies in Frontier History*. Oxford: Oxford University Press, pp. 73–84.

Lee, K., and Leung, W. (2012). The Status of Cantonese in the Education Policy of Hong Kong, *Multilingual Education*, 2(2), pp. 1–23.

Leibold, J. (2007). *Reconfiguring Chinese Nationalism: How the Qing Frontier and its Indigenes Became* Chinese. New York: Palgrave Macmillan.

Leibold, J. (2016). Han Cybernationalism and State Territorialization in the People's Republic of China. *China Information*, 30, pp. 3–28.

Lenin, V. I. (1914). *The Right of Nations to Self-Determination.* https://www.marxists.org/archive/lenin/works/1914/self-det/ (accessed on January 13, 2023).

Leow, R. (2022). The Patriarchy of Diaspora: Race Fantasy and Gender Blindness in Chen Da's Studies of the Nanyang Chinese. *Twentieth-Century China*, 47 (3), pp. 243–265.

Lightfoot, S. (2008). *The Chinese Painting Collection and Correspondence of Sir James Stewart Lockhart (1858–1937)*. Lewiston, NY: Edwin Mellen Press.

Lijphart, A. (1984). *Democracies: Patterns of Majoritarian and Consensus Government in Twenty-One Countries*. New Haven, CT: Yale University Press.

Lo, H.-M. (1976). *The Correspondence of G. E. Morrison.* 2 vols. Cambridge: Cambridge University Press.

Luk, B. H.-K. (1991). Chinese Culture in the Hong Kong Curriculum: Heritage and Colonialism. *Comparative Education Review,* 35, pp. 650–668.

Luo, J. (Lo Chia-lun 羅家倫), ed. (1954). *Geming wenxian* [革命文獻 Revolutionary documents], vol. 5. Taipei: Zongtongfu disanju yinzhu gongchang.

Mark, E. (2018). *Japan's Occupation of Java in the Second World War: A Transnational History*. London: Bloomsbury Academic.

Martin, W. A. P. (1896). *A Cycle of Cathay or China, South and North with Personal Reminiscences*. New York: Fleming H. Revell Company.

McCormick, F. (1913). *The Flowery Republic*. London: John Murray.

Mullaney, T. S. (2011). "Introducing Critical Han Studies." www.chinaheritagequarterly.org/019/scholarship/019_han_studies.inc (accessed on September 16, 2022).

Noonan, R. (2003). Grafton to Guangzhou: The Revolutionary Journey of Tse Tsan Tai. In: K. Tseen, ed., *Locating Asian Australian Cultures*. New York: Routledge, pp. 101–115.

Ong, A., and Nonini, D., eds. (1997). *Ungrounded Empires: The Cultural Politics of Modern Chinese Transnationalism*, London: Routledge.

Qin, X. (秦孝儀), ed. (1989). *Guofu quanji* [國父全集 The complete works of the founding father], vol. 2. Taipei: Jindai zhongguo chubanshe.

Reid, G. (1921). *A Christian's Appreciation of Other Faiths: A Study of the Best in the World's Greatest Religions*. Chicago, IL: The Open Court Publishing Company.

Richard, T. (1915a). Letter to Tse Tsan Tai on March 19. Author's personal collection.

Richard, T. (1915b). Review of Tse Tsan Tai's 1915. *The Chinese Recorder*. April.

Rhoads, E. J. M. (2000). *Manchus & Han: Ethnic Relations and Political Power in Late Qing and Early Republican China, 1861–1928*. Seattle: University of Washington Press.

Schiffrin, H. Z. (1968). *Sun Yat-sen and the Origins of the Chinese Revolution*. Berkeley, CA: University of California Press.

Sleeman, J. H. C. (1933). *White China: An Austral-Asian Sensation.* Sydney: J. H. C. Sleeman.

Snyder, T. (2022). "The Making of Modern Ukraine. Class 1: Ukrainian Questions Posed by Russian Invasion." YaleCourses. www.youtube.com/watch?v=bJczLlwp-d8.

Sun, Y. S. (1897). *Kidnapped in London: Being the Story of My Capture by, Detention at, and Release from the Chinese Legation,* London. Bristol: J. W. Arrowsmith.

Sun, Y. S. (1914). "Zongli zhi Xinjiapo gepu Hongmen tongzhi lun Zhonghua gemingdang zi fucong dangkui wei weiyi tiaojianshu" [總理致新加坡各埠洪門同志論中華革命黨以服從黨魁為唯一條件書], July 29. In: J. Luo, ed. (1954). *Geming wenxian,* vol. 5. Taipei: Zongtongfu disanju yinzhu gongchang.

TNA FO 17/1718 (1896–1905). "Chinese Revolutionaries in British Dominions. Sun-Yat-Sen, Kang-yu-wei, etc., (Kidnapping of Sun-Yat-Sen by the Chinese Legation)."

Tsang, S. (2004). *A Modern History of Hong Kong.* London: Bloomsbury Academy.

Tse, T. T. (1899). "The Situation in the Far East." (時局全圖) Cartoon Source: https://zhuanlan.zhihu.com/p/58384230 (accessed on September 5, 2022).

Tse, T. T. (1905). "On the Removal of Works of Art and Relics." In *Comptes Rendus Du Congrès International d'archéologie. 1re Session.* Athens: Impr. "Hestia," C. Meissner & N. Kargadouris, pp. 372–373.

Tse, T. T. (1909). "An Ethnographical Question," *China Mail,* June 30, p. 5.

Tse, T. T. (1912). Letter to Sir James Stewart Lockhart on September 9 including political resume and political biography. In: S. Lightfoot (2008), pp. 151–156.

Tse, T. T. (1914). *The Creation: The Real Situation of Eden, and the Origin of the Chinese.* Hongkong: Kelly & Walsh, Ltd. 1914. Harvard

Library. https://i f.lib.harvard.edu/manifests/view/drs:5C116629$1i (accessed on August 29, 2022).

Tse, T. T. (1915a). Flyers, author's personal collection.

Tse, T. T. (1915b). "The Cradle of the Human Race. The Cause of the Deluge and the Change in the Antediluvian Polar Regions. A Reply to 'The Japan Chronicle'." Reprint from *The Japan Chronicle* by Kelly & Walsh in Hong Kong, December 9.

Tse, T. T. (1916). "Sir Hiram S. Maxim: An Appreciation," *South China Morning Post*, November 27.

Tse, T. T. (1917a). *Shijie yuanshi zonggang. Zhongguo huangzhong laiyuan* [世界元始總綱. 中國黃種來源]. Chinese ed. of *The Creation: The Real Situation of Eden. The Origin of the Chinese*. Containing "Proofs of the Deluge." Hongkong: Tsun Wan Yat Po.

Tse, T. T. (1917b). "Proofs of the Deluge, The Upheaval and Subsidence of Continents, and the Change in the North Polar Regions. A Reply to Alfred H. Crook, M.A., F.R.G.S." Reprinted from *The South China Morning Post*, November 12.

Tse, T. T. (1918a). "The Real Situation of 'Eden'. Proofs of the Deluge and the Great Upheaval of Central Asia. Origin of Loess deposits, Salt Lakes, Salt Marshes & Deserts: A Reply to The Roman Catholic Encyclopaedian Society of Macao." Reprinted from *The South China Morning Post*, April 20.

Tse, T. T. (1918b). "China in the Time of the Deluge. Origin of the Crustaceans of Taihu Lake of China. China The 'Shinar' of Genesis. Why the Ancients of The West Failed to Discover China: A Reply to Notes of the Royal Asiatic Society." Reprinted from *The Shanghai Times*, July 4.

Tse, T. T. (1919). "Truth of the Bible and the Dean of Lincoln's Disbelief: Historical, Geographical & Scientific Proofs of the Truth of the Biblical Record of Eden and the Flood." Reprinted from the Hongkong Daily Press, April 30.

Tse, T. T. (1920a). Loess and the Deluge – Chinese Turkestan the Cradle of the Human Race – Cause of Upheaval and Subsidence of Continents, Change in North Polar Regions, and Sudden Freezing of Northern Asia – Fallacy of the Ice Age: A Reply to Alfred H. Crook, M.A., F.R.G.S. Reprinted from the Hong Kong Daily Press, April 1.

Tse, T. T. (1920b). Letter to Rev. H. R. Wells in London Mission on November 6 from Hong Kong.

Tse, T. T. (1922). "What Was the Colour of Our Primitive Ancestors? The Real Mountains of Ararat." Reprinted from the *Hongkong Daily Press*, January 11.

Tse, T. T. (1923). "Origin of the Mongolian Desert, and Its Prehistoric Fossils." Reprinted from the *North China Star*, November 7, by Kelly & Walsh in Hong Kong.

Tse, T. T. (1924). *The Chinese Republic. Secret History of the Revolution* 中華民國革命秘史. Hong Kong: South China Morning Post, 1924.

Tse, T. T. (1928). *Ancient Chinese Art: A Treatise on Chinese Painting*. Hong Kong: South China Morning Post, p. 16.

Tse, T. T. (1937a). Pamphlet, Xie Shudetang 謝樹德堂編訂, comp. *Zhonghua minguo geming zhenxiang: Xie Sheng'an (Tse Tsan Tai)* [中華民國革命真相: 謝聖安(謝纘泰)].

Tse, T. T. (1937b). Authorization letter for Clara B. Mitchell, September 1. Author's personal collection.

Tse, T. T. (1937c). Letter to Clara B. Mitchell via YWCA Hong Kong, July 25.

Wagner, R. (2012). Don't Mind the Gap! The Foreign-language Press in Late-Qing and Republican China. *China Heritage Quarterly* 30/31, June/September. www.chinaheritagequarterly.org/features.php?searchterm=030_wagner.inc&issue=030 (accessed on September 20, 2022).

Wang, D. (2005). *China's Unequal Treaties: Narrating National History*. Lanham, MD: Lexington Books.

Wang, D. (2007). *Managing God's Higher Learning: US-China Cultural Encounter and Canton Christian College (Lingnan University), 1888–1952*. Lanham, MD: Lexington Books, 2007.

Wang, D. (2020a). *Longmen's Stone Budahas and Cultural Heritage: When Antiquity Met Modernity in China*. Lanham, MD: Rowman & Littlefield.

Wang, D. (2020b). Ten Things We Need to Know When Teaching about Early China. *Education about Asia*, 25(2), Fall, pp. 5–11.

Wang, D. (2021). *The United States and China: A History from the Eighteenth Century to the Present*. Lanham, MD: Rowman & Littlefield.

Wang, Y. C. (2022). "Sun Yat-sen." *Encyclopaedia Britannica*, November 8. www.britann ca.com/biography/Sun-Yat-sen (accessed on December 7, 2022).

Waterhouse, H. B. (1932). Tse Tsan Tai: The Chinese Revolutionary. *Grafton Daily Examiner*, September 24. Reprinted in *United China Magazine*, October 1933, p. 490.

Wilbur, C. M. (1976). *Sun Yat-sen: Frustrated Patriot*. New York: Columbia University Press.

Wilensky-Lanford, B. (2011). *Paradise Lust: Searching for the Garden of Eden*. New York: Grove Press.

Yu, G. T. (1991). The 1911 Revolution: Past, Present, and Future. *Asian Survey*, 31, pp. 895–904.

Zarrow, P. (2012). *After Empire: The Conceptual Transformation of the Chinese States, 1885–1924*. Stanford, CA: Stanford University Press.

Zou, Y. (2014). An English Newspaper for British and Chinese: The South China Morning Post Study (1903–1941). PhD thesis, Lingnan University, Hong Kong.

Index

agency 98, 99

Ah See family 3–4

Aisin Gioro 27

ambition of Tse Tsan-tai 5, 69, 107

Ancient Chinese Art. A Treatise on Chinese Painting (Tse Tsan-tai) 199; Development 201–204; Foreign criticism 217–218; masters 211–216; origin 201; schools 209–211; Technique 204–209

Anderson, B. 10, 22, 62

anti-Chinese racism 2

Anti-Footbinding Society 120, 129

anti-Manchu ethnic cleansing 26

anti-Manchu racism 27, 28

antiquities and geoculture 40

antiquities protection 71–8

appreciations for Tse Tsan-tai's works 105–106

Archaeology 55, 57, 58

atheism 64

Austin, D. A. 2

Australia 1, 5, 220

Australian Chinese 3, 89, 90, 91, 92; Chinese Australians 1–6; Chinese migrants in 220

Australian and New Zealand Army Corps (ANZAC) 91

Austria 59

Baptism 5, 57, 107

Belgium 59

Benton, G. 220

Bergere, M. C. 21, 43, 98

Bertie, F. 222, 223

Biographical sketch of Tse Tsan-tai 106

Blake, H. A. 43, 129, 133, 221

Bolshevik Communism 89

Bolshevism 42, 47, 50, 93, 97

Borodin/ Gruseriberg, M. 48

Boshan Wei Yuk 78

Boulger, D. C. 222

Boyd Kaye & Company 17, 80

Brady, A.-M. 26

Brenan 222

Brest-Litovsk peace negotiations 25

Britain, xv 8, 9, 12, 23, 35, 45, 47, 59, 78, 86, 88, 93, 111, 148, 156, 182, 222

British Foreign Office 16, 34

British Hong Kong 1, 9, 12, 14, 17, 26, 30, 33, 34, 39, 55, 58, 69, 70, 74, 78, 87, 89 *see also* Hong Kong

brotherhood of man 29. 58, 64, 67, 68, 197

business career of Tse Tsan-tai 80–84

Calvin, J. 54

Cameron, N. 36, 228

Cantlie, J. 14, 15, 35, 41, 42, 46, 114, 223

Canton (Guangzhou) 7–9, 24–26, 34, 35, 41, 44, 48, 77, 88, 103, 104, 112, 113, 127, 128, 135–136, 141, 223, 225

Canton- Macau Railway Convention (1904) 18, 80–81

Canton River 18

Capitoline Wolf 66

caricaturist 73

Carroll, J. 11–12, 13, 88

Castelo Branco 81

Chadwick, O. 16

Chamberlain, J. 37, 221

Chan Fun 109

Chan Kam-to 115

Chan Siu-pak 113, 114, 131, 132, 226

charlatanism 67

Chau Chiu-ngok 109

Cheng Jiongming 48

Chen Huanzhang 65

Chen Jiongming 91

Chen Qiyou 89

Chen Tianhua 28

Cheung, G. 9, 232

Cheung Tsoi 120; Chiang Kai-shek 89, 90, 98; China 12, 18, 37, 56; and the curse 97–100; becoming a republic 153–155; Tse Tsan- tai's arrival in 108–109

China Mail 6, 71, 106, 111, 112, 113, 120, 129, 132, 133, 139, 142, 143, 144, 161

Chinese Australians 1–7

Chinese colonization 11

Chinese Communist Party (CCP) 8, 26, 37, 50, 99, 227

Chinese Empire 9, 10, 36, 62, 102

Chinese national anthem 159

Chinese nationalism 13, 58, 68, 78, 88, 93, 98, 224

Chinese paintings 72, 76, 203, 225

Chinese Patriotic Mutual Improvement Association 17

Chinese Republic. Secret History of the Revolution (Tse Tsan-tai) 5, 21, 22, 87, 101, 227; advent of the Manchus 102–103; ambition 5, 107; Anti-Footbinding Society 120, 129; Appreciations 105–106, 143. Arrival in China 108–109; betrayal 18, 140–141; Biographical sketch 72, 106; Canton, second attempt to capture 103, 127, 128, 135–136; China becoming a republic 153–154; Chinese national anthem 159; Commonwealth Government 92, 103, 127–128; difficulties and dangers 109–110; Empress Dowager's coup d'état 119, 121; Hongkong Chinese Club 120; Kang Yu-wei 16, 34, 44, 115, 116–117, 119, 120, 121, 123, 124, 125, 126, 127, 136, 144; Kang Yu-wei and Tse Tsan-tai, meeting between 115–116; King Lien-Shan, rescue of 129–146; last of the Mings 101–102; Li Hung Chang's trap 132–133; Manchus, abdication of 153–166; manifesto to Emperor Kwang Hsu 113; martyrdom of Kang Kwang-jin 122–123; Maxim, H. S. 17, 86, 88, 145–146, 147, 148; Meetings at headquarters 104–105; Morrison, death of 165–166; Morrison, interview with 136–138; Morrison, meetings with 139–140; movements for independence 103–104; national flag of the republic 159–160; organizing the revolution 112–113; parties unification 115–123; Party split up 114–115; political cartoon 125–126; political confession 118–119; "Po Wang Whui" Society 126–127; President of Provisional Govt. 113–114; Reid on political situation 160–162; revolution 146–152; Richard on China 158–159; rottenest government in existence 138–139; S.C.M. Post, Ltd. 141–142; seed germinates 110–111; Smith's remarkable letter 154–157; Sun Yat-sen elected Provisional President 147–148; Ta Tung Movement 133–134; Tse Tsan-tai and Kang Kwang-jin, meeting between 117–118; Tse Tsan-tai meets Mrs Archbald Little 129–131; Tse Yet-chong, death of 142–143; union and cooperation 123–127; Wei Chow Movement 131–132; World's Chinese Students' Federation 143–144; Wuchang Revolt and Li Yuan-hung 146–147; Yangtze Provinces, progress in 123–124; Yeung Ku-wan, assassination of 134–135; Yeung Ku-wan and Liang Chi-chao, meeting between 124–125; Yuan Shih-kai, death of 163–165; Yuan Shih-kai elected president 162–163; Yung Wing, death of 157; Yung Wing's advice 148–152; Yung Wing's scheme 144–145

Chinese Revolutionary Party 49

Chinese Turkestan 28, 54, 55, 56, 60, 64, 66, 167, 168, 169, 171, 174, 181, 183, 197, 201, 210

Chi Yu 190–191

Chow, Vivian Yung 90–93

Christianity 39, 57, 59, 60, 64, 65, 67, 86

Chueng, P. C. I. 83

Chung Kwok Po Co. 80

Chu Yuan-chang (Hung Wu) 101

Clarence and Richmond Examiner 3

Clarke, P. 70, 228

Clementi, C. 11

C. L. King & Co. 80

Cole, G. 35

Colin McD. Smart 88, 132

Collyer, W. R. 223

colonial cosmopolitanism 29, 58

colonialism 1, 10, 48, 88

Columbus, C. 54

Commonwealth Government 92, 103, 127–128

Communist Party 8, 26, 37, 50, 99, 220

Confucianism 65

Confucius Academy 65

cosmopolitan public sphere 87

Couchman, S. 220

Courland 25

Cowen, T. 88, 113

Cradle of the Human Race 166, 167, 168, 169, 170, 171, 202, 230

Creation: The Real Situation of Eden and the Origin of the Chinese (Tse Tsan-tai), *The* 55, 166, 172–173, 219; beginning of civilization 176; Cradle of the Human Race 166, 169–171; Garden of Eden, 168, 169, 170, 171; peopling of the world 173–176

creation myths 62, 64, 65, 67, 68

Crown Colony of Hong Kong 1, 34, 98

Cunningham, A. 70–71, 80, 88, 92, 105, 129, 135, 138, 139, 140, 141, 219

Curzon 24, 38

de Azevedo, Jose 81

Dietler, M. 57

Disporic Cold Warriors (Tien-wen Kung) 220

divine recognition 60

Duncan, C. 5, 6, 23, 71, 75, 81, 83, 85, 86, 88, 102, 106, 111, 112, 161, 225, 228

East Asia 6, 7, 8, 47, 57, 87, 91, 99, 226

Economist Intelligence Unit 32

Edgerton, W. E. 223

egalitarianism 91

Empress Dowager's coup d'état 119, 121

England 5, 40, 73, 77, 107, 110, 113, 165, 219

English Law 36

ethnonationalism 73

Europe 6, 8, 18, 24, 27, 29, 30, 45, 53, 55, 57, 58, 59, 60, 63, 64, 65, 66, 67, 69, 72, 74, 75, 76, 78, 79, 81, 110, 123, 130, 146, 148, 152, 164, 175, 182, 186, 187, 198, 19, 202, 203, 204, 207, 217, 218, 222

Evens, C. 70

Executive Council of Singapore 44

Far East 33, 113, 161

Fitzgerald, J. 2, 3, 4, 5, 26, 48, 91, 94, 220

Five Patriarchs of China 177

Fuhi (Henoch) 177, 178, 179

Hwang Ti (Arphaxad) 177, 190, 191, 192; Nü Wa (Noah) 177, 179, 185; Shen Nung (Shem) 177, 189, 190; Yao (Reu) 177, 192, 193, 194, 195, 196, 197

Foreign Enlistment Act 34, 223

France 59, 222

Francisco Tse Yet 159

Fran Koch 74

fratricidal war 60, 67, 198

friends and associates of Tse Tsan-tai 84, 85, 86, 87, 88, 89

Fuhi (Henoch) 177, 178, 179

Fukumoto, M. 132, 133

Fung Shan 147

Garden of Eden 54, 55, 60, 64, 66, 67, 167, 168, 169, 170, 171, 174, 195, 197, 202

Genesis 53, 54, 55, 64, 65, 66, 166, 168, 169, 170, 171, 172, 173, 174, 178, 179, 180, 183, 188, 190, 197

geopolitics 56

Germany 24, 25, 54, 59, 74, 161, 222

Goodnow, F. J. 32

Gourley, E. 38

government versus nation 30–33

Grafton 1, 3, 4, 5, 90, 107

Grafton Daily Examiner 3
Great Britain 47, 93, 111, 148, 156, 182
greatness 58, 162, 200, 212
Great Revolution 31, 103, 145
Greenway, C. C. 5, 107
Guangdong 1, 4, 7, 8, 18, 34, 43, 48, 71, 78, 88, 92, 107, 143, 227
Guangxu emperor 39
Guomindang (GMD) 8

Hale, B. A. 71, 88, 148
Hale, E. 32
Hamburg Tung Kee 82
Han Chinese 14, 26, 27, 28, 29, 61
Han Dynasty 211
Harston, J. Scott 141
headquarters, meetings at 104–105
H.E. Chang Pat Sz 83
Hing Chung Whui 103, 111, 114
historical determinism 98
Hoiping District of China 18
Ho Kai 43, 88, 111, 112, 113, 121, 125, 131, 133, 136
Holcombe, A. N. 33, 47
Hong Kong 1, 3, 4, 5, 7, 8, 9, 10, 11, 12, 13, 14, 15, 16, 17, 19, 24, 25, 26, 30, 33, 34, 35, 39, 41, 43, 44, 55, 58, 69, 70, 71, 73, 74, 75, 76, 77, 78, 80, 81, 82, 83, 84, 87, 88, 89, 92, 93, 98, 100, 166, 199, 221, 225, 226, 228, 229 *see also* British Hong Kong
Hongkong Chinese Club 120
Hongkong Daily Press 54, 71, 105, 110, 111, 129, 130, 134, 135, 137, 138, 139, 141, 142, 143, 146, 148, 154
Hongkong Telegraph 71, 106, 111, 113, 134, 137
Hordern, A. 5
House of Commons 37, 222
Huainanzi 224
Huang Zunxian 65
Hucker, C. O. 68
Hu Han-min 78, 225
Hung Chuen-fook 103, 126, 127, 135, 136, 139, 140, 141, 142
Hung Chun-fui 126, 127
Hung Wo 126
Hung Mun 90, 91
Hutcheon, R. 69, 70, 81, 220
Hwang Ti (Arphaxad) 177, 190, 191, 192

illiberalism 88
Imagined Communities (Benedict Anderson) 10
independence, movements for 103, 104

industrialist, Tse Tsan-tai as 80, 81, 82, 83, 84

international society 143

Japan 8, 18, 23, 28, 30, 42, 44, 46, 49, 56, 65, 71, 78, 87, 89, 91, 106, 110, 114, 115, 119, 120, 121, 123, 124, 125, 127, 128, 131, 132, 133, 134, 156, 161, 215, 218, 222, 226

Joffe, A. 48

Jones, C. S. 14, 15, 35, 42, 46, 223

Journal of Chinese Revolutionary Progress 23, 227

Kai Ho Kai 88, 111, 125

Kalevala 64

Kang Kwang-jin 115, 117, 118, 119, 120, 121, 122

Kang Youwei 6, 34, 40, 43, 44, 79

Kang Yu-wei 16, 34, 44, 115, 116, 117, 119, 120, 121, 123, 124, 125, 126, 127, 136, 144, 222

Kang Yu-wei and Tse Tsan-tai, meeting between 115, 116

Kayloe, T. 21

Kelly & Walsh 166, 224

Kemenade, W. V. 97

King, A. Y.-C. 12, 13, 14, 65

King, F. H. H. 70, 228

King, S. 90, 92

King Lien-shan 129, 130, 135; betrayal 140, 141; Canton, second attempt to capture 135, 136; Li Hung Chang's trap 132, 133; Little, Tse Tsan-tai meeting with 129, 130, 131; Morrison, interview with 136, 137, 138; Morrison, meetings with 139, 140; rottenest government in existence 138, 139; S.C.M. Post, Ltd. 141, 142; Sir Hiram S. Maxim 145, 146; Ta-ung Movement 133, 134; Tse Yet-chong, death of 142, 143; Wei Chow Movement 131, 132; World's Chinese Students' Federation 143, 144; Yeung Ku-wan, assassination of 134, 135; Yung Wing's scheme 144, 145

Ki Yat, F. 83

Kiyofuji, Kōshichirō 43, 44

Knudsen, R. A. 25

Kojiki 65, 68

Kollecker, A. 141

Kowloon Peninsula 8, 221

Ku Kai Chih 203

Kuk Kong Coal Mining Co. 83

Kung, C.-W. 99

Kuomintang (KMT) 8, 37, 48

Kwang Hsu 113, 129, 150, 228

Lattimore, O. 29

Lau In-bun 109

League of Nations 25

Lee, K. 11

Leibold, J. 61, 62

Lenin, V. I. 24, 25, 48, 49

Leow, R. 23, 220

Leung, W. 11

Leung Lan-fan 115, 117, 120

Leung Wan Kwai 82

Liang Chi-chao 119, 121, 124, 127

Liang Qichao 39

Lightfoot, S. 15, 18, 71, 72, 75, 76, 83, 84, 220, 221, 225

Li Hongzhang 41, 43

Li Hung Chang 87, 132, 133

Lijphart, A. 221

Li Ki-tong 83, 127

Li Pak 127, 130, 131, 135, 136, 137

Li Ssu Hsün 209, 211, 212, 213, 214

Lithuania 25

Little, Alice 228

Little, Archibald, Tse Tsan-tai meeting with 129, 130, 131

Li Tzu-cheng 101, 102

Liu, F. W.

Li Yuan-hung 146, 147; Wuchang Revolt and 146, 147

Lo, H.-M. 70

Lockhart, J. 15, 54, 71, 72, 73, 74, 75, 76, 77, 78, 79, 83, 87, 108, 220, 225

Loh Yu 191

Lo Man-yuk 109

London 17, 34, 35, 36, 39, 41, 45, 47, 70, 71, 104, 106, 114, 120, 136, 137, 138, 145, 148, 153, 154, 155, 160, 161, 222, 226

Loong Hung Pung 4, 90, 91, 92

Lü Haihuan 81

Luk, B. H.-K. 9, 11

Luk King-fo 110, 120

Luo, J. 49, 50

Macartney, G. 221

Macartney, H. 33, 35, 38, 221

Mackinder, H. J. 56, 57

Malaysia 8, 23, 175

Manchu dogs 28

Manchurian mineral resources 18

Manchus, 22, 102–103

Manchus; Abdication of 153; China becoming a republic 153, 154; Chinese national anthem 159; Morrison, death of 165, 166; national flag of the republic 159, 160; Richard on China 158, 159; Smith's remarkable letter 154–157; Thos. H. Reid on political situation 160–162; Yuan Shih-kai, death of

163–165; Yuan Shih-kai elected president 162–163; Yung Wing, death of 157

Manchu Tartars 5, 6, 102, 107, 109

Man Ning Patent Medicine Co. Ltd 75

Man U Tong Co. Ltd 80

Mark, E. 12

Martin, W. A. P. 59

martyrdom of Kang Kwang-jin 122–123

Maxim, H. S. 17, 85, 88, 145, 147, 148

May, F. H. 75

McCormick, F. 9, 11, 14, 27, 28, 30, 31, 42, 79, 99

Ming China 27

Ming Dynasty 6, 14, 102, 144

Ming restoration 6, 24

Mitchell, C. B. 84, 219, 227, 228, 229

Miyazaki, Torazō 43, 44

Modern Standard Chinese (Putonghua) 11

Morrison, G. E. 70, 88, 104, 136, 137, 138, 139, 140, 142, 144, 146, 148, 152, 157, 160, 162, 163, 164, 165; Death of 165; interview with 136–138; meetings with 139–140

Mount Tai 72

Mullaney, T. S. 220

Nako Nisi Ju Taro 44

Nanjing (Nanking) 14, 42, 92

Nara Hala 27

national humiliation 33, 36, 37, 46

Nationalism 10, 13, 18, 22, 26, 28, 45, 57, 58, 62, 65, 67, 68, 73, 78, 87, 88, 90, 93, 94, 98, 220, 224

Nationalist Party 8, 26, 37, 49, 89, 90

national self-determination 24–25, 62

Nation versus government 30–33

Ng Lo-sam 135

Ng Sui-sang 135

Nihon Shoki 65

1911 revolution 2, 8, 14, 15, 18, 21, 22, 23, 26, 28, 33, 46, 50, 62, 77, 89, 91, 99, 228; anti-Manchu ethnic cleansing during 26; Britain 33; British Hong Kong 33; Hong Kong 34–35, 39, 41; Nation versus government 30–33; Qing China 33, 36; racism and nationalism 26–30; Sun Yat-sen (1866–1925) 41–50; Taiping heritage 23

Ning Tiaoyuan 28

Nonini, D. 99

Noonan, R. 3

"no Political Party in China" 86

Nurhachu 102

Nü Wa (Noah) 177, 179, 184, 185, 188; great antiquity of Chinese 186–187; origin of the Chinese and religion of the Chinese 188–189; real Mount Ararat 185; religion of the Chinese 188; re-peopling of the world 185–186

Ong, A. 99

Opium Wars 8

Outer Mongolia 48, 62

Padre Jacob Lao 95, 159

Pan Gu 65

parties unification; Anti-Footbinding Society 120, 129; empress Dowager's coup d'état 119, 121; Hongkong Chinese Club 120; Kang Yu-wei 116–117; Kang Yu-wei and Tse Tsan-tai, meeting between 115–116; martyrdom of Kang Kwang-jin 122–123; political confession 118–119; Tse Tsan-tai and Kang Kwang-jin, meeting between 117–118

party split up 114–115

Pearl River Delta 7, 9

People's Republic of China (PRC) 80, 91, 99, 219

Petrie, T. 71, 88, 148

Playfair, G. W. 70

Po Ching 75

Poland 25

Polemicists 23

political agenda of Tse Tsan-tai 89

political cartoon 125–126

political confession 118–119

"Po Wang Whui" Society 126–127

Po Young 75

Provisional Government 113, 135, 136, 147, 149

Puyi 15

pyramidology 67

Qin, X. 49

Qing China 1, 9, 16, 33, 36, 42, 78, 94, 221

Qing dynasty 15, 21, 102

Qing Empire 4, 14, 18, 24, 27

Qing government 4, 8, 11, 33, 82, 221

Qing regime 8, 16, 34

Quan Wah & Co. 80

racial purity 1, 2

racial self-consciousness 28

racism and nationalism of Tse Tsan-tai 26–30

radical reformist 40

Red Tower 82

Reid, G. 58–59

Reid, T. H. 111, 113, 120, 129, 141, 160–162

revolution, organizing the 112–113

Rhoads, E. J. M. 27

Richard, T. 40, 70, 85, 88, 120, 122, 123, 133, 137, 158–159

Ring des Nibelungen 64

Romulus and Remus myth 64, 66

Royal Geographical Society 56

Russia 23, 25, 26, 28, 40, 45, 47, 48, 56, 59, 142, 145, 222

Russian Socialist Party Programme 25

sage adviser 70

Salisbury 35–36, 38, 222

San Francisco 91

Sao-ke Alfred Sze 94

Schiffrin, H. Z. 37, 39, 45, 229

science and technology 81

scientific evidence 67

S.C.M. Post, Ltd. 141–142

secularization 64

See, J. 4, 106

See Yap 7

Shanghai 5, 40, 44, 49, 71, 75, 76, 77, 81, 82, 83, 85, 91, 106, 119, 120, 122, 129, 134, 137, 143, 147, 148, 155, 158, 222, 226, 227, 228

Sheng Xuanhuai 81

Shen Nung (Shem) 177, 188, 189, 190

Shewan Tome's & Co. 80

Singapore 41, 43, 44, 49, 113, 114, 139, 223

sino-centrism 27, 62, 78

Situation in the Far East (1899 cartoon), The 125

Sleeman, J. H. C. 3, 220

Smith, D. Warres 71, 88, 129, 130, 137, 138, 148, 154–157

Snyder, T. D. 63

South China Morning Post (SCMP) 22, 69, 70, 80, 105, 141, 142, 143, 145, 148, 199, 220, 227

Soviet Bolshevism 42, 97

Soviet Russia 25–26, 43, 50

spirituality 58, 217

sportsmanship 91

state-sponsored nationalism 26

Steam Navigation Co. 109

Stephen King Jung Sao 92

Sung dynasty 214

Sun Yat-sen 2, 14, 15, 16, 18, 19, 21, 25, 30, 31, 34, 35, 37, 39, 41, 42, 43, 44, 45, 46, 48, 49, 50, 77, 88, 89, 90, 91, 92, 94, 98, 103, 104, 111,

112, 113, 114, 115, 118, 120, 127, 128, 130, 131, 132, 133, 135, 137, 139, 142, 143, 144, 147, 151, 152, 154, 157, 161, 223, 227; elected Provisional President 147; political autobiography 46; Zhonghua Gemingdang 49

Swettenham, A. 223

Swettenham, F. A. 41

synarchy, kernel of 13

Sze Kin-yu 134

Taiping heritage, 23

Taiping Rebellion 26, 221

Taiping Uprising of 1851–1864 4, 14

Taiwan 8, 32, 91, 98, 99, 219, 228

Taiwan Strait 98

Tak Sau 134

Tang Dynasty 211, 215

Tang Shao-yi 131, 148, 150

Tang Tsai-chang 134

Ta Tung Movement 133, 134

Ta Tung Palace 212

Ti Kuh Kao Sin 194

"Tse Tsan Tai: His Political & Journalistic Career" (Chesney Duncan) 85

Tse Tsi-shau 140, 141

Tse Yet-chong, death of 142–143

Tsung Teh 102

Turkish Republic 66, 225

Uchida, Ryōhei 43

United China Magazine 91, 92, 93, 95, 227

United Front government 24, 26

United States 9, 18, 23, 27, 31, 60, 86, 91, 93, 94, 115, 120, 124, 130, 131, 132, 137, 138, 143, 145, 157, 221

universalism 58

universal peace 18, 29, 58, 64, 67, 95, 197, 200

usurpers 24, 103, 126, 156

van Kemenade, W. 97

Versailles Peace Treaty 25

violent illiberalism 88

Volkhovsky, F. 45

voluntary disclosure of Tse Tsan-tai 78

Voretzsch, D. G. 74, 225

Wagner, R. 70

Wang, D. 4, 8, 37, 40, 46, 56, 57, 65, 68, 80, 88, 224

Wang, Y. C. 43, 224

Wang Wei 209, 213–214

Ward, A. G. 70

Waterhouse, H. B. 3–4, 220

Wei Chow Movement 131–133, 134

Weihaiwei 71, 73, 76
Wilbur, C. M. 45
Wilensky-Lanford, B. 54
Wilson, W. 25
Wing Kee & Co. 80, 83
Wing On Co. Ltd 75
Wolseley Sun-helmet 17
Wong Kwok-u 109
Wong Shing 112, 114
Wong Wing-sheung 112, 113, 114
World War I 24, 25, 55, 58, 60, 83
World War II 12, 25, 80
World's Chinese Students' Federation 143–144
Wuchang Revolt and Li Yuan-hung 146–147
Wu Lien-teh 143
Wu San-kwei 101, 102
Wu Tao Tzu 204, 215–216
Wu Ting-fang 155

Xinjiang 55, 56, 157

Yamato clan 68
Yangtze Provinces, progress in 123–124, 126
Yao (Reu) 192, 194; China's indigenous civilization 195–196; origin of the Jews 194–195; Universal peace and the brotherhood of man 196–197
Yaumati Steam Launch Co. Ltd 84
Yee Hing 4, 90, 91
Yeung Ku-wan 34, 103, 109, 111, 113, 114, 115, 118, 119, 120, 121, 123, 124, 124, 125, 126, 127, 128, 130, 131, 132, 133, 134, 135; and Liang Chi-chao, meeting between 124–125; assassination of 134–135
Yip, H.-M. 220
Yow Lit 114
Yu, G. T. 220
Yuan Shih-kai 32, 105, 146, 147, 148, 150, 153, 154, 159, 160, 162, 163, 165; Death of 163; elected president of the Republic 162
Yuan Shikai 49, 70, 77, 79, 225
Yung Ku-wan 131
Yung Wing 27, 88, 130, 131, 133, 134, 135, 137, 138, 139, 143, 144, 148, 149, 151, 152, 157, 221, 223; advice 148–152; death of 157; scheme 144–145
Yunnan Petroleum Co. 83

Zarrow, P. 64, 65
Zhonghua Gemingdang 49–50
Zou, Y. 81, 227
Zou Rong 28